Virtue Based Management

Dr. Jean-Francois Orsini, OP

This book is dedicated to all those who contributed to my education, formation and growth, personally, professionally, culturally and spiritually. This starts with my dear family, remarkable members of the Dominican order, both first and third orders, and my professors and professional supervisors.

CONTENTS

Page

Preface   xvii

1. Part I - The Who and the What
   - The Christian Manager and Work.....................25

   Management and Work
   Machines at Work
   Animals at Work
   True Work

- 1. - The wonderful Human Person –
Human Nature and the Christian Manager. 29
   Human Work
   The Person
   The Souls
   The Human Soul
   Human Acts

- 2. Human Nature and the Behavioral Sciences 36
   A Matter of Knowledge
   Philosophy of Science
   The Sciences and Ethics

- 3. - Destination Happiness - Ultimate End and the
Christian Manager...43
   Common and Erroneous View of Human Needs
   The End of Human actions
   Ultimate ends
   Christian ultimate end
   Prescribed patterns of behavior
   Ends and choices
   Ends and love

- 4. Behavioral Sciences and Human Needs................51

Models of Human needs
Of Particular Needs
Need for Safety and Security
Need for Love and Need for Affiliation
Need for self-actualization, for Achievement and Creativity
Psychometrics and their use

- 5. - Preparing the Outfit of the Voyager
- Growth in Holiness and the Christian Manager. 59
Kant and the Ethics of Pure Reason
The Goodness of God
The Objectivity of Christian Ethics
Personal Sanctification
Following Christ
Voyage to the Supernatural order
Actual Grace and the gifts of the Holy Spirit
The Infused Virtues
Faith Hope and Charity

- 6. - The Most Precious Gear
- The Virtues and the Christian Manager..................................72
The Nature of Virtues
Characteristics of Habits
On Acquiring Habits
Virtues and Vices

- 7. Prudence...77
Modern Dangers to Prudence
Nature of Prudence
Prudence in Business
Prudence and Conscience
Prudence and Business Ethics

- 8. – Justice...86
Justice and Rights
Justice as Virtue
Justice and the "Other"
Justice as Obligation
The Three Justices
Justice and Private Property
Justice in Business
The Just Manager

- 9. – Fortitude..101
The Nature of Fortitude-Courage
The Parts of Fortitude
Courage and Work
The Courageous Manager
The Courageous Corporation

- 1O – Temperance..108
The Nature of Temperance
Sex and Food
Curiosity
The Temperate Manager
The Temperate Corporation

- 11. - What kind of Action - The Nature of Work......................116
The Four Parts of Work
The Relative Importance of the Parts
The Four Dimensions of Work   The Christian Aspect of Work
Work, Justice and Mercy
Work and Providence
The Work of the Manager

Part II: - The Busy Village - Work and the Managing of
Organizations and Businesses..123

- 1. - Double Perfection and Sweet Success - The nature of business..123
Business as the Establishment of New Work
Business as Environment for Work
External Cooperation with a Business
Marketing Function: a Financial Imperative
Marketing Function: a Social Imperative
Marketing function: source of perfection
Developing the Marketing Imperative
The Second Justification of Business
The Second Business Perfection
Innovation and Change

- 2. - In the Image of Man - The nature and function of
organizations..138
What is an Organization
The Functional Levels

Vertical Divisions and Mission
The Hierarchical Levels
The Operational Level
The Strategic Level
The Transactual Level
The Soul of the Organization
The Problems of Organizations
Strategic Problems with Organizational Structure
Strategic Problems with Long-term Planning
Strategic Problems with Rational Management

- 3. - A Wheel within a wheel - The social impact of organizations......153
What Organizations Owe Human Beings
Promoting Human Dignity
The Christian Status of Organizational Employees
The Christian Function of Organizational Employees
Only Status Viable for Organizations
Promoting Human Dignity Outside the Organization
Responsibilities of Ownership
Ethics of Organizations vs. Business Ethics
Organizations Unethical by Design
Organizational Ethics more Fundamental than Business Ethics
The Roots of Business and Organizational Ethics
The business organization as good citizen
Mediating organizations

- 4. - What is our Agenda ? - Strategic planning for organizations......174
Strategy and Vision
Strategic Planning and Managerial Style
Strategic Plan and the Organizational Brain
Strategic Plan and the Organizational Will
The Snake-shaped Strategic Process
More Strategic Resolve
Military Strategy
Boldness of Vision
Idealized Planning
Strategic Planning as a Permanent Activity
Strategy and Operations

- 5. - Checking the course - Controls......188
The Black Fords
Controls as Navigation System

Controls of Corporate Structure
Long-term vs. Short-term Control
Controls and Strategy
Specific Controls
Controls as Police
Controls and Correction
Controls as Re-organization
Reaction against Standard Setting
Reaction against Evaluations
Reaction against Correction
The Nature of Human Resources
Work Design and Human Performance

- 6. - How to Think - Decision Making and the Staff function............201
Japanese Decision-Making
The Social Impact of Decisions
Society Impact Decisions
Metaphysics and Social Sciences
Decision-Making and Mathematics
Epistemology and Decision-Making
Human Acts and Decision-Making
Prudence and Decision-Making
The Staff Function

- 7. - Causes of the Business Organization................................218

Part III: - People at Work –
Organizations and the Managing of People...............................221

- 1. - Who is in charge here - Authority of Managers.....................221
Authority and Similar concepts
The nature of authority
The Christian view of Authority
Authority, Nature and Grace
Fundamental issue about authority: God
Fundamental issue about authority: Property

- 2. - Variety of Persons - Psychology and Management...................231
Personality in Management
Personalities and Psychology
The assumptions of Secular Psychology
Personality and Charity

ix

Overcoming Personality Differences
Managing Different Personalities

- 3. - What is going on here - Perception and Management............... 242
Flawed Perception
Sensation and Perception
Species
Perceptual Selectivity
Perceptual Organization
The ethics of advertising
The dilemma of advertising
Perception and Managers
Perception vs. Awareness

- 4. - Loving what we do - Motivation and Management.................250
Theory X and Theory Y
The Pluses and Minuses of Theory X
The Pluses and Minuses of Theory Y
First Conclusions
Qualifiers of Theory Y
The brave new manager-less worker
The brave new moral athlete worker
Motivation and ESOPs
The basis of workers motivation
Education
Decentralization
Beyond the basic conditions of workers motivation
Motivation and Love

- 5. - Corporate Solomons - Conflict resolution and Management.........264
Conflicts within and conflicts between
Conflicts over what
Types of Organizational conflicts
Conflicts over goals
Conflicts over means
Managing conflicts

- 6. - Picking the Best and Brightest
- Selection and Appraisal of Personnel......................................272
Subjectivity
The search for objectivity
Tests and more tests

Emotions and making a living
The Right to Subjectivity
Hiring and the Christian Manager
Business Ethics and Employee Evaluation

Part IV: - The Dynamics of Management
- Integrating the People in the Organization............................285

- 1. - Rainbow - Individual Value Systems and Corporate..............286
Value Systems
The nature of values
The exchangeability of values
Systems of values
Ethics, attitudes and behavior
System of values and worldview
Given values and desired values
Values System and Action Plans
Values System and Life Plans
Difference in Value Systems
Domains of Reference
Understanding and Interest
Individual values and Organizational values
The Organizational Values Information System

- 2. - Following the flow
- Change : The Development of Human Resources
and the Development of Organizations....................................301
Change and human beings
Change in organizations
Personal change and value systems
Change, virtues and values systems
Change management in individuals - the "scientific view
Managing change in organizations -Organization Development
Sensitivity training
Sensitivity training as business evil
Sensitivity training and Society
Organizational change - a true Value approach

- 3. - Each age has its problems
- Managing the Growing organization 318
Growth and development
The five phases of growth

Phase 1 - Creativity
Phase 2 - Direction
Phase 3 - Delegation
Phase 4 - Coordination
Phase 5 - Collaboration
Pattern not immutable
The issue of small corporations
Virtues
Theology of work and management

- 4. - The Sky is the Limit - Innovative Management.........................328
The Cortisone story
The process of invention
Virtues and invention
Inventing and thinking
Inventing, value systems and ethics
The management of invention
Institutionalizing creativity
Innovation
The difficulties of innovation'
Breakthroughs
Innovative management

- 5. - Providing Objects of Admiration – Leadership.............................345
Great men
Other theories
Situational theories
Path-goal leadership theory
Scientists' angst
The managerial grid
Back to basics
Authority and society
Authority, Society and society's goal
The leader's virtues
Morale
Born leaders
Forming leaders
Calvinism and business

- 6. - Trail Blazing - Entrepreneurship......................................363
The nature of entrepreneurship
The entrepreneurial philosophy of life

Bias against entrepreneurs
Paradoxes and Christianity
Psychological traits of entrepreneurs
Entrepreneurial perception
Generalists
Effectiveness and efficiency
Need to act
Blacks and Koreans
The parable of the talents
Different sorts of talents
Liberalitas
Cultivating the economic talents
Fear and entrepreneurship
Providence and entrepreneurship
The entrepreneurial imperative

CONCLUSION..383

Perfection, efficacy and the business life
Management and morality
Capitalism
Cardinal Ratzinger – Pope Benedict XVI
The Church and Capitalism
What Adam Smith really said
Two justices
General justice
A new economic theory
Conclusions for policy
Churchmen
Antonism

REFERENCES AND FURTHER READINGS.....................403

INDEX..411

ABOUT THE AUTHOR..440

Ethics and management

"Ethics offers a necessary descriptive conceptual framework for management. Ethics helps understand what management really is. But ethics is also descriptive in a different plane: most managers, most of the time, and as they perform most of their tasks are quite ethical."

"Ethics on the other hand, also offers a necessary prescriptive norm for management: the more a businessman, manager or employee is ethical at work, the more he will be effective."

Ethics and the economy

"The more businesspeople, managers and employees are ethical, are well versed in the ethical content of all business decisions and are actively seeking to perfect themselves in the virtues on the job, the more successful their personal businesses, the better working the economic system and the more prosperous a country."

Ethics and virtues

The cardinal virtues, the central axis of this book, belong to the Church because they belong to human common sense and wisdom. To oppose the re-introduction of the virtues in management under the argument that they would introduce "religion" in secular matters is poor reasoning. It is inaccurate and is proof of poor scholarship. It would further cause a tremendous loss as it would suppress a very successful and tested approach that helps human beings and belongs to human patrimony, that of Catholics and other Christians, that of Jews and that of pagans.

PREFACE

"The fifth major component of the general theory of management is value theory. Reduced to more commonly accepted terminology this refers to the theory of business responsibility or the social responsibilities of business enterprises. It is considerably broader than the term 'business ethics' commonly implies. It embraces the ethical implications of business enterprise but goes beyond that. Value theory has yet to make its major contribution to management science. There are few names for us to mention in this field for it is a very underdeveloped field of inquiry. Outstanding contributors are Peter Drucker, Richard Eels, Clarence Walton and C. West Churchman."

"As value theory evolves it will be its major task to provide a set of values which will (1) define management as a science and not simply subjective art; (2) define the ends and goals of business enterprise and management (so far all we have asked of science is that it help define the means of achieving culturally prescribed ends and goals); (3) define the social and public responsibilities of management and business; and (4) integrate the diverse themes found in management principles, human relations, decision theory, and behavioral science. The major function of value theory will be to integrate the other major components and weave their themes into a coherent body of management theory.

"This is obviously a key and strategic role that we are assigning to value theory. The lag we witness in the development of value theory, however, is the primary reason why a general theory of management has not yet been developed."

W. C. Frederick,

"The Next Development in Management Science: A General Theory," Journal of the Academy of Management, Sept.1963.

Professor Frederick had the vision of a Value theory of management. He believed that the place this theory would have in the whole body of management would have to be preeminent. We agree.

We must acknowledge that decades after these words, very little has been done in the way of developing this value theory.

Our proposition is that all attempts to develop such theory have been unsuccessful because all have been too shy to handle the matter as required.

First, the values we are talking about are not plucked out of thin air or borrowed from some obscure but academically revered thinker. They are values commonly shared, or at least recognized, in the Western world. They are Christian values.

Second, these Christian values must be articulated and systematically presented in a manner that is consistent so they can relate, without being forced, with the major themes of management. Such a system exists: it is the philosophical system developed by Thomas Aquinas.

Here is the Creed of John D. Rockefeller, Jr.

"I believe in the supreme worth of the individual and in his right to life, liberty, and pursuit of happiness"

"I believe that every right implies a responsibility; every opportunity an obligation; every possession, a duty.

"I believe that the law was made for man and not man for the law; that government is the servant of the people and not their master.

"I believe in the dignity of labor, whether with head or hand; that the world owes no man a living, but that it owes everyman an opportunity to make a living.

"I believe that thrift is essential to well-ordered living and that economy is a prime requisite of a sound financial structure. whether in government, business, or personal affairs.

"I believe that truth and justice are fundamental to an enduring social order.

"I believe in the sacredness of a promise, that a man's word should be as good as his bond; that character -- not wealth or power or position -- is of supreme worth.

"I believe that the rendering of useful service is the common duty of mankind and that only in the purifying fire of sacrifice is the dross of selfishness consumed and the greatness of the human soul set free.

"I believe in an all-wise and all-loving God, named by whatever name, and that the individual's highest fulfillment, greatest happiness, and wildest usefulness are to be found in living in harmony with His will.

"I believe that love is the greatest thing in the world; that it alone can overcome hate; that right can and will triumph over might."

The breadth of the Creed that this great captain of Industry claims to be pertinent to business life is impressive. The elements of this Creed that are not commonly treated in modern management manuals are also noteworthy.

It is necessary, to have a framework, or philosophy, within which to place the this Creed's elements and then to place them in relation to modern propositions of management. When this framework is completed, it is necessary to show how movement from one element to another is possible.

The philosophy of St. Thomas Aquinas is the closest to an official philosophical system for over a billion Roman Catholics world-wide. It has solid roots in the past as it borrows heavily from the wisdom of Greece and the pre-Christian world. It shares a vibrant life today under the name of neo-thomism. One eloquent witness of the life and potency of neo-thomism comes from surprising quarters. Official Soviet texts of philosophy ascribe to neo-thomism what amounts to the philosophical guardianship of the "general processes of the development of Western ideology in the XXth century."

This book does not pretend to deliver a wholly developed Value theory of management. Much academic work, philosophical as well as scientific, would be necessary before such presentation could be available.

The book only tries to give thumb-size presentations of key points that a neo-thomistic theory of management would have to include. It also endeavors to offer a panoramic view of the subject.

Hence some points are presented without discussion, while others are more developed which may not seem to be central to the argumentation. But this writer has found that the latter points really need to be cleared up.

The fall of the Soviet empire has open the eyes of the world and has revealed that their economic system was not workable. However, the "free market" system has not yet won over the hearts of everybody. The moral case for this free-market system has not been properly made. This book intends to bring heavy ammunition to eventually win this fight.

Indeed, the subject matter of this book touches the raw power of a nation to grow and develop starting with what really motivates each individual. Each one of us has had the experience of commenting casually to an otherwise calm person about a matter of politics or religion with explosive results. This book is aiming at the same trigger mechanism. It relates to the most private and protected inner powers of individuals to be motivated, creative and productive, as well as to the method of channeling these human powers in well-designed organizations.

In its death throes, the Soviet Union attempted to liberalize its political ideology in the hope of boosting the national economy. In China, the relatively fast advances of the economy in some regional pockets and segments of the population have triggered a popular outburst and demand for greater democracy. It is obvious to impartial observers that democracy and greater economic development require free markets and freedom for managers and organization employees to make individual decisions.

It is no coincidence that the most prominent groups demanding more freedom in many Communist nations are religious groups, most of them Christians. Communist governments should realize that within these groups is nurtured the true seed of their country' genuine development. This book aim at channeling the intellectual and spiritual energies of these religious groups more directly toward the goals of economic development.

The Third World would also have much to gain from the perennial ideas presented in this book. Experts now acknowledge that previous development activities, conducted through public programs and under public authority have, in fact, achieved little.

Mr. Hernando de Soto, in his book "The Other Path" has shown that the solution must reside in the economic and managerial empowerment of each private individual of the Third World, no matter how puny his efforts or how trivial his projects seem to Westerners. We believe that Third World entrepreneurs are perfectly capable of assimilating and implementing the ideas presented herein. I have long thought that Church leaders, including Catholic bishops, in poor countries, should delve on these concepts and educate the souls of their people to promote economic growth and political harmony, rather than letting socialist ideas under the form of "liberation theology" prevail and keep the people and these nations down.

However the book has primarily been written for individuals in our world, whether undergraduate students or seasoned executives; whether business tycoons or persons who are only concerned with "making a living."

Many in our Western are worried about the economic competitions from Japan, China and other Asian countries. It is high time we understand that the Asians succeeded because they rely on basic and profound values to motivate themselves in their managerial and industrial efforts. If we are too shy to refer to, much less pursue, our deepest Christian ideals to direct our behavior, then we have already given up in the competition. Ironically, these Christian values are what made us the economic superpower the Japanese wanted to copy. If we return to these values, then we cannot but prevail again.

We know executives with great experience in the business world who have resolved to study the manner in which the two powers of God and Mammon interact. They make this study their chief interest.

We know also very religiously oriented individuals with a great love for Our Lord and a great concern for their families who are seeking some light on the proper attitude to adopt in the world of work. They can find in these pages reasons for performing effectively in the secular world while at the same time making great strides in their spiritual life and contributing to the development of their family life.

In this Western world and upon the end of this century, ethical issues and problems of civilizations have been entwined and are more prominent than ever. A new affluence and new technical advances may be partly responsible for these troubled times. Individuals who are affluent or enjoy personally an impressive scientific knowledge have eagerly accepted and adopted the perennial ideas presented in these pages.

In management as in life many problems are properly handled when given the proper priority. More than anything, this book will have been successful if it improves, ever so little, the priority of its readers and the culture of its time.

It is our hope that many will see the powerful potential of the ideas set forth in this work and become interested in developing them, and to make them better known, whether in the academic world of business schools, schools of philosophy and theology, or in the practical world of businesses. We would be most happy to correspond with such individuals and bring our assistance to their projects.

The First part of the book starts with a review of philosophical and theological notions that are absolutely necessary to understand the more technical presentations which follow.

Further, we have taken the ideas presented a few steps beyond Church teachings to arrive at a full blown theology of work. In this manner, philosophical and theological concepts will later mesh smoothly with the tenets of the discipline of management.

Thus even the readers who possess a good grounding in philosophy and theology would gain in reading this part and see how it evolves for the purpose of readying themselves to study issues of management from a Christian perspective.

In particular this first part deals squarely with the conflict between science and philosophy as well as theology as they each claim they know man best.

The second part considers issues and themes of the sociology of business and of work. It shows how it is possible to extend, and still respect, the elements of a theology of work from the individual to the collective dimension.

The third part then reexamines individuals, qua individuals, busy at work within business organizations. We reexamined the familiar themes of the psychology of management from our Christian perspective.

The fourth part puts it all together studying individuals and organizations impacting on each other while they evolve together and even re-generate their mission, outlook and structure.

The Conclusion re-viewing the import of what has been covered, presents new propositions for businessmen, managers and employees, naturally, but also for the hierarchical Church, political analysts and citizens at large.

The author acknowledges that he was sitting on the shoulders of giants, and grateful to them, when he conceived and put together these theses that are but strands of ideas that these giants previously developed so well and so conveniently for our purpose.

At the Wharton School, I want to thank Hasan Ozbekhan, Russell Ackoff who might be a little surprised of how their ideas turned out, considering that neither is Christian. I want to thank also Ross Webber and Andy Van de Ven who helped me through that difficult ordeal. Among my Dominican friends, I am most indebted to Fr. Bart de la Torre, OP, who always supported me on these dangerous waters and Fr. Pierre Conway, OP, who looked in the entire manuscript for errors against the teachings of St. Thomas. I want to thank Jean-Loup Dherse and Capt. Tad Stanwick USN (Ret.) who supported me in insisting on the relevance and the necessity of this approach in the business realm. I am most grateful to Fr. Bertrand de Margerie, S.J. for the time he took looking through the manuscript and his precious suggestions.

I am most thankful to Dean Jude Dougherty of Catholic University of America School of Philosophy, Fr. James Downey, OSB, Executive Director of the Institute on Religious Life, Dr. William May, a theologian greatly admired by the Pope, and Fr. Michael Scanlan, TOR, President of the Franciscan University of Steubenville for their most precious and insightful suggestions and support.

The manuscript would not have turned into a book without the help of several friends. To Veronica Frazier, I am most indebted who revised the whole manuscript and made it fit for public consumption. Fran Griffin should take much credit as she edits my newsletter and has tried to modify my style.

I am the sole responsible for any error, weak spots or confusion that still remains.

PART 1.

1. - The Who and the What -- The Christian Manager and Work.

Management and Work

The first understanding of "work" by managers is that it is an activity, done by others, that they are to understand, supervise and organize. Indeed, the job of managers is to ensure that the work being done under their authority and responsibility is well defined, that it is designed to attain a given objective, that it is correctly planned, structured and implemented.

This is not the only reason why managers should be interested in work. Indeed, the job of manager itself is work. It is a specialized type of work.

To understand this special type of work we need first to understand the general nature of work.

Because "management" is also some type of work -- just as much work as the work of the employees -- the comprehension of that fact by managers helps them understand their employees better and bring them closer to the people who work with and for them. It helps them relate with their employees; it helps them see the bridges that exist between managers and employees. And it helps them communicate better with these employees; it helps them use these bridges so that they can have exchanges. By understanding the common elements and objectives of their different works, manager-employee relationships will be well adjusted and productive.

In addition, "management" includes an educational and training function. Managers need to educate and train their employees to understand what they are doing and to perform their work better.

When managers properly educate and train their employees on the nature of work, and the similarity between the manager's work and the employee's work, several good results can be expected:

1/ solidarity within the organization between managers and employees 2/ an understanding on the part of the employee of the function of management. In turn, when the employee understands management, he will better understand 1/ the authority and responsibilities of his or her direct supervisor, also 2/ how to help one's supervisor to meet these responsibilities, and hopefully be rewarded for it, and 3/ how to qualify him or herself to handle his or her superior's job and earn the promotion to replace this supervisor.

Now, what is the nature of work? Does what we understand by "work" in everyday language help us to understand the nature of work?

Machines at Work

Power Station No. 10 in the Rocky Mountains sits on top of a major dam. In the control room, engineers sit on padded chairs and seem to spend most of their time exchanging jokes. Once in a while, though, they glance at the dials in front of them. Most of the time, they seem satisfied with what they see, but occasionally they proceed to turn a knob here and push a lever there.

Should we conclude that these engineers are not working? The huge pumps below are transferring tons of water from one chamber to the next. Sensors are registering pressures at different water depths, and informing the colossal gates about how much water they should release to maintain a pre-determined pressure. Other dials indicate how much electricity is being produced when the masses of water push on the blades of the turbines and make them spin.

These machines are producing enormous amounts of work, converting hydraulic power into electric power. The science of physics has developed a method of measuring work; thus we know that the more the masses of water are shifted from one place to another, the more work is being done.

According to this mathematical definition of work, the human engineers who only, occasionally do something as simple or seemingly effortless as pushing a level or turning a knob, are not doing much work.

Animals at work

A line of 5OO ants is being stretched all the way between the small anthill that they call home and the first line of bushes dozens of feet away. The ants' activity is very purposeful. They leave their home, head for the bushes. There they cut into precise pieces some new tender leaves that their leadership has found particularly appealing. They hold these leaves between their mandibles and head back home in a single line. The piece of leaf is so large over their body that they look like sailboats. Once arrived at the anthill, they discharge their leaves and return, again in a single, very orderly line, towards the bushes and the leaves.

Are these ants working? They may not extend objectively a very great amount of work as the pieces of leaves are so tiny that they do not amount to much. But shouldn't we consider the relative weight of these leaves to the weight of these ants' bodies?

Besides, the ants are not machines. Clearly they have an objective and that they are capable of taking initiatives when necessary to ensure that the objectives are met. Where there is an accident on the transport line -- a larger animal having stepped on the line and killed a number of ants -- the following ants, after a moment to appraise the situation, initiate a detour around the bodies of their dead brothers. When a burst of wind blowing on the piece of leaf makes an ant topple over and let go of its burden, the insect gets back on its feet, reloads its cargo and returns to the procession. These ants must certainly be working. They have an objective, and are able to correct any problems that would prevent them from attaining it.

True Work

In truth these machines and these ants are not working. The Holy Father made it plain:

"Work is one of the characteristics that distinguish man from the rest of creatures, whose activity for sustaining their lives cannot be called work. Only man is capable of work and only man works, at the same time by work occupying his existence on earth. Thus work bears a particular mark of man and of humanity, the mark of a person operating within a community of persons. And this mark decides its interior characteristics; in a sense it constitutes its very nature."

Pope John Paul II's encyclical "On Human Work" (Laborem Exercens), 1981

Maybe we are just accustomed to think that machines work and that animals work. What the Pope tells us is that there is really no comparison between human work and the work of animals and machines. In other words, we cannot draw many useful conclusions about human work when we study the work of machines and animals. If we really want to understand something about human work, then we should understand something more about what it is to be human.

1. - The Wonderful Human Person -- Human Nature and the Christian Manager.

Human Work

We are accustomed to say that, for example, a horse works hard, while machines work efficiently. But the pope tells us that they do not really work. Only human beings work. We will never understand what work really is until we understand why only human beings work.

What is so special about human beings that gives true work such hidden and powerful meaning? What is it that we must understand about this human being that affects work in ways that the "work" of a machine or of an animal cannot be affected?

"Man has to subdue the earth and dominate it, because as the 'image of God' he is a person, that is to say a subjective being capable of acting in a planned and rational way, capable of deciding about himself and with a tendency to self-realization."

Pope John Paul II's encyclical "On Human Work" (Laborem Exercens), 1981

The Person

Each man, each human being, is a "person," that is to say, he is a 1) "subjective being" -- an independent individual -- 2) who can act 3) by thinking through his actions in advance, and 4) by making independent decisions, including which best course of action to take, and, 5) by so doing, this human person becomes a better person.

If that were not enough, man is a person because he is made in the "image of God." There is something divine about being a person.

Theologians suggest that human memory images the Father, human intellect images the Son and human love and will images the Holy Spirit.

Man is a person because he has a rational soul and freedom of choice. No machine, no animal can claim the same attributes.

The Souls

The ancient Greek philosopher Aristotle, who was not a Christian, gave us a true understanding of man. The best theologians, over the ages, then set this admirable, rationally derived understanding within the framework of Christian revelation.

Man is the union of a body and of a soul. The body is what we see, the soul is the principle that makes this body operate. When the soul has left the body, not only does the body not function, but the man is not a complete man, and God has provided for the resurrection of the bodies after Judgment Day.(1)

To say that man is soul and body is to say something that goes against three opinions. One opinion views the body as an instrument, a possession that can be used and abused at will.

The second opinion is that the body is some sort of appendage, possibly the vehicle for leading our lives before the departure to heaven, but nothing otherwise of great consequence.

The third opinion is that bodies and souls are somewhat loosely paired, that they are interchangeable. This false opinion has led some to the idea of reincarnation. Specific bodies and souls are on the contrary made for each other and complement each other as no other body and no other soul can. Transgenderism is an absurdity. A male has a male body and a male soul. A female has a female body and a female soul.

Now, let us take another look at the soul. Philosophers and theologians tell us that there are three classes of souls because there are three classes of living beings; viz. the vegetative soul, the animal soul and the human, or rational, soul. Each soul has its own proper manner of operation.

The vegetative soul has the function of growth, nourishment and reproduction. The animal soul, in addition to the latter functions, has passions and mobility. The human soul – in addition to the animal soul - has reason, or intellect -- i.e., the capacity to think -- and a will -- i.e., the capacity to make choices. A human being is a person because he has both an intellect and a will.

Because it is intellectual, the human soul is immortal, according to the same principle that ideas do not die and cannot be killed. The human soul needs the body to grow and develop but can exist independently of the body. In particular, the mind needs the brain to grow and develop but will be independent of the brain after death.

Vegetative soul	Animal soul	Human soul
Growth	Growth	Growth
Nourishment	Nourishment	Nourishment
Reproduction	Reproduction	Reproduction
	Passions	Passions
	Mobility	Mobility
		Intellect
		Will

Figure 1

Thus one important notion is that the different souls, within the three classes, are like Russian dolls for which the next smaller soul is contained in the next larger soul. Thus an animal's soul includes the qualities of a vegetative soul. Indeed, an animal enjoys all the functions of a plant: the animal grows, feeds and reproduces itself.

The Human Soul

The soul of a human being incorporates again the functions of a brute animal soul (and naturally also the functions of a vegetative soul). A human being is mobile like an animal. It has passions such as fear, anger, sexual desires like an animal.

A very important notion about souls is that a living creature must use the functions of his higher soul to function correctly. Indeed, a plant just stays where it was born limited to reproduce itself by scattering its seeds in the wind or having bees pick up the pollen off its flowers. A plant also receives its nourishment from the ground where it stands and its water from the rain that falls at its feet.

A brute animal has to use its mobility to feed and reproduce itself. It has to hunt. It has to fight to keep a territory. It has to run to survive from predators. The animal must seek a mate and have relations with this mate.

The animal also uses its "passions", e.g., fear, anger, desires. Instincts trigger fear in the lamb at the sight of the wolf; the fear commands the lamb to flee. The female of the species knows anger when some predator threatens her litter. Hunger pains motivate brute animals to graze, hunt or otherwise seek food. The animal must utilize its natural function of mobility and its passions to survive as an individual and as a species.

Man also has to utilize his higher functions. He cannot rely on his natural physical defenses to stay alive.

Prehistoric Man, who had neither claws nor beak nor fangs, nor instinct, had to use his intellect to hunt and defend himself against a world of wild creatures. He did admirably well. He prevailed. Likewise modern man, by natural design, cannot use his mobility and his passions to subdue

32

other men, or nature, to survive in the "civilized" world.

Man's reason must be in control of his body, his passions and his acts. Man's passions are essentially similar to the passions of the brute animals. He feels pain, fears, has anger, desires, etc... However, to control those passions properly, man needs to govern them with the guiding light of his rationality and by exercising his will.

Men and women have been designed to behave rationally. Thus the moral law stems from natural law: the lower functions of the human person must be controlled by his higher functions. For men and women to behave otherwise represents a defect of operation within them. Further, for humans to behave like brute animals, places them lower than brute animals. Brute animals are supposed to behave like brute animals by design. Humans who behave like brute animals are functioning under a corrupted operation of their own nature.

Controlling one's passions means properly using or suppressing them depending upon the requirements of a given situation, according to rational principles.

It is all right to have anger when we have witnessed an injustice and to use this anger, and the adrenaline that comes with it, in order to give us the strength to perform the acts necessary to correct this injustice, provided we are not otherwise uncharitable in doing so. It is all right to have fear in a certain situation, so that we are extremely prudent in that situation, provided we remain rational and not let this fear paralyze us.

It is all right to have desires as long as they are under the control of our intellect. "Under control" does not mean repression of the passions; rather, it means operation of these passions according to reason.

We need to satisfy our appetite for food every day, because our body, as well as our social nature (indeed eating in company is a very important social act) requires it. It is all right to satisfy sexual desires with one's spouse when mutually desired, provided that there is openness to new life.

We know that desires for food must be satisfied on a daily basis. However, desires for sexual contact, which exist for the reproduction of the species, can have their satisfaction postponed indefinitely by any one member of the species without harm to the individual or the species, provided other members of the species produce sufficient offspring. The high level of emotionalism attached to the so-called "sexual revolution" has done much to blur this clear-cut reality.

It is biologically factual that man operates better when his rationality controls the manifestations of his animal soul. It is also morally true.

Human Acts (Sum. Theo. Ia.IIae Q. 6-21)

Human work falls under the categories of human acts. What do philosophers mean by human act? They mean that this act is a voluntary act.

Human acts require the operation of the will. In other words, a simple bodily operation like yawning, in that sense, is not a human act because it is involuntary, although it is indeed an act performed by a human being. Acts performed by humans which are not human acts, like yawning, have no bearing on the morality of the person. However, they are good in themselves for they contribute to the well-being of the human individual.

A voluntary act is an act in which the human being chooses. This person will choose a thing or a course of action which is preferable to him over another thing or course of action.

John, the mail clerk, is running out of stamps, but he still has many first class cents stamps. He decides to stamp all the mail with several first class stamps.

Situation 1: John is choosing to use only first class stamps because he does not want to go out in the rain to the post office.

Situation 2: John is choosing to use first class stamps rather than do nothing because the mail has to leave in 3 minutes.

In situation 1, John preferred to use the first class stamps instead of going to the post office in the rain to get the proper stamps. In situation 2, John preferred to use the stamps rather than miss the deadline. We may say that in Situation 1 what motivates John is the aversion of discomfort and the rain; in Situation 2, it is the desire to meet the deadline. Each person chooses what he loves over what he does not love or loves less; if he loves properly, he will choose well.

The will is thus called the "appetite of the intellect," for it prompts the human being to seek what he perceives as a good thing or act, what he "hungers for" so to speak.

Neither the rain nor the deadline limits the choices of John. They are simply factors to be considered before choosing. The rain in Situation 1 presented John with the choice of buying new stamps or using basic first class stamps. He made the choice independently. He did not have to choose to use the first class stamps. A voluntary act is a free act in which circumstances do not interfere directly with our freedom to choose.

Further, a human act has a moral dimension. It is a good act if it measures up to sound reason. Human acts that fall short of what they ought to be are, to the extent of their failure to measure up, evil acts.

If John, in Situation 1, does not buy stamps in the rain for the simple purpose of avoiding personal discomfort, then his act of using first class stamps is evil. If, in the same situation, he reasonably considers that the risks of catching a cold or get soaking wet do not warrant the saving of a few cents, his act is good. The intention of the agent and the quality of the act are essential elements in the voluntary aspect of an act.

Using first class stamps and walking in the rain are not essentially evil acts. Therefore, the circumstances of this type of act are important to determine their moral content. However, there are other acts that are evil in the absolute, like killing an innocent life. Killing an innocent life is an intrinsically evil act.

As the moral quality of the act supersedes the intention of the agent or the circumstances, killing an innocent life is evil in all circumstances. Intention and circumstances may modify the responsibility of the agent but do not change the objective fact that an intrinsically evil act is evil.

Lack of intention, like in the case of an accident, definitely reduces responsibility. Misguided intention does not reduce responsibility. The intention to kill an innocent life to achieve a good -- like abortion for the sake of the mother's mental health -- does not lessen the responsibility of the agent at all. Evil means cannot be used this way to attain good ends.

The sphere of operation of the agent cannot solely define the morality of human acts. They are also dependent on a more comprehensive and objective understanding of what is right and wrong in God's creation. We need to preserve innocent life as it is a gift of God. Only He can take back what he has given.

2. Human Nature and the Behavioral Sciences

The vision of human nature presented to us by theology is not the only one offered to our study. Scientists today also study human nature within the behavioral sciences, a term coined in the 1950's at the Ford foundation.

The behavioral sciences include anthropology, psychology and sociology. The behavioral sciences, in turn, are part of the social sciences, along with economics, history and political science. Generally, the behavioral sciences are defined as the "scientific study of human behavior."(2)

The sub-discipline that takes the conclusions of the behavioral sciences and applies them to the world of management is called "organization behavior." Most books on management that are used in business schools are written within the field of organization behavior. Most popular self-help books for managers also draw heavily on organization behavior ideas and literature, even if they approach their subject and treat it in a much lighter manner. We are thinking of books like "In Search of Excellence" and "The One Minute Manager", etc.

Behavioral scientists also define their field by its scientific methodology. They contend that only they have a scientific approach to human behavior in work settings, much better than a philosopher, a theologian or a simple practicing manager can ever gain.

Because the behavioral sciences are so pervasive, it is important for a Christian manager to understand where they fit in relation with his faith and his practical experience in the field of management.

Basically these sciences claim that philosophy and theology are of little help in understanding management and people in managerial settings. The behavioral sciences are still imprinted with the anti-religious bias of their founders who include people like Freud, in psychology, and Durkheim and Auguste Comte in sociology.

A matter of knowledge

These thinkers also defined themselves as "positivists," that is their approach to knowledge is that nothing exists which cannot be positively experienced. While this is a good approach for some types of scientific research, positivism went beyond and was really a philosophy of life. Nothing exists, they claimed, which cannot be investigated by their methodology. This is a narrower view than the philosophy of materialism. As we know, the most famous ideology based on materialism is Communism. Positivism is even narrower than Communism in its understanding of the human experience.

Apart from philosophy and theology, the bias of behavioral scientists negates a large section of human life and experience.

Should behavioral scientists be consistent, they should admit that their approach would promote the idea that art does not really exist because it is so subjective. Similarly, the legal process and the way it gathers proof has a doubtful utility, because legal proofs, such as eye-witness accounts or deductive conclusions are not valid for positivists. These proofs cannot be repeated by other researchers in the same field. Thus their conclusions cannot be granted universal validity.

Perhaps if the behavioral sciences accepted eye-witnesses as elements of proof they would have to accept the witnesses of the life of Christ. Since they do not, they can dismiss the data of revelation as irrelevant to their methods of research.

Even those subjects that the behavioral researchers accept are not left unscathed by their methods. For their research method often suffers from the defect of "reductionism." The concepts that the scientific methodology of the behavioral scientists set itself to test often need be simplified to the extreme. They are "reduced" to very simple ideas; for example, a variable proxy for how "open" a management style is may be the angle, the number of degrees, in the opening of his office door. If the door is opened wide, the manager has a very open style of management; if it is very narrow, he has a closed style of management. This reductionism casts a grave doubt on whether the studies are really meaningful.

Should the Christian manager throw away all studies done by modern management scientists then? No, because as in all complex human matters, including the behavioral sciences, there is a mixture of good and bad. What is important is to replace organizational behavior in its proper perspective and to develop for ourselves an intellectual "filter" which will help us tell the good studies and insights on management from the bad.

Philosophy of Science

The discipline in which a scientist reflects on what it is to be a scientist and perform scientific activities is called philosophy of science. Interestingly, scientists in the natural sciences, like physics and chemistry, geology and astronomy are usually more interested in the philosophy of science than behavioral scientists.(3)

It may be that since natural scientists do not have the human being as the object of their research, they feel that they have to return to what at least one human being, knows and how he knows it.

The behavioral scientists tend already to have answered these questions by using the methodology of their own disciplines for this purpose.

Let us now study the distinctions between the philosophy of psychology and the science of psychology. Both methods of inquiry have the same object, which is man. But the science is interested only in the behavior, potentialities and modes of operations of men. The philosophy is interested in acquiring knowledge of the most fundamental elements of man and what distinguishes men from other things that exist. The science of psychology studies chiefly what man does. The philosophy of psychology studies chiefly what man is.

There are also differences in methods. Philosophy is grounded on data that are part of common experience. Science uses data drawn from special experience, in particular through the method of scientific experiment. The tools used by philosophy are that of common sense; that is, they are reasoning tools that anyone can utilize. The tools of science are specialized tools, like a microscope, a spectrograph or statistical methods, for which special training is required.

Philosophy asks the more fundamental questions about man: where he comes from, what is his relationship with the rest of the universe, what is his real nature. But some particular questions may be asked about men which science is concerned with: do men enjoy working in the ABC company? Would program X make men more efficient at their job?

A parenthesis: theology takes up the mode of discourse of philosophy but introduces the data of Revelation. Therefore, when philosophy asks: where is the origin of man, theology answers: he is a creature of God. But theology picks up again the philosophical discourse when it goes on to compare this human creature with other creatures and with nature and with God. The interpretation of the Bible always goes hand in hand with a philosophy, whether it is simplistic or very advanced, or anywhere in the middle.

A note of warning here: the modern decline of the discipline of philosophy has tended to make us view many human questions as theological or religious questions. Thus, the question of the existence of God is viewed as a theological question but it really is a philosophical question. It belongs to the sub-field of philosophy called theodicy. Theology gives this question on the existence of God specific answers.

God can be discussed without making the discussion a religious discussion. In particular, the question of the existence of God belongs in the philosophy of science, on the origin and purpose of the universe. However, it is the teaching of Aquinas that many elements of knowledge that could be acquired independently of revelation by only a limited number of persons, over a long time, and with an admixture of error, have been revealed by God for the greater benefit of all.

Returning to philosophical psychology and scientific psychology, there are two spheres of research about man.

Historically, all scientific studies have grown out of philosophy. When a new narrow set of questions is asked about man, a new behavioral science is created. For example the question: "What are the actions of man in society?" has led to the development of sociology. But only philosophy can answer the basic questions: "What is the nature of man?" Therefore, the addition of all the specialized sciences together can never suffice to respond to basic questions on the nature of man, because the questions do not belong to the sphere of their inquiry.

The Sciences and Ethics

One very important conclusion on the distinction between what the behavioral sciences can teach us about man at work and what philosophy and theology can teach us is that ethics has no place in the behavioral sciences.

Ethics is a discipline of philosophy and is concerned about what man should do, how he should behave, in view of what he is. The behavioral sciences only analyze how man is already behaving and what circumstances may modify the way he is behaving. The sciences can thus modify human conduct and behavior from the perspective of what is called "human engineering," never from perspective grounded in genuine ethical concerns.

41

"Business Ethics" is a new discipline in business schools that purports to make students more aware of ethical issues in management. Unfortunately, it is taught after the other disciplines of management are taught. It comes like an afterthought: "Oh, well, dear students, I almost forgot: make your decisions as competent managers but please do not forget to behave ethically." The error here is that ethics, and philosophy, comes after science when it should be the other way around.

The worker and the manager should have a good philosophical understanding of what it is to be a human being at work, and of what is proper behavior for such human being, before they can be taught proper bookkeeping techniques, for example, or how to have their sales force more effective by winning more points at sales contests.

The more fundamental questions, which belong to philosophy, should be answered before the more peripheral questions that are studied by scientists.

There is a historical reason why the proper order is not kept. In pluralistic societies such as America and Europe, there is a reluctance to discuss points of philosophy and theology.

Unfortunately, because they are not discussed in public, they are not discussed in the privacy of our own homes either.

Each one needs to develop his own view about management and ethics, based on his own philosophy and belief.

Otherwise, the philosophy and beliefs of the non-believers are imposed on all of us, by default. Non-believing scientists would then impose their views on these matters by a type of cultural imperialism.

There is another set of consequences resulting from non-believing scientists imposing their values on the general population that is even more dramatic: the general population divides their lives between two sets of values: the values they have at home and the values they are taught to follow on the job.

The mental health of people at work is thus greatly endangered and the effectiveness of their work is also very impaired.

This situation in the western world needs to be compared to the situation in a country like Japan. The great majority of Japanese belong to the Shintoist religion that proclaims that their emperor is godlike and that they belong to a very special race. These are the values they hold at home. The values they are told to hold on the job are the same. Therefore they should work for the economic strength and national security of Japan and to show the supremacy of the Japanese people.

Unhindered by philosophical inconsistencies, Japanese workers and managers appear to be more effective at their jobs than Western workers and managers.

The vision of human nature is most important, for it provides us with a standard. Ethics and good behavior start with a good understanding of the standard of human behavior. No one can be expected to behave properly until he has a fairly solid understanding of what is proper behavior. The behavioral sciences, as they are now taught and articulated, have destroyed the sense of a wholesome understanding of human nature, both at the individual and at the cultural levels. These must change in order for a proper and Christian understanding of human work to prevail again.

3. Destination Happiness -- Ultimate End and the Christian Manager

A Common and Erroneous view of Human Needs

"Behavior is directed to obtain wants that will satisfy needs... We cannot see another's needs directly; we can only infer their existence by observing that people want various goods and conditions and act in order to obtain them. These wants can usually be described by the wanter; they are numerous, ranging from such material specifics as bread and chrome-plated baubles to such abstract states as security, love, prestige and power. Although wants are apparently limitless, needs are not. They are relatively few, but these basic drives motivate behavior in quest of a much larger number of wants"

"Management" Ross. A. Webber (4)

This is a typical view of modern management theorists who belong to the school of thought that Needs are what drive our behavior. There is an incredible number of errors in such a position. It will be easier to untangle the knots in this very mechanical and uninspired view of man when a balanced presentation of the ends of man is presented.

The end of human actions

A philosopher and theologian are interested in what is the "end" of man, and what is his "ultimate end." Basically, most of this question can be treated with Aristotle's book: the Nichomachean Ethics.

"Every art and every inquiry, and similarly every action and pursuit, is thought to aim at some good; and for this reason the good has rightly been declared to be that at which all things

44

aim."

Thus begins the Nichomachean Ethics, one of the two treatises of Aristotle -- who has been called The Philosopher -- on ethics. All human acts and deeds are performed with an end in view and this end is perceived by the agent -- the person who performs the act – to be good. The key word here is "perceived."

The agent may be wrong, in other words. The burglar sneaks into a house to steal some objects of value. To appropriate such objects of value is good, in the view of the burglar. But is it objectively "good"? Certainly not. It remains that even the end of this action is a type of good. What is necessary to establish whether an action is really good? For Aristotle, an action to be good must correspond to an improvement of the person performing the action. We know that, ethically, to steal does not improve the quality of being of a person; on the contrary. It is a bad action.

The action of the burglar is still aiming at a good. He wants that TV set and these jewels and they are good to him and to own them is also good. He does not care about becoming a better person.

If the burglar was really convinced that his action is bad, he would not commit it. Knowledge of the good is, for Aristotle, an important element of ethics.

Ultimate ends

Let's go back to simple acts. Why do I tie my shoes? To be dressed. Why do I want to be dressed? To be presentable when I go to work. Why do I go to work?

Human actions can be ordered in different levels of importance. Each action has an end and different ends have different levels of importance. Wouldn't it be most interesting to see what the ultimate end of human action is? Why look for an ultimate end? Because this end would subordinate all the other human actions. It would give them meaning. Also, by knowing the ultimate end of man, we could save time by ignoring unimportant goals and shooting directly at the main target.

With this idea in view, different possible ultimate ends are paraded before us by philosophers to inquire whether they could be the ultimate end. Thus health, riches, power - commonly viewed as ultimate ends by many individuals who do indeed organize their lives to attain these ends - are examined. Aristotle always comes to the same conclusion: health, riches, power are means to other ends. Health has for its end the state of being without illness. Riches satisfy ends related to hunger, aesthetics, security, entertainment, etc. Power is a means to gain what the specific power can bring.

No, concludes Aristotle, there can be only one single ultimate end. This end is happiness (eudaimonia). Happiness must exist and we understand what it is, for we have a word for it. Happiness is also defined as the satisfaction of all needs and wants and the enjoyment of all that is good.

Christian Ultimate End

Aristotle had a hard time convincing his audience of his definition of happiness. St. Thomas Aquinas, who picked up the Greek's philosophical development, brought it to its Christian conclusion. Happiness is sharing in the beatific vision; it is being face to face with God.

The ultimate end of man is to be saved and to come into the

presence of one's Lord and Creator for He only is the source of all good things. Nothing else will satisfy the soul of man until he has reached that end and can rest in that vision. The philosophy of the pagan Greek has helped to explain in logical terms the propositions of the Christian faith.

Prescribed patterns of behavior

Now that the Christian knows that his ultimate end is the beatific vision, or salvation if you prefer, what must he do to attain it? This goal is quite remote - actually it is very remote as it belongs to a different order, the order of grace - and it seems impossible to attain by mere human power.

Religion indicates to us what to do to attain this goal: we need to follow Christ and obey his Commandments. We need to live a virtuous life by obeying all the commandments of the Decalogue and the commandment of Love which Christ himself gave us.

In parenthesis, Aristotle defined "happiness" in part as "living well," which included living a virtuous life. Similarly, patterns of truth have been distributed throughout creation and human affairs by God who, by giving all individuals in turn the chance to follow them honestly, offers them different ways and roads to come to Him.

Ends and choices

Now that we have the general rule of behavior, how are we to apply it right now and right where we are? How are we to apply this obligation to the numerous little responsibilities that we seem to have all the time?

47

To each of these responsibilities, we can conceive different plans of action. I need to tell this employee to straighten up or to leave us. How am I to do that? What words should I use ? Where should I tell him? Should I yell or be calm? Should I do it in writing? Should I tell him in front of his peers? So many decisions for a single responsibility. And I have so many other responsibilities I must attend to.

To each of these decisions, the different courses of action can be either ethically good, ethically bad, or ethically neutral. How am I to tell?

Well, as a Christian I would try to imagine what Christ would do in a similar situation. In other words, I would try to use a criterion borrowed from my ultimate end to organize the end closer to me that I have to reach now; i.e., talking to the employee. But there can be different ways to do even that. A well-timed word of encouragement in front of his peers could be useful, or a complete review of his behavior to be conducted behind closed doors may be wise.

I may even decide that I do not have to straighten up this employee. Why do I want to do that to begin with? For his own good? For the good of the firm? For my own career as a manager? Well, I may conclude that he is in the wrong place to begin with and he should not be reprimanded, only let go. Or that the firm should have to put up with him the way he is. Or that it does not make any difference to my career how I am going to resolve this situation.

It is part of the human condition to have a very wide latitude in making choices, of selecting ends. There are very few choices that I have to make. I have free will. I can make the wrong choices, naturally. The three roots of wrong choice, or sin, are ignorance, malice and passion and I have many occasions to yield to these.

My free will may not be 100% free. There are limits. If I am prisoner and asked to talk or be tortured, I can always refuse to talk. The threat of torture is indeed constraining, but there are instances of people who do not talk under torture.

A correct understanding of free will must also include the fact that the willingness to do something good is good itself. As all good things come from God, a good decision that I make comes from God. But I am not an inert instrument. I can refuse and that bad decision to refuse definitely comes from me. Free-will is therefore fundamental to cooperate with the goodness of God and there is merit to it.

There is one end that I have to follow because of my human nature, it is to love God, the source of all good things. Even if I do not know this fact, even if I do not know God, I tend towards Him as my ultimate end. "Thou hast made us for Thyself" cries Augustine to the Creator; "and our hearts will be restless till they rest in Thee."

Ends and love

Ends are objects of action but what directs us to these ends and motivates us to seek these ends is love.

Every created power has a basic tendency to be attracted to its appropriate object. The eye is naturally designed to see. It has a natural desire for light. The intellect has a natural desire for truth. The will has a desire for the good. The sensual appetites have a desire for their object: the digestive power for food, the sexual system for sexual union, etc.

The intellect decides which desires need to be satisfied and consequently which power need be exercised. The sensual appetites are attracted by material substances. The intellect can only view the good in terms that are non-material. When the stomach has hunger pangs, the intellect knows what it is and decides to look for food. The stomach does not know food in general and cannot plan to seek food in general. The intellect controls this situation. On the other hand, if concrete food is presented to me, my appetite for food may draw me to this particular food. It will be the determination of my intellect to decide whether it is a good idea to eat this food at this moment.

Thus the intellectual desire for food and the sensual desire may be out of step with each other. I may put more food on my plate than I can eat. My intellectual appetite for the food is greater, more greedy, than my sensual appetite for the physical food.

Popular wisdom has a phrase for that: my eyes are bigger than my stomach.

There are three kinds of love: first the love of concupiscence, or of lust, for anything that is useful or agreeable. Then, friendship is divided into two kinds of love: love of another for our own sake, because this friendship is pleasurable and useful, and love of another for the sake of this other, which is perfect love.

Love seeks union with the object of that love.

It is better and more effective to say that Love is the source of human behavior, rather than need. Indeed "need" seems to relate to an almost mechanistic demand on the part of what would be the human machine. "Need" also does not reflect the fact that some people may desire that the desires may be eschewed and not satisfied.

"Need" further does not relate to the fact that human nature has several appetites, some of which may licitly be satisfied without much fuss, while others must be satisfied in more controlled circumstances.

"Need" and wants are concepts that do not explain the differences between the sensual, or intellectual, appetite for specific objects and the intellectual appetite for a whole general class of objects perceived as goods.

4. Behavioral Sciences and Human Needs

To have stated the flaws and limitations that the concept of needs have to describe human behavior is not enough. We have to follow the behavioral scientists in their search for understanding of needs, a search that takes them quite a distance and has important consequences for management, as it is taught, and for managers, as they are asked to function in a business setting.

Models of Human needs

Behavioral scientists have postulated the existence of needs.

But as these needs are not material, the scientists – as materialists - have no real proofs that they exist. They have been obliged to develop different theories of needs. (5)

The first debate among behavioral scientists concerning needs considered the question of how many needs there are. The answers ranged from 3 to 20. The consensus was that all needs can be reduced to 3 types: 1) Existence needs that relate to the biological necessities of life, 2) Relatedness needs that deal with the relationship with other people and 3) Growth needs that express personal development. Existence, Relatedness and Growth gave the name of the ERG model.

Growth

Relatedness

Existence

Figure 1

The ERG model is the most popular model with behavioral scientists. The runner up is a model that includes 5 needs, with the added characteristic that they are arranged in a hierarchical fashion: 1) physiological, 2) safety, 3) love, 4) esteem and 5)self-actualization.

Self-actualization

Esteem

Love

Safety

Physiological

Figure 2

This model implies that the lower needs must be satisfied for the human being to be interested in pursuing higher level needs. Food is the first type of need, then when food is not a worry, the subject would be motivated to find a shelter, etc. At the end of the line this individual would be motivated to seek ways to self-actualize, provided his self-esteem was well taken care of.

It is a little bit unsettling to have such basic elements of human nature picked out of thin air. It would seem clear that scientists should not have to play this sort of guessing game about such an important subject. They should have some solid criteria to make such an important determination. Since their discipline is incapable of providing such criteria, it is quite obvious that it would have to be provided from outside the science. As we already stated, the criteria need to be provided by the philosophy of psychology.

This said, let us take a closer look at these theories.

The hierarchy of the 5 needs has some appeal. However, how can one understand the behavior of people who, eschewing food and shelter to the point of losing weight and undermining their health, devote most of their time to pursuing their love, whether romantic love, love of money and power, or spiritual love?

What is the self-actualization need that the model proposes? Is it another way to say that individuals who have everything want to make themselves gods? Apparently, this need of self-actualization being the last is limitless. To self-actualize without limit seem really to indicate that it would be normal for us to be interested, at this level of needs, to become gods.

There are many other remarks that can be made about this 5-Need model. The 5-need model is not really accepted by the majority of scientists and the ERG model is preferred.

Of Particular Needs

The ERG model is retained, not because it is a better description than the 5 needs model but because it is simpler. 3 needs are simpler than 5 needs. The fact that the 3 needs model is not absolutely hierarchical is not really a problem to behavioral scientists. It may be understood as a confession that they do not know how to establish a hierarchy of needs. In addition it could tell us that they are not really

53

interested in models of human needs.

The behavioral scientists who have spent the most time studying needs have worked on specific needs rather than on a model of needs. The ERG model is a rather handy means of filing away the different particular needs that have been investigated by these people - no more, no less.

Thus the existence needs include the needs for safety and security. The relatedness need includes the needs for love, affiliation,, social-esteem, and power. The growth need includes the needs for self-esteem, competence, achievement, and creativity.

Needs for Safety and Security

Description of the needs for safety and security includes the rational prudent and conscious needs to be safe at home or on the job. The need extends to offspring and employees. The "construct" of Need of Security (that's the way behavioral scientists call an idea that they are going to define and study scientifically) includes also the gamut of behaviors about security exhibited by people who display such a need at an extreme level. For example it would include people who organize their life principally around their need to be safe.

Individuals with such needs may be encountered in modern inner cities where the crime level is high and we can consider such people normal people. But cases considered by the scientists in their studies go beyond examples of individuals with normal fears. Indeed, they include the different cases of phobias where security seems to be the prime element of classification of the phobia.

Indeed, when behavioral scientists, here psychologists, examine a specific human trait, their procedure is not to sit down and think logically of what are the different elements that make this trait human in its essence, as a philosopher would. Instead, they corral a number of interesting real cases, that is human-being-patients, who have some bearing on the subject and study them.

Whatever the scientists are going to find about the need for security of that particular group of people - if they believe they have properly "randomized" their sample (made sure the people they examine are representative of the population as a whole) - they are going to publish it as the universal definition of the need of security for the whole human race.

A disquieting prospect is that, psychiatrists being who they are and psychiatry being what it is, chances are great that the groups of people they are going to concentrate on in their studies of specific needs will include cases of abnormal psychology. The conclusions they will provide with their study will mingle normal behavior and abnormal behavior. Caring deeply for their patients and being afraid of being called "judgmental," the clinical psychiatrists will keep the distinction between normal and abnormal behavior fuzzy in their studies, if they even consider making such a distinction.

For the Christian with a scientific bent, there is an anguishing possibility that Need for Security as a construct will then be defined as including cases of sheer cowardice as well as pathological abnormality, including brain damage cases and cases where severe mistreatments appear in the patients' history.

Nonetheless, Need for Security may be an interesting concept and may be useful for industries in the locksmith business or the insurance business, for example, to establish psychological profiles of customers.

Psychometric profiles or any substantial conclusions that may be drawn from such studies should be used by businesses in a Christian fashion. In particular, they must take particular care of not reinforcing

55

vices and of not pushing sick people beyond the threshold of sanity. On the contrary they should reinforce courageous behavior and isolate pathological clients for medical referrals.

Need for Love and Need for Affiliation

This need, which is really only the Need for Affiliation (Love is much too unruly a concept to be investigated by scientists) is the target of studies by other types of behavioral scientists, sociologists and social psychologists.

The professional bias of sociologists is that individual human beings are somewhat conditioned by the society around them and its culture. In the general scheme of things, there is not really such a thing as a valid belief and ultimate truth, only concepts that are agreed upon by social consensus, they believe.

Sociologists take great pleasure at describing the herd instinct in a specific group. For example, they show how teenagers like to concentrate around malls and "hang-outs," share the same taste for jeans and other fashionable pieces of clothing, use the same vocabulary and share the same outlook on life. This need to conform to the standards of a group is explained by the need to be accepted by the group.

Again this tendency is normal up to a point. Because it is normal, it can be dealt with as part of managerial reality and decisions must be made to take that reality into account. But to the extent that specific manifestations of this tendency are abnormal, they cannot be exploited.

Thus some teenagers may simply seek the company of their peers to acquire socializing techniques that will help them in their adult life to deal with others. Other teenagers come from broken homes and seek in their peer groups a second home. They will be much more attached to

56

these groups that will offer them their principal source of affiliation. Other teenagers may seek to join teen gangs because their view of life is "kill or be killed" and they have quickly concluded that they want to be on the side of the powerful, rather than on the side of the weak and of the victims.

Need for Self-Actualization, Achievement and Creativity

Need for Self-Actualization corresponds to "be all you can be."

It insists on the value of the individual and its personal search for aggrandizement, and it does not make any judgmental decisions on whether such aggrandizement is indeed an aggrandizement, or rather a corruption of the individual.

Need for Achievement, sometimes for some authors, include self-actualization and creativity, but in fact it is most always a construct that is defined in terms of competition. To achieve is usually understood as to become "king of the hill." In that sense, the concept of achievement is not only different but even opposed to the concepts of self-actualization and creativity, for one has to compete where others have already selected the hill.

Naturally we all feel that we can learn more, do more, be good at more things. But more is not necessarily better. What is tragic about these needs is that there is no real criterion by which to measure whether specific conditions of self-actualization, and creativity are really conditions of betterment or not.

One can select to be a better Nazi in his search for self-actualization. Another becomes a work alcoholic in his search for achievement. To beat anyone at the office, to put in more hours than anyone else really can give an edge! A third may be looking more particularly in those directions that should shock people in order to be more creative. The more disgusting his artwork, the fewer other artists are likely to follow that method of expression and the more unique, thus creative, he finds himself.

Psychometrics and their use.

The advantage of these different needs is that they have been studied in considerable depth by quite an impressive number of people. In particular, different questionnaires and tests have been developed that purport to measure these needs, and different individuals do respond differently and consistently to the best of these tests. Up to a point they seem to be valid. (6)

Our purpose is primarily to question what these tests really measure and how to use the results from such tests.

The same techniques that have been utilized to develop the tests may also be utilized to measure "constructs" that are developed according to criteria that are genuinely Christian. For example, the individual questions that comprise a test can be written in such a mode that deviant behavior cannot be assimilated with normal behavior. If it appears that normal and deviant behavior cannot be distinguished from answers to the main body of questions, perhaps a methodological precaution is to include a preliminary stage to the test where the degree of normality and abnormality of the respondent's behavior is first tested.

The customer who seeks primarily cavity-fighting capabilities in his toothpaste has a strong need for security. Once research has established that fact, it does not mean that it is proper to exploit this need to the extreme. Instead, we can design a marketing plan on the premises that, given that this segment of the market is mostly interested in security, which need we will naturally cater to, how can we introduce other dimensions and other natural needs to "relate" to these potential customers?

We can deal with an employee who sees in his job primarily a source of security with an approach that will respect that fact but will not exploit the employee on that basis. The incentive system to be developed by management and to be used for this employee may not ignore his attitude of job-as-security but will try to entice the employee to grow in the other dimensions of the job for a broader development of his personality..

Similarly for the market segment who are primarily interested in the fact that toothpaste is important for their social life, this finding need not be exploited one-dimensionally. Employees who also view their jobs primarily as a means to socialize should not be taken advantage of on the basis of this personality trait.

5. Preparing the Outfit of the Voyager -

Growth in Holiness and the Christian Manager

Now that the Christian at work has understood the nature and agreed on the identity - God - of his ultimate end, he is ready to undertake the voyage towards this end. We have found on the way that each one of us has different personality characteristics that set us apart from one another as well as a human nature that bonds us together. These characteristics and human nature somewhat channel the choices that we make at work and as managers. These limitations do not impair our will in what is the most important of all its exercises: the choice towards spiritual perfection.

Kant and an Ethics of Pure Reason

At this point it is useful to take a better look at this ultimate end. We stated that the only end that is not a means to another end is happiness. For a Christian, this happiness is being with God.

A brilliant but misguided philosopher, Immanuel Kant, took exception with that ultimate end, even though he was a Christian himself. We mention him because he has strongly influenced the field of ethics, and professors of business ethics may more readily acknowledge that they are followers of Kant than of any other single philosopher.

That's how important Kant is.

Kant thought that a person's salvation or the beatific vision that person might enjoy was too selfish an ultimate end for human beings and too subjective a base on which to establish a system of ethics. Kant, then, thought up something he called the "categorical imperative" according to which an ethical act must have the potential to be universalizable. Stealing is wrong because if everybody stole, society could not function properly. So went his reasoning. (7)

In parentheses, if we push Kant's ideas to their farthest conclusions we must think that Kant also voided many humble acts from any ethical content, which is a very dangerous situation. To choose to be a baker is not an ethical action for Kant, because if everyone were a baker, there would be too many bakers in society and society would not function. The choice of a vocation, among other decisions, had thus no ethical dimension for Kant.

The problem is that Kant was the first one, in a Christian culture, to displace God from the central place in ethics that He had occupied since the beginning of Christian civilization. Kant replaced Him with Duty. Kant was the first major philosopher of the Christian civilization to secularize ethics. His avowed goal was to develop an "ethics of

60

reason." But pagans like Plato and Aristotle did not know the Christian God and they built their ethics as rationally as they could and without any hidden agenda - theirs was really an ethics of reason. Now, in this post-Christian era, any ethicist who wants to pretend to be rational and a good ethicist uses Kant, knowing that he will be saved from having to bring God in the ethical picture. This is being quite misguided.

The Goodness of God

Kant took away from the Christian ethics as he found it the sweet obligation to be ethical that comes from our friendship with the God of Love and replaced this obligation with the impersonal and cold obligation of duty.

Before the Christian era, ethics was in some way an art. "If you want to live well, here are a few hints on how to do it," a Greek philosopher would say, "I have built a system of ethics for that purpose."

When Christianity came, ethics received its compelling obligation from the Ten Commandments softened and justified by the Law of Love. Kant sought to keep the compelling obligation of Christian ethics in his ethical system but dropped the law of Love.

If secular ethics professors are fond of Kant and use his philosophical system, the general public is generally feels that Kant's ethics - which it seldom knows as such - really presents an unacceptable burden. Kant's ethics is one of the prime reasons why the average person becomes very defensive when the subject comes to ethics. Even in this world that thinks itself as Christian, Kant's ethics has warped the public awareness of the true dimension of ethics.

The Objectivity of Christian Ethics

Indeed any guide of spirituality will encourage his student to follow Christ and love God, not for his, the student's own salvation, but ultimately for the Goodness and Glory of God.

The Glory of God reintroduces universality in a spiritual journey. It is the search for happiness and for salvation that may lead us to the threshold of adopting a Christian ethics. But seeking God's Glory is the door that reopens for us the proper perspectives.

It asks us to see around us God's creation. This creation is the handiwork of God. Anyone who takes on the road of spiritual growth is required to develop a keen sense of praise to God for his creation. By praising God and His creation we acquire a healthy sense of objectivity as concerns our own person.

Wayfarers on the road of spirituality must learn to praise God and to thank God. As God can be seen in his creation, all of natural creation is a great teaching aide in the spiritual life.

This creation is also marked by obvious blemishes that are the effects of evil. Another purpose of the spiritual life is to deplore these blemishes, to strive hard to eradicate them, and to fight the evil that caused them.

Students of spirituality must also petition God to redress injustices and provide us the strength to cope with evil. They also need to learn and confess their own shortcomings as they grow increasingly aware that these personal defects of theirs contribute to the total sum of evil in the world.

Personal sanctification

"You, therefore, must be perfect, as your heavenly Father is perfect" (Mat. 5:48); "To all... who are called to be saints" (Rom. 1:7); "It is God's will that you grow in holiness" (1 Thess. 4:3).

After the Goodness of God and salvation, the end of the spiritual life is thus the sanctification of one's own soul. Please note that Christ does not suggests us politely to a life of holiness. To take the road towards sanctification is an obligation for all Christians, for all human beings.

This sanctification is made possible in the sharing of sanctifying grace in this world. Perfect Union with God, on the other hand, will have to wait for it is possible only in the other world.

So if we cannot attain perfect union in this world what can be attained? The answer is that the purpose of the spiritual life is not so much to attain any definitive goal as to strive towards an objective: "You shall love the Lord your God will all your heart, and with all your soul, and with all your mind, and with all your strength" (Mark 12:30). This is indeed the agenda of the spiritual life.

There are 3 grades in the process of personal sanctification. They correspond to the stages of birth, growth and maturity. They are also called the purgative, the illuminative and the unitive. In the first stage one needs to learn how to make a complete break from sin, in the second stage one gains new light for the spiritual life, in the third one seeks simply to be united with Christ.

It is important to note that there are no doors between the stages. Rather, it is totally habitual for our spiritual life to consist of a combination of elements from each of the three stages, at the same time.

In the first stage we need to purify the different components of our person: our external senses, our interior senses, our passions, intellect, and will. Throughout our spiritual life we can rely on the help of the sacraments, the meritorious effects of our good works and our prayers. We should never be satisfied but continuously pray for our growth in holiness.

Following Christ

"It is in Christ and through his blood that we have been redeemed and our sins forgiven, so immeasurably generous is God's favor to us. God has given us the wisdom to understand fully the mystery, the plan he was pleased to decree in Christ, to be carried out in the fullness of time; namely, to bring all things in the heavens and on earth into one under Christ's headship" (Eph. 1:3-15)

To help us understand how we can follow Christ, we can start from the description that Christ gave of himself: "I am the way, the truth, and the life" (John 14:6).

Christ is the way to God. We can only be holy in Christ, and to the extent that the life of Christ is in us. He is the only way to go to the Father. He is also the personification of true sanctity.

Christ is the truth for he is the Incarnation of the eternal wisdom of God. Through Christ we can share in all his wisdom and knowledge, as master and teacher. And, as Christ, we are called to become true children of God.

Christ is the life for several reasons. As our redeemer, He obtained for us eternal life. Christ is also the Source of all graces. Lastly, Christ is the head of the Mystical body to which we are called to belong to obtain life. Naturally, the head determines the life of the whole body.

"Through him, with him, in him, in the unity of the Holy Spirit, all glory and honor is yours, almighty Father, forever and ever." This sacred formula makes us tend towards the Glory of God through our participation in the mystery of Christ by living through Christ, with Christ and in Christ.

Close to us in the order of creation, we have the privilege to have Mary, who is a powerful mediatrix with her son. As Christ humbled himself and spent many months in the womb of Mary, we must follow Him also in becoming her children and accepting her as our spiritual mother. We do well to honor Mary. Christ, out of his divine gratitude for the young woman who accepted to be His mother, honored her more than He has honored any other creature as He made her "full of grace."

To follow Christ, we must then also follow Him in His filial relationship. As we must obey Him in all things, we must take very seriously, responsibly and lovingly the statement He made on the Cross: "This is your mother."

We must love Mary for Christ's sake.

Voyage to the supernatural order

To share the life of Christ, we need to progress towards a dimension with which we are not familiar: the supernatural dimension. This is impossible for us alone. But it is possible for God to bring us to this dimension. (8)

God does it by giving us and all His children something called Grace. Grace belongs to the supernatural order but can reach us in the natural world. Grace is in some way our transportation vehicle from this world to the supernatural world. As the soul gives shape to our natural life, sanctifying grace gives shape to our eternal life. Not to be in the state of grace is to be dead to eternal life.

To be in a state of grace is to be in a situation of friendship with God. Grace is also an incremental dimension of that friendship which can be acquired according to... the economy of grace.

Grace is infinitely precious; it is good and, as it belongs to the spiritual world, it is limitless. Thomas Aquinas said that the minimum degree of grace in one individual is greater than the natural good of the entire universe.

Besides the Blessed Sacrament, there is nothing more precious in this world than individuals in the state of grace.

The good news is that this extremely powerful and precious thing is readily available to us. The love of God gives us grace. God offers us his friendship. All we need to have grace is to accept the love of God for us. God wants us to have grace and He will move us to accept it. But we can refuse it. A mortal sin is a sin by which we firmly refuse grace and therefore die to eternal life, even if our material life seems unchanged.

Love brings the lover and the object of that love together. Because of His love for us, God draws us to Himself through grace. As God leaves us freedom of will, He takes great care that His love is not to be compelling. We will not be attracted to God automatically unless we accept His love.

If we do accept His love, grace does many marvelous things for us. Grace makes us adopted children of God. Grace makes us true heirs to God's Kingdom. Grace makes us coheirs with Christ. Grace gives us supernatural life. Grace makes us just and pleasing to God. Grace gives us the capacity for Supernatural merit. Grace unites us intimately with God. And grace makes us living temples of the Trinity.

Actual Grace and the Gifts of the Holy Spirit

In the process of bringing us over to the supernatural life, God does not simply make our souls holy by one stroke, but He also proceeds to make us function as holy persons must function. He changes the way we operate so that our actions become more holy.

"There shall come forth a shoot from the stump of Jesse, and a branch shall grow out of its roots. And the Spirit of the Lord shall rest upon him, the spirit of wisdom and understanding, the spirit of counsel and might, the spirit of knowledge and the fear of the Lord. And his delight shall be in the fear of the Lord" (Isaiah 11:1-3)

This quotation from the Bible is the usual quotation for the foundation of the doctrine of the gifts of the Holy Spirit. The gifts are free gifts on the part of God to help us become more holy. The gifts stay with us as long as we are in the state of grace.

The gifts operate in the supernatural order and the Holy Spirit is the primary agent. In other words they operate in us only when the Holy Spirit so desires. We cannot call upon them to operate. And they do not operate according to a human mode.

Some gifts affect our intellect. Of these a number affect the manner in which we know the truth:

- Understanding: "gives us a deeper insight and penetration of divine truths held by faith, not a transitory enlightenment but as a permanent intuition".

- Knowledge: "to judge rightly concerning the truths of faith in concordance with their proper causes and the principles of revealed truth".

- Wisdom: "to judge and order all things in accordance with divine norms and with a connaturality that flows from loving union with God."

Another gift affects our intellect but in relation, this time, not to the things we know but to the things we do:

- Counsel: "to render the individual docile and receptive to the counsel of God regarding one's actions in views of sanctification and salvation."

A gift affects our intellectual appetite, or will:

- Piety : "to give filial worship to God precisely as our Father and to relate with all people as children of the same Father.

The remaining gifts affect our sensual appetites:

- Fortitude: "to overcome difficulties or to endure pain and suffering with the strength and power infused by God" and

- Fear of the Lord: "to avoid sin and attachment to created things out of reverence and love of God."

The Infused virtues

Grace also gives us infused virtues. The virtues are what make us function properly and we will treat them in detail in the next chapter. The infused virtues give us energy and promptness to do virtuous acts. We feel uplifted and transported by this energy.

Here's how the infused virtues work. Our mind has assessed the terrain that we need to cover in our spiritual journey and has prepared itself for the trek we would have to undertake to cross it. But the infused virtues pick us up and make us fly over this terrain. It is exhilarating and naturally very convenient.

The difference between the infused virtues and the gifts is that only the Holy Spirit decides when the gifts are going to operate. We may be in the middle of another occupation while receiving a specific gift. On the other hand, we receive the infused virtues when we are ready to perform a certain act of moral goodness and we find that this act is much easier to perform than anticipated. Contrary to what happens with the gifts of the Holy Spirit, it is we who initiate the operation of the infused virtue.

One difference between the infused virtues and the virtues that are not infused is that the infused virtues are a gift of God. The regular virtues we must acquire by practice; we have to pay our dues to possess them.

Also another difference between the two types of virtues relates to their cause: I can acquire the virtue of temperance regarding drinking, and that is good for me as man. The infused virtue of temperance concerning drinking is aiming at my goodness as a child of God.

In addition, acquired virtues operate according to the light of reason. Infused virtues operate according to the light of reason illuminated by faith.

Faith, Hope and Charity

There two are classes of virtues that can be infused: theological virtues and moral virtues.

Faith, Hope and Love are the theological virtues. They are principles by which we are ordained directly to God as our end. Only God can infuse them into the soul. There is, consequently, no such thing as an acquired theological virtue. We cannot grow in those virtues all by ourselves.

On the other hand, the infused moral virtues direct us regarding the means of our end who is God.

Faith enables us to know God as first truth. Faith means that we know that the ultimate reality in the universe is infinite goodness. Faith means that we know that this goodness is a person, an intelligent and loving being. This person is God. Faith requires an assent of our intellect to what is proposed for belief by the Church. We can grow in faith by believing more intensely in the truth revealed to us and its relevance to our everyday life.

Hope makes us desire God as the supreme good for us. We hope in God through our will. Hope reinforces in us the notion that this supremely intelligent and loving being is available to us, that He is reachable. Through hope we know that we can be on the side of this infinite goodness and share in His existence.

In our growth in hope we must avoid falling in the two opposite extremes contrary to hope: presumption and despair. We avoid presumption when we are fully convinced that we are nothing without God. We avoid despair when we have completely understood that God can forgive the worst of our failings. We grow in hope in becoming detached from the things of this earth, when we become more easily comforted in difficulties by spiritual things, and it is easier for us to do good.

Charity is a supernatural virtue infused by God into the will, by which we love God for himself above all things, and ourselves and our neighbor for God. Charity unites us with God in the love of friendship, that is to say in Charity. We love God because he is God, not because of what He can do for us. In Charity we commit ourselves to infinite goodness.

The intellect and the will operate differently in respect to Charity.

The intellect raises up lower things than itself by comprehending them and, so to speak, by honoring them and giving them an intellectual form. But the same intellect lowers things greater than itself by trying to understand them. This is why by trying to understand God we make God smaller than He really is.

On the other hand, the will degrades itself by cherishing what is below itself. But it enhances itself by loving what is above itself, especially God. A consequence of this very point is that the inferior created things that we may love, we need to love them in God, through God and for God.

To strive for charity is the ultimate goal of Christian perfection. In this goal we attach ourselves to God ever more tightly. We do not necessarily grow in charity by performing more acts of charity but by increasing the intensity of our love of God.

The three theological virtues are distinct. In particular, when we commit a mortal sin, we immediately lose the virtue of charity -and the state of grace. But we may keep our faith. A good thing so we may be move to contrition leading us to confession and regain that virtue.

In the chronological order of spiritual growth, the first theological virtue is faith, by which we know that our goal is God. The second is hope, by which we desire to meet our goal. The third is charity by which we attain our goal.

However, in the order of perfection, charity is the most excellent virtue. "And the greatest of these is love" (1 Cor. 13:13). Only charity may remain after our death. Hope is the second most perfect as it is more closely related to charity.

6. The Most Precious Gear - The Virtues and the Christian Manager.

The soul has to discover that its proper end is God. The theological virtues put the soul in the proper direction towards that end. It remains that the operations of the soul should also be transformed so that the entire person can start on his journey toward God. The moral virtues are what will transform these operations of the soul.

"If one loves justice, the fruits of her works are virtues; for she teaches moderation and prudence, justice and fortitude, and nothing in life is more useful for men than these." Book of Wisdom 8:7

It is time to realize that these virtues, prudence, justice, fortitude and moderation are indeed those qualities that are more useful to us than anything else. In particular these virtues are the most useful to managers. And indeed the central axis of this book will be on these virtues.

Now this quotation of the Bible on the cardinal virtues is actually more recent, by at least three centuries, than a writing of Plato, a non-Christian philosopher, on the same virtues. When Agathon in Plato's "Symposium" makes a speech on Love, he organizes his speech in four parts around the cardinal virtues. Agathon does not explain where these notions of virtues come from. We are to understand that his listeners would have found the notions of virtues, even then, old hat.

The cardinal virtues, the central axis of this book, belong to the Church because they belong to human common sense and wisdom. To oppose the re-introduction of the virtues in management under the argument that that would introduce "religion" in secular matters is poor reasoning. It is inaccurate and it is proof of poor scholarship. It would further cause a tremendous loss as it would suppress a very successful and tested approach that helps human beings and belongs to human patrimony, that of Catholics and other Christians, that of Jews as well as

72

that of pagans.

The Nature of Virtues

We could have developed the notion of virtues in the subchapter on the Nature of Man, for virtues and habits, of which they are a species, belong there. But it is preferable to treat this subject in the fresh light of spiritual growth that we have just encountered. (9)

Indeed, it is in the nature of man to be a creature of habit. Man has the powers to do many different things. Any single man does not use all his powers. He prefers to limit himself to exercise only a certain number of powers for which he develops ease, grace and pleasure in action. He develops habits of using his powers in specific and similar ways.

Habits are stable dispositions to do certain things in pre-determined ways. It may strike my fancy to help a blind person to cross the street today because I feel like it. I have the disposition to be helpful today. If I have this disposition most of the time, it is more than just a disposition, it is a habit.

I brush my teeth with the same hand, by laying the toothpaste always in the same fashion and I do so in the same room and at the same time of day, every day. This is a habit. I also know a few things about subjects of science. This is also a habit. The latter is an intellectual habit. I used my head to learn how to brush my teeth. All habits are possible because of the rational character of the human species.

Characteristics of habits

We all remember our first day in school, or our first day on a new job. It was very hard because we had to do many things that we had never done before. To acquire a new habit is quite difficult and certainly very taxing on our intellectual abilities. Once it has become a habit, we do not even think of what we are doing, because it almost "comes naturally." Habits are very useful.

If we, as members of the human species, all have basically the same powers to do a great number of things, our habits are however witnesses of trials and efforts that we ourselves went through as individuals. We can take credit and blame for them. Habits are very personal.

If we, as members of the human species, have powers to do certain things, in a sense we - each one us - do not really have these powers until we have developed a habit to act upon them. It is a faculty of the human species to be able to read and write, but individual men can actually do it only if they have spent quite some time training and exercising their reading and writing habits. There are no short cuts. Habits are necessary to be able to utilize human powers. They must be developed to perfect the powers to act.

Thus, habits are somewhat midway between the powers and actions. The habit of writing is beyond the simple human ability to write and somewhat short of the specific action of writing.

On Acquiring Habits

The process of acquisition of habit is a very deliberate process. It takes quite some time like forming hot iron into a sword. The first strikes do not seem very effective but little by little the metal takes the shape the blacksmith intends to give it. Similarly habits do not disappear in an instant. Habits are quite enduring.

The process for the acquisition of habit is repetition of the action for which the habit is developed. One learns how to read by reading, how to lay brick by laying bricks.

Different men develop the same habits differently. Some individuals have more intellectual abilities and learn how to write faster. Some individuals are not hampered by a vivid imagination which make others think of all kind of dangers and they thus develop the habit of courage more easily.

Once a habit has been developed it displays three different characteristics: (1) uniformity - it is capable of operating so smoothly and uniformly, it really looks like a machine; (2) propensity - once we have acquired a habit we have a tendency to exercise it at the tip of a hat. Actually, it often takes an act of will to curb one's habit. If in the winter, I have the habit to take my coat off the rack before going out, I have to learn in the spring to stop doing so. Because of this propensity, habit has been called "second nature"; (3) pleasure - we can think of a dancer who knows his number so well, or the skier who slaloms down the same slope all day long so well that they scream with contentment after completing the dance or the descent, even though we might wonder why they do not get bored doing the same thing repeatedly.

Virtues and Vices

In the matter of habits, as in the matter of perfection, if we are not progressing, we are deteriorating. We can progress by meeting more difficult challenges; but being satisfied by a certain level of quality in one of our habits and never seeking new challenges will inevitably lead us to slip backward in our proficiency.

Habits may be modified by acts of other habits. A well-practiced memory is quite useful for the habit of science. But if I am growing to become a coward, my sense and habit of justice are going to be seriously undermined.

There are good habits, for example whether to wash one's teeth or be knowledgeable. And there are bad habits, such as swearing or littering. Good habits, in relation to man's ultimate destiny, are called virtues. Bad habits, in relation to man's ultimate destiny, are called vice. A vice is not something that has an existence of its own. It is the absence of a virtue that alone has a true existence of its own.

Aristotle's definition of moral virtue is "a quality that makes its possessor good and his work good."

There is a profusion of virtues and vices. For each thing that man can do – that is as human acts which require the use of the will -he can do well or badly. There are consequently vices and virtues related to the exercises of all these human powers.

The rational character of man is what makes habits possible. But habits can be acquired both for intellectual powers and for lower powers. Good habits of the intellectual powers are called intellectual virtues. Good habits of the lower powers are called moral virtues.

Indeed, the true essence of morality is not to develop good habits of the intellect, but good habits for our sensual powers. Perhaps it is more difficult for us, whose senses are in a great state of confusion, to keep in rein our lower powers than our intellectual powers. Further, as we will see, our moral habits have a strong impact on our intellectual habits. Thus, if ultimately we want to develop genuine intellectual virtues, we have to come around and develop solid moral virtues first.

Intellectual virtues are more limited in scope than moral virtues. I can be a good mathematician but a bad person. The virtue of the science of mathematics is somewhat limited to what I do. But if I am just, I am just as a person. The moral virtue of justice affects what kind of person I am.

GENDER	POWER	SPECIES	OBJECT
		understanding	first principles
Intellectual	Speculative Intellect	science wisdom	proximate causes ultimate causes
	Practical Intellect	art prudence	things to be made things to be done
	Will	justice	human acts to be rectified
Moral	appetite of flesh	temperance	mild passions to to be moderated
	appetite for aggression	fortitude	emergency passions to be moderated

The Virtues of Man

7. Prudence

The great number of virtues that exist have been traditionally regrouped within four categories: prudence, justice, temperance and fortitude, the four cardinal virtues. Each one of these virtues, in other words, indeed constitutes a category that contains a great number of related virtues. The cardinal virtues are called cardinal because the other virtues "hinge"- the meaning of the world cardinal - on them.

The first of these cardinal virtues is the virtue of prudence. It is not the first virtue arbitrarily. It is the first virtue because it must exist before any other virtue, even any other cardinal virtue can exist. There can be no justice, courage or temperance where there is no prudence. And in addition, there can be no faith, hope and charity where there is no prudence. The virtue of prudence is indeed very important.

Joseph Pieper, one of the great contemporary philosophers even claims that "nothing less than the whole ordered structure of the Occidental Christian view of man rests upon the preeminence of prudence over the other virtues." (10) If God the Father to whom the concept of Being, existence, is related, precedes the Son, who is the Truth, the mind of God, He, in turn precedes the Holy Spirit, who personalizes the Good. Thus, Prudence, which is related to Truth, precedes the moral virtues that are related to the Good.

Of all the moral virtues, prudence is the most intellectual. And one cannot be ethical who does not exercise his intellectual faculties even to be ethical. In a sense, one cannot be ethical before one knows "what's what" about the world. Thus many of those individuals who fight for a cause may have a strong sense of justice but lack prudence when they insist that their cause should prevail at the cost of more important values.

Modern dangers to prudence

We must note here that the trendy and typical sign of corruption of traditional Christian values has often been the fact that justice is being given precedence over prudence. This results in a false justice, a justice that is not rational, therefore not human and not ethical.

For example, the fight against apartheid, which is indeed a true and noble fight for justice, was much too often translated into one single action that strongly defies rationality. Many groups around the planet who claimed to be anti-apartheid demanded that foreign companies leave South Africa. This action was not only puzzling but also infuriating to many anti-apartheid South Africans who insisted for years that they did not want foreign companies to leave their country because these companies actually contributed to the improvement of their living conditions and to the dismemberment of Apartheid.

Lawrence Kohlberg, famous for the many studies on the moral education of children which he developed from a totally anti-Christian perspective, wrote in "The Humanist," the publication of the secular humanists, that - scorning the "boy-scout bag of virtues" - there is only one virtue and that this virtue is Justice, totally disparaging the importance of the virtue of prudence. Kohlberg died committing suicide after having strongly influenced the educational philosophy in the West.

Nature of Prudence

Prudence is quite different from what we usually understand today by prudence. The classical virtue of "prudence" corresponds more to what we would call today "good judgment." Several connotations to the modern meaning of prudence indeed have to be reviewed and discarded before we can truly understand the cardinal virtue of prudence.

Prudence is not some sort of cowardly and conniving attitude and behavior, aiming at preserving one's feeble strength. Modern understanding sees too often prudence as some sort of faculty for intrigue and a less than courageous attitude. Modern understanding also grants some wisdom to prudence: "Soon I will be driving my car, it is prudent that I do not drink too much."

What is prudence? "Prudence is the apprehension of objective reality, especially in the concrete aspect of this reality as it relates to ways and means to attain practical objectives."

The different "parts" of the virtue of prudence are the following: (1) deliberation, (2) judgment and (3) decision. Indeed prudence does not relate to a simple movement of the intellect but to a more complex process. These will be studied in the chapter on decision-making. Also, in each of these parts exist possibilities of perfect action and faulty action. The theory on prudence naturally also contains a presentation on the human powers to be perfected in order to improve on prudential judgment. These will also be presented in the chapter on decision-making.

Prudence in Business

Prudence in business is the skill necessary to select means in order to attain desired business ends. Briefly we can note that that skill is useful both at the qualitative as well as quantitative level.

Qualitatively: a new means to attain a known end can be really useful, especially if one had no previous practical means to attain this end and it can thus open a new industry. Quantitatively: a more efficient means to attain an end can make a business more competitive and ensure its success.

An accounting system and a management information system (MIS), which organize means and ends, cannot be developed without the virtue of prudence which prioritize the hierarchy of accounts or data.

Thus it is absolutely remarkable that prudence, or "good judgment," was considered the number one cause of business success in a very enlightening study.

A number of successful businessmen were polled on the question of which factor, in their opinion, was the most important to their business success. Among the choices of potential sources for business success offered them in the questionnaire were "social contacts", "personal wealth", even "marrying the boss's daughter", etc. all elements that the general population would more readily select as indeed determinant elements for success. (11) These successful business persons instead named "good judgment".

As an example, let us follow a typical strategy that a top managerial team could use for the development of its business activities.

- We can start by postulating that to be successful in business one has to have a product that everyone desires, and so to satisfy this desire at a price which allows a comfortable profit.

- Step two: one needs to have some sort of protection on the exclusivity of this product that everyone desires, otherwise competitors will jump in, slash the prices, and there will be no way to be successful at it in a business way.

- Step three: among other means of legal protection, patents are prominent legal means to this purpose.

- Step four: a great majority of patents are under-exploited and can be had for little cost.

- Step five: if we do a good job putting a deal together, we should have no difficulty finding the extra financing required; the rational value of the deal would be easily communicable, for example, to a bank.

Hence we should first secure the financing and then go through each of the above identified steps as a way to become successful.

Now all these different steps towards a business plan require already some serious knowledge about patents, manufacturing, marketing, business law, etc. and how to combine these different elements into a plan. The knowledge of these disciplines and combination of elements is part of the virtue of prudence.

But prudence is also involved at the second level of activities and perhaps the most important: the practical implementation of the plan. How do I evaluate financing partners? What kind of industry do I want to be involved in? How do I select an inventor with a good patent in that industry? Where do I get the financing for a pilot plant? How do I get some up-front contracts to fill comfortably my order book so to put me solidly in business? How do I hire personnel? etc.

The development of the strategic business plan can be learned in business school, or from books. It can be learned as a purely intellectual endeavor, or it can it can be learned from experiences during which prudence, as a virtue, will be thoroughly exercised. The implementation part of the plan requires hard work, which we'll see later is related to the virtue of courage. But successful implementation depends mostly on making the "right calls," that is, exercising correctly the virtue of prudence at the most practical level.

In consequence, the virtue of prudence is indeed the crucial determinant of business success.

The virtue of prudence in business is acquired by first developing a great familiarity, beyond the mere intellectual apprehension, with the different elements of business decisions. These elements must be known not only in their principles but also in their concrete aspects. Furthermore, the virtue of prudence in business is developed by making a great number of such business decisions involving these elements in different configurations.

One businessman can specialize in certain business domains, for example in retailing, or the airline industry, or steel making. But no business person can avoid learning about the principles of the components of the business decisions in their specialties, about the concrete aspects of these components. And no business person can avoid practicing making such decisions if he indeed wants to become a better business person.

Prudence and conscience

It is important to note here that the very practical application of prudence to concrete cases consists exactly in what we also call "conscience": i.e., to decide in the general scheme of things whether some applied decision is correct or awry, and what it would take to make it correct.

To develop in oneself the sense of morality, we must develop the desire to do the moral thing and to acquire the habit to do the moral thing. We cannot do either if we do not see, in a particular circumstance what is the moral thing to do. Prudence and our conscience help us to see that. However prudence needs to be perfected and conscience needs to be formed.

A grave confusion exists these days about conscience. It is believed by many that the principle of freedom of conscience allows for the making of decisions of conscience without any need for objective criteria. Granted that conscience is a decision-making power belonging to individuals, still the elements of the decisions and the principles according to which the decisions are to be made must be objective and must relate to reality. Until they are, we do not have a free conscience but a pitifully unformed conscience, in other words, a shapeless intellectual organ.

The liturgy of the Church used to include the words: "God, Thou showest the erring the light of Thy truth, that they may return to the way of justice."

Truth and prudence come before justice. The wicked are not so much people who take the position that they are against any form of justice; on the contrary they often speak loudly in favor of certain forms of justice but, as their sense of justice is awry, as they believe they can have justice without the truth about God and nature, some of the forms of "justice" they promote are at odds with true justice.

The "justice" of having homosexuals practice their behavior unhindered by society is a true injustice against God and nature.

Prudence and Business Ethics

Good intentions do not at all suffice for justice. They do not suffice for businesses to be good businesses. They do not suffice for the detractors of business to be in the right. Indeed, it is much too often the case that self-appointed "reformers" of business are moved by a subjectively developed sense of justice, without firm ground in prudence.

The instinctive and correct reaction of business people, faced by such reformers, is to refuse even to dialogue with these people who not only know very little about the business world but, obviously, know very little about virtues and human nature, since they know so little about prudence. Some reformers of good faith but poor understanding of the business profession seem to have forgotten that prudence is an essential part of any profession and thus have led themselves to believe they can reform a profession they know very little about without studying its inner prudence. Very few channels of communications are possible between businesses and these all too numerous members of the anti-

84

business establishment.

In the discipline of moral philosophy one exercise consists in examining real moral cases to present an analysis of the situation, identifying the moral principles applicable to the case and pronouncing judgment on the goodness or badness of the acts described in the case. This difficult exercise was too often improperly conducted and gave a definitely pejorative connotation to the name "casuistry," the name of an otherwise legitimate and praiseworthy exercise. (12)

The temptation of bad casuistry was to provide simplified guidelines and poorly developed analysis for judging the ethics of individual cases, thereby negating the value of prudence. In its deformed form, casuistry was an academic and doctrinal failure. Today, however, a new secular casuistry is emerging. Harvard Business School is proud of its "case method" but do not seem to see the inherent dangers of this pedagogical tool.

Now, casuistry was also developed as an aid to the teaching of ethics, specifically the training of confessors. Interestingly, the argument that the case method is only a means to start the dialogue between teacher and student was also used claimed in casuistry.

The inescapable fact is that in both old-time casuistry and the case method, there is an implicit belief that ethical judgment can be rendered or approximated on a case as presented in an academic setting.

Prudence involves cases to be resolved in the here and now, not in the abstract. Prudence is the virtue, or good habit, of seeing the right method for solving an ethical dilemma, when one is personally involved - emotionally and materially or financially - in the situation. Prudence cannot be taught academically. The decision maker must have "a dog in the fight".

"A moral theology that relies too much upon casuistry necessarily becomes a 'science of sins' instead of a doctrine of virtues, or a theory of

85

the Christian idea of man" writes Pieper.

Is it not true that most business ethics courses have structures that make them more akin to courses in the science of corporate sins than courses that teach positively and constructively decision-making to executives?

"A merely casuistic moral theology assumes the immaturity of human beings. Moreover, it intensifies and perpetuates this immaturity," continues Pieper. This can also be said about business ethics taught by the case method.

Pieper concludes: "The classical Christian doctrine of the preeminence of the virtue of prudence is essentially opposed to all falsifying, moralistic, or casuistic regimentation of the person who is called upon to make decisions. The first of the cardinal virtues is not only the quintessence of ethical maturity, but in so being is also the quintessence of moral freedom."

A true Christian doctrine applied to the ethics of the business world is less moralistic and allows for more moral freedom than secularist approaches to business ethics as encountered almost everywhere today in business schools and corporate seminars.

8. Justice

Justice and rights

A right comes into existence when something is due someone. Justice is concerned with rights.

For Justice is the virtue which observes the rights of all. Indeed, injustice exists when someone is cheated of something to which he is entitled.

How do we practically know that something is due to a person? What establishes rights? The answer is: the law. But, how can that be? Have we not seen numerous cases of people demonstrating and opposing the laws of a country because they are unjust? Certainly! Also, when we say "the law" we mean several things: the laws of men or a nation or international laws, the laws of nature and the laws of God, or divine laws. When individuals oppose the laws of their countries and they are in the right, it is because they are inspired by natural law or divine law.

Rights thus come before justice. But where do rights come from in the law?

If I do a given job I have the right to be paid. But do rights only come from what we do? Certainly not! There are also rights that do not depend on what we do but on who we are.

In particular, some rights come simply from the fact that I am a human being. Civil rights and human rights are derived from this source. Persons have special rights that brute animals do not have.

The rights of persons are derived from natural law and divine law. Natural law states that human beings are above animals because only the former are rational. Divine law states that human beings are made in the image of God and they should be respected for that great dignity.

Human beings are also persons with an intellect and a will and should be respected and allowed due exercise of their intellect and will. These exercises are precisely the rights that totalitarian regimes do not respect since the thinking and the deciding is made for all by the government, usually under the principle of "scientific socialism." Totalitarian philosophy considers that people should be happy to have the thinking and the deciding done for them, by experts, and to be left free to enjoy the "socialist paradise."

Not only do we now know that societies built on these principles do not work, but we also know that human beings suffer terribly by not being left free to exercise their natural powers of thinking and deciding.

Rights that come from natural and divine laws are inalienable rights. No human laws can suppress them. Prudence in government must be thoroughly penetrated by this axiom. Prudent politicians must know about natural law and divine law before they are ready to call for justice and the satisfaction of rights.

Justice as virtue.

"Justice is a virtue whereby a man renders to each one his due with constant and perpetual will."

Aquinas quotes at this point a pagan Latin philosopher, Cicero: "Good men are so called chiefly from their justice." Pagans were conscious of the perceived preeminence of justice.

Further, when divine Scripture talks of the just man, it means the holy man, the good man. In this sense it certainly appears that justice is the first of the cardinal virtue.

Is not justice competing with prudence for the first place among the cardinal virtues? To that question, there are several answers.

Justice and the "other."

Justice is the only virtue that truly turns us, students of the spiritual life, towards others. Alone of the cardinal virtues, it perfects us in our relationship with others. It implies some acceptation of objectivity, on our part, as concerns our relative importance - or lack of importance - in the general population, a willingness to forego our natural tendency for self-centeredness.

Justice as virtue forces us to appreciate the other as "other" instead of denying this other full human dignity because of his differences with us. Nazis "liquidated" people because they were different. The process is always the same with injustice. First the Nazis worked hard at proving that non-Aryans were truly different. This done, they then had no problem recommending their "liquidation."

Today, it seems very often that general opinion, led by the media, views as "others" those people who claim as their own the traditional Christian culture.

The terrible wrong of class struggle is that each class sees the other class as "others," as not quite human beings. The temptation of the rich is to let themselves be appalled at the poor quality of life that the poor are willing to put up with. The rich are easily drawn to think that the poor may not really be human beings if they do not enjoy what would appear to the rich to be some items of first necessity. "How can they live in such dirty and run-down housings - they must be some kind of animals." The fact that the poor seem to put up with their dismal environment, instead of gaining the sympathy of the unjust rich is the very cause that motivates the unjust rich to ignore the needs of the poor.

The temptation of the poor, on the other hand is to think that all the rich "are not like you and me, they are different," as F. Scott Fitzgerald framed it. Essentially, the poor cannot believe that the rich are not naturally inclined to give up all their riches to the poor. If they only knew how much the poor would like to receive these riches!

"Certainly, if the rich were as human as the poor are, they'd be much more generous!" Or so goes the reasoning of the unjust poor. "If the rich are so insensitive, they are not quite human and they can be fought."

Present culture pretends to protect the handicapped and many laws have been passed and ramps have been built for handicapped people. On the other hand, present culture also advocates the abortion of future handicapped children, as "damaged" children.

Again, if they are different they can be destroyed is the modern world rationale.

Justice as obligation

Because justice brings us to recognize what we owe to others, it is the virtue that brings out the most forcefully the idea of obligation in ethics.

The notions of debt and of duty are very similar. A debt may be incurred toward an individual. It can also be incurred toward society at large. We indeed must all contribute to the public good.

Many ethical systems, including the systems of Immanuel Kant and most of the modern academic systems of ethics, insist on the importance of duty. These systems are called "deontological systems of ethics." Practically, they reduce ethics to the study of moral duty and obligations. The deontological approach to ethics is necessarily restrictive.

Deontology is to be opposed to another approach, the teleological approach to ethics, which is the approach used by Aristotle and Aquinas, which consists in the search of good objectives (which are at a distance; tele in Greek means "at a distance": television, telephone), and then to understand and promote the behavior necessary to attain these objectives.

Deontological systems of ethics are really upside down approaches to viewing the matter of ethics.

If I am ready to meet my moral obligations, I am displaying the proper attitude required to become a just person. This is an attitude that can be publicly recognized as the proper disposition of an ethical person, or at least of a person who seriously strives at being ethical. The public places a great value on the fact that I feel an obligation towards others.

Justice is also a virtue that aims at the best organization of society. When I spend efforts at rewarding people who have done well or to punish other people who have done some evil, I am working at improving society. Objectively, the good of society is better than the good of any individual, including my own good. Working at improving society should be the real motivation of the ethical Christian person. By doing justice, this Christian person is principally motivated by following Our Lord's request that we pray and act so that "His Kingdom Come." To act for justice is simply to act towards reestablishing creation as it would have been before the Fall of Adam and Eve and the advent of original sin.

The three justices.

There are three forms (or parts) of justice. Each distinctive form is so important that we could almost say that justice covers three virtues. The distinction between the parts is crucial because their confusion can be very misleading and weakens the whole idea of justice.

The first part of justice is between individuals (commutative justice). The second part of justice is from the community towards the individual (distributive justice). The third is from the individual towards the community as a whole (legal justice or general justice). As mentioned, students of the spiritual life are chiefly interested in legal justice, but must be concerned with the other parts of justice.

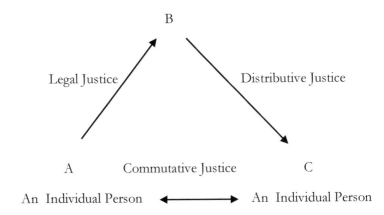

The Social Whole

B

Legal Justice   Distributive Justice

A   Commutative Justice   C

An Individual Person   ←——→   An Individual Person

A Schematic Representation of the Basic Forms of Justice

In addition, the philosopher John Finnis teaches that each individual must go beyond a general concern that distributive justice is effective in his community. Indeed, the willingness to commit oneself for the cause of distributive justice is akin to sharing in the spirit of solidarity and working for the furtherance of the common good.

"Few will flourish, and no one will flourish securely, unless there is an effective collaboration of persons, and co-ordination of resources and enterprises (including always, in the notion of collaboration and co-ordination, patterns of mutual restraint and non-interference)." (13)

Ideologies of the left insist on a limited and erroneous form of distributive justice. Interestingly, their proponents hold this only for non-Communist countries. In Communist countries, the ideologues of the left believe that the priority be reversed: it is what individuals owe to the Communist state that is really important. Conservatives are also very interested in civic duty: what individuals owe to society. Being in the military is a high form of legal justice being rendered.

Justice between individuals, on the other hand, is mostly a justice of respect of contractual agreements and of another person's rights. In matters of justice between individuals, what is owed is exactly equal to the amount of the debt. Between individuals, justice is a matter of tit for tat.

On the other hand, in matters of distributive justice, the justice owed by society to an individual is more than a matter of tit for tat. The community itself is indebted to the individual according to the degree that the individual has been serving society. Society is more indebted to its citizens who are the most active and constructive on the social scene than to people who have never contributed significantly to society.

Distributive justice is therefore very often proportional to the rank that someone has in society. For it is the mark of healthy societies that the social rank corresponds to the rank according to which individuals effectively contribute to the common good. In such societies a "Noblesse Oblige" attitude prevail.

A society should honor more its generals than its private soldiers for example. If generals do not truly merit the honor given them the issue is not one of distributive justice but of the way the army promotes its generals.

In the case of a foreign invasion, society must protect the buildings which contribute the most to the common good, including bridges and roads but also those private industrial installations which contribute the most directly to providing the goods which will best help the people withstand the foreign aggression, like bakeries, dairy plants and weapon manufacturers.

All citizens, under distributive justice, have the basic right to be protected by the police and the army, to be treated fairly by the justice system and the laws and to share in the cultural and material heritage of the nation.

Who decides what someone has contributed to society? The government decides. The leader decides. From justice comes the notion of authority, as a source of rights to implement distributive justice. Communism ultimately denies this authority to governments when it insists that the "dictatorship of the proletariat" should prevail and that even Communist governments should one day be abolished. Naturally they also state that it should not be done immediately but when "Le grand soir" (the big evening) will arrive and there will a permutation of the classes the poor (the proletariat) being on top and the rich on the bottom of society. Apparently that has not yet happened in any socialist country so the people in power are safely there.

Wrongly pretending that no one has definite authority over the citizenry and thus denying natural law, Communism ironically has been instrumental in the establishment of the most authoritarian "Nomenklatura", i.e., class of the governor-citizens, which rules over the governed- citizens.

Distributive justice in our modern minds is negatively affected by the notion of "income redistribution." Most democratic countries have adopted the principle of tax rates that are not proportional but increase with the levels of income. For many people, distributive justice simplistically means to take money from the rich and give it to the poor.

The definition of distributive justice is that "something is given to

94

the private individual insofar as what belongs to the whole is due to the part."

The aggregated income of the citizens does not automatically belong to the government, or to society as a whole, in democratic countries; therefore it cannot be redistributed to the citizen on the authority of the government. Consequently, the principle of non-proportional taxation cannot find its roots in the principle of distributive justice. It comes rather from a practical compromise between the greed of the rich and the envy of the not-so-rich.

Non-proportional taxation is in sum a corruption of the Christian principle that morally obliges the rich to perform corporal works of mercy: feed the hungry, shelter the homeless, cloth the naked, among others. It is a corruption because non-proportional tax laws are not promulgated under the principle of Christian brotherly love and therefore do not promote Christian brotherly love; they often are used as justification to many rich for not performing works of mercy. In this sense, therefore, these laws can even prevent Christian brotherly love.

It is proper for governments to have programs to offer the poor with the wherewithal to provide for their basic needs. But the plethora of distributive justice programs have not succeeded to "bring the poor out of their poverty" after the decades of the President Lyndon Johnson's "War on Poverty". Could it be that these programs will never succeed as long as we think that charity can be farmed out to the government? Would it be that these programs do not count for us to comply with our moral obligation of charity to the poor?

Justice and private property

It is in his treatment of Justice that Aquinas provides his justification for private property.

There are three reasons why private property can be maintained as a legal right.

The first reason is based on the motivation of individuals: one works harder if one can keep the fruit of his work. The second reason is between oneself and the community: disputes can be better resolved if each one knows what he owns. The third reason is related with society as a whole: a society in which private ownership exists is a more stable and affluent society.

However, God established the rule that all the things of this world belong to all human beings as a group (not each thing individually which can stay in the state of private property). That is to say that the use of the good material things of the world must be beneficiary to each and all.

This is principle is called the "universal destination of all created goods."

This stated, it remains that we must have a principle of organization to distribute efficiently these goods among men. The principle of private property - a principle recognized by the Church with the provision that the use of things must have a social dimension - is the organizing principle and happens to be much more effective than a system where the Church or the government would have to precisely decide where go each item of property.

However, private property should never be understood in a very narrow manner and especially it should never be understood in abstraction of its being principally a legal mechanism for the efficient distribution of goods to men. In particular private property should not be used to defraud the common good, as when a piece of property is wantonly destroyed by its owner so that it can benefit no one. In French law, it is illegal to destroy banknotes.

Another accepted interpretation of the social destination of privately-owned goods is that, while such goods can be kept as private property, their utilization must have a social purpose. It is a teaching of the Church that privately owned goods should be used in a manner that benefits the common good of society. Lest anyone be tempted to defraud the rich in virtue of this latter principle, we must hastily mention that this principle of the social destination of goods has never been used, to our knowledge, by the Church to defraud anyone, but it may have been invoked for the purpose of recommending uses for specific items of properties so that they could become marginally more profitable for society.

Justice in business

Justice in business can be viewed from the point of view of an employee, or from the point of view of an organization. From these two levels of analysis several relationships exist that should reflect a spirit of justice.

At the level of the employee and manager, the rights of other employees and managers in the organization need to be respected. The rights of people outside the organizations such as employees of other firms, competitors, suppliers, or customers, all stakeholders, also need to be respected. These rights include matters concerning just wages, honesty in the quality and quantities of products and services to be delivered, as well as the dignity of the status of these individuals encountered in business settings, as human beings and as working people.

Still at the level of the individual employee, general justice, under the form of loyalty, demands that the employee support the organization. Also, justice requires that, in cases of malfeasance on the part of the organization towards the general public, employees have the duty to take the necessary steps to protect this general public.

But they must be extremely cautious before taking any such step, known as "whistle-blowing." They must be absolutely sure that there is indeed malfeasance of intention and great damage being done to the general public.

Most employees usually have to assume that they do not have the great picture of what their firm is doing or what the industry is all about. They cannot consider that they know better than top management as relates to the justice of an activity, except in the rare cases when the company has committed an intrinsically evil action.

Employees must also delay "going public" until they have tried all avenues for obtaining reliable information on the nature of the firm's activities and for obtaining redress on activities of dubious justice. Before coming out against their company, it is a good idea to also seek the advice of a knowledgeable and unbiased third party.

Businesses should implement distributive justice for their employees within the company. The rights between two employees in a dispute and/or the negative effect that each party would cause the company should be assessed from the perspective of distributive justice. "Sexual harassment" cases come under distributive justice.

Businesses should operate in a spirit of commutative justice in their relationship with their competition and suppliers. They should be good citizens and follow the precepts of general justice towards the community and the nation, thus fulfilling their obligation of general justice.

The just manager

In addition to these prescriptions to abide by just principles in a setting that happens to be a business or commercial setting, managers are well advised to cultivate the virtue of justice for the sake of improving their company's management policy and their own managerial skills. Indeed, the attitude associated with a great level of sensibility to the needs of others is an attitude that is most important for business success.

In developing the corporate strategy of a company, one of the phases of that exercise is the assessment of "threats and opportunities" to the business. A spirit of justice is precisely the right attitude necessary to hone the sensitivity required to carry out this strategic exercise as it should be.

The environment of businesses is changing every day. Changes may be imperceptibly happening every given day. But changes need be assessed regularly, otherwise they will turn out to be major changes in the long run. The outside environment of a business can change: the social, technological, political and cultural levels. Businesses need to know how they relate with society at these levels and how they are situated in relationship to the trends that exist at each of these levels. Preferably, they should be one step ahead of the trend, unless there are practical and ethical reasons not to be.

Innovation in a company, whether the development of products or services, cannot be done in a vacuum. Corporate innovations need be related to changes in the outside world. Innovation is a necessity. Many companies have disappeared which did not know how to innovate. Innovation must be a good adjustment between the psychological resources of imagination of some members of the corporation and the sociological realities of the corporate environment.

A company in the buggy-whip business should not be allowed to promote a R&D policy supporting, say, the fiber-glass buggy whip without testing the idea in the market place. It needs to take a peek at the outside world and realize that buggies are disappearing.

Business organizations also change internally. Changes in

organizational structures, in personnel rotation as well as changes resulting indirectly from outside pressure will transform an organization, its resources and capabilities, from within. To ignore the changes and to expect that well established policies will bring about the same effects that they always did may be a sorely misled assumption. Corporations with an increasingly higher percentage of female personnel need to establish new or different policies about "fraternization" between employees.

The empathy that is necessary to be truly just is precisely the necessary element that will make the difference between a mechanical implementation of the "threats and opportunities" and an effective and comprehensive gathering of data on information that are of crucial importance for the survival and success of a business.

At a more immediate level, the manager who feels the empathy of justice will also be more in tune with the changes in his work team and divisions and will be more capable of adapting his own behavior to correspond to these changes. He will not only preserve his job but greatly enhance his career in the organization.

This empathy of justice cannot be faked. The ability to genuinely get in someone else's shoes to see the world from that perspective can be cultivated as any virtue can be cultivated.

But the Christian needs to go beyond justice. The desire to make changes so that the living conditions of the owner of the shoes can be improved also needs to be cultivated. One cannot clearly see the world from the perspective of the "other" if one has no real interest in improving the view that this "other" will have. We need to "love our neighbors as ourselves" to truly be in their shoes.

Under the spirit of justice we respect others as the "others" that they truly are with their full rights and dignity. Under the spirit of charity, we treat these others as ourselves. And under the spirit of charity, the others will be better treated. Charity fulfills the demands of justice and goes beyond.

9. Fortitude

The Nature of Fortitude-Courage

Fortitude, or courage, presupposes some vulnerability. Therefore, an angel cannot be brave. Naturally, the ultimate vulnerability is death. Courage, ultimately, means being ready to face death.

Courage also means facing a hardship, which can be as difficult to face as death, to achieve something or preserve something of value. Within the Christian religion what has to be preserved is more precisely one's obedience to Christ. For a Christian the ultimate proof of courage is martyrdom. All Christians are not called to martyrdom, but all Christians are expected to stand ready to die for Christ. This ultimate proof is expected of all in the same manner that charity, as bountiful as possible, is expected of all Christians.

Short of martyrdom, courage means an attitude of firmness that must exist in all the virtues. In the present culture, the lack of interest in courage is evidenced everyday by, among other marks, the prevalent idea that we should have an open society in which all opinions will be available and where we expect good opinions and Truth to prevail by themselves, without necessary involvement on our part. A society that defends this non-committal notion of a market place of ideas is a society without understanding of the virtue of courage.

On the contrary, the first psychological attitude that comes with courage must contain the understanding that all that is worthwhile is not attainable or, if attained, will not be preserved without effort. This attitude underlies the next necessary attitude of the courageous person which is the readiness to expend this necessary effort.

"It is for the sake of the good that the brave man exposes himself to the danger of death." The brave man must know the good.

To know the good in a concrete situation, the brave man needs therefore to possess the virtue of prudence.

Furthermore, the brave man must have the desire to do the good; he must have justice. Courage is subordinated to prudence and justice.

Naturally to modern ears to state that prudence must ordain courage is a very strange proposition. We can only make such a proposition because we have already developed in the previous pages the true nature of the virtue of prudence.

Also, courage, to be a virtue, must be ordained to justice. "Fortitude without justice is a lever of evil," wrote St. Ambrose. History is full of seemingly courageous warriors who brought blood and terror to whole nations. The unjust wars of those awesome warriors are the proof that their courage was in fact no courage, for, not being ordained to justice, it was no virtue.

To be courageous one needs be able to experience fear. And one cannot experience fear if one does not love. I cannot fear to lose my life if I do not care for my life. "He who fears the Lord will tremble at nothing" (Eccles. 35:16).

The parts of Fortitude

Of passive courage and active courage, it is passive courage, or endurance, which is the closest to the true virtue of courage.

Active courage or the virtue of being able to oppose evil is naturally an expression of courage, but passive courage contains, in addition, another important part of courage which is the virtue of patience. And no one can be truly virtuous without having the virtue of patience at a high degree. Patience is, in many ways, the test of true virtue.

Alas, patience, is not very much in fashion nowadays because patience is the typical virtue of neither youth nor of this youth- oriented society.

"Just anger" is another part of the virtue of courage, and, for other reasons, it is a virtue that is also not very much in fashion. The ability to experience at a very high level the injustice of a situation sends the adrenaline that surges in us the passion of anger. When someone is able to harness his anger and direct it to make himself better and exhibit a courageous behavior it is evidently a virtue. When the mother sees her children in danger, she is ready to stand up to the wild beast.

Just anger is not appreciated in the Anglo-Saxon world where raising one's voice seems to be the ultimate sin as it invades the hushed surrounding of someone's comfortable privacy. It is a virtue much better understood in the Latin, Asian and African worlds.

"Meekness" is part of the virtue of courage. Like courage it strikes an even balance between aggressive behavior and cowardliness. To turn the other cheek is part of meekness and is also an expression of patience, typical of the Christian who is in this world but not of this world. "The prince of the world" is the devil. Therefore the role of the Christian cannot be to prevail in all the competitions that are open in this world, unless he acts in ways that are not distinguishable from the ways of those who are true heirs of the devil.

However, meekness does not necessarily mean turning the other cheek. "If there was harm in what I said, tell us what was harmful in it, but if not, why does thou strike me?" (John 18:23). The most patient of men, Jesus Christ, made this reply when struck in front of the high priest at his trial. This time, it was not necessary for Christ's plan of Redemption, nor in view of His commitment to obey His Father, that he be stricken that particular blow. He therefore did not need to be patient about it. He was justified in courageously rebuking the man for the injustice of his blow.

Courage and Work.

In the proceedings of an annual conference of the Society of Industrial Psychologists, one author complained that although they had made great strides in their studies of the psyche of the worker, they still had not been able to develop a valid concept of "effort."

The irony of this admission is that in reality "effort" is the central concept that industrial psychologists are supposed to be dealing with. Corporations do not pay the salaries of industrial psychologists primarily for the betterment of the psychological health of their employees. Corporations pay psychologists above all to make sure that the employees are going to keep their noses to the grindstone, that they will keep up their level of "effort." (14)

Courage is, in a narrow perspective, the principal virtue that must be understood by specialists in the whole field of work and management. Laziness, indeed, is a vice that comes directly in opposition to courage. Hard work is thus a part of the virtue of courage. Christian psychologists who understand that relationship between work and courage have a better grasp of managerial reality and can be more effective in improving managerial problems related to work attitudes.

If they were really consistent in their intention to watch the bottom line and really understood their interest, corporations would more readily use Christian industrial psychologists rather than secular industrial psychologists. Only the Christian industrial psychologist has the key to employees' effort.

In work, courage is the willingness to do something that is difficult but good or worthwhile, in spite of the fatigue or negative consequences for the body or mind of the worker. Difficult work can be of different natures: it can be strenuous work that is taxing for the muscles; it can be dangerous work and taxing for the nerves with the additional risk of physical accident; it can be boring work, repetitious work, that is demanding for the worker's patience; it can be intellectually difficult work and a burden for the brain of the worker.

The courageous manager

Work can also be dangerous career-wise, that is the manager may take a chance with his career pursuing a line of activities.

Such an intellectual work effort that is potentially dangerous for one's career is called an initiative. Good corporations naturally will encourage the taking of initiatives, by rewarding successful initiatives and by not sanctioning initiatives that failed and were undertaken within acceptable limits of prudence.

Good corporations understand that businesses being in a sea of constant change, new procedures, and new ways of doing things must be developed and instituted if they want to keep adapted to changes. These new methods need to be developed by trial and error after they have been subjected to a normal level of reasoned analysis.

Analysis is not enough. Pushing analysis to the extreme is not useful in the business world. New techniques have to be tried and tested with reality because businesses exist in the world of the practical.

The development of some new techniques involves whole teams within a corporation and their refining may be the object of reasonable level of organizational planning. Other techniques only involve the responsibilities of a single individual worker or manager. The latter should then stand ready to conceive and implement some of the new approaches to do his job.

The courageous corporation

In addition to the courage of work teams and of individual employees and managers, courage can be institutionalized in the corporation.

Courage is the attitude with which one is ready to fight for preserving or for attaining a good thing that can be attained. In corporations, part of the strategic effort consists in investigating and listing new areas of business that the corporation, as a whole, could be involved with.

It would be a sort of institutionalization of courage in corporate settings to develop programs to systematically and pro-actively try and enter these new business fields.

Programs in innovative management, innovative technology and/or innovative businesses are basically going to be successful, if and only if the virtue of courage is well appreciated and shared within a corporation.

Magnanimity, which means having a great mind is a part of the virtue of courage. A magnanimous person tends to great deeds and neglects little things. A magnanimous corporation would be interested in great projects and pass over little projects in which its energies could be wasted. A magnanimous corporation would more specifically manage its portfolio of programs in a way that would call for the concentration of its resources in really challenging programs.

Magnificence which means doing great things at great, or proportionate, but reasonable, costs is another part of courage. Magnificence can be translated in corporate strategy into a vision of challenging programs. The program to place a man on the moon was an effort in magnificence on the part of President Kennedy. Similarly some corporations are corporations with vision, when others are perfectly content to struggle with the mundane. A magnificent corporation would have a corporate strategy staff who would not be afraid of launching great programs, but at the same time the corporation would have a very well developed cost accounting and project auditing system to avoid wasteful expenses and a very savvy director of finance who would know how to bring down as low as possible the cost of capital for the firm.

Perseverance is another part of courage. A corporation perseveres after it has given itself a well-defined objective, would stay with it and would not be easily swayed from its resolve.

A corporation may decide to increase its Research and Development expenditures and for a time this decision will be costly. It will require much courage to keep this objective until new technologies start to come out of the R&D department and before it will be able to earn its keep.

Another corporation may have a revolutionary new product and decide to undertake a significant level of advertising expenditures to familiarize the general public with the product. Again, early results from this program may be disheartening.

A third corporation may develop programs to develop the understanding and the acceptance of the virtuous life among its employees and managers. The short term effect of these programs may require a strong soul at the corporate helm. Still, in business as in the life of the individual, the same reality ordains: "He who loves his life will lose it." Courage is the quality that is necessary to let go the self-centeredness, the love of self, the "way things are done here" and to risk extending oneself towards new and promising horizons.

10. Temperance

The Nature of Temperance

If courage is, in the narrow sense, the virtue which keeps in check the human passions of aggressiveness and fear, temperance, in the narrow sense also, keeps in check the passions towards sensuality. Courage is the virtue that ensures that our powers as mobile animals are under the control of reason. Temperance is the virtue which puts into the control of our intellect our magnificent ability to feel our surroundings thanks to an extremely complex nervous system.

Pieper tells us that the etymology of the word temperance indicates that the ancients had a much broader view of this virtue:

"In St. Paul's First Epistle to the Corinthians (12,24f) we read:

> Deus temperavit corpus. 'Thus God has established a harmony in the body, giving special honor to that which needed it most. There was to be no want of unity in the body; all the different parts of it were to make each other's welfare their common care.' The primary and essential meaning of 'temperare,' therefore, is this: to dispose various parts into one unified and ordered whole."

Aquinas says that the second meaning of temperance is "serenity of the spirit." In other words, temperance should not be viewed primarily for its negative aspects of keeping the passions under check, but for its positive aspect of allowing the intellect to perform freely from any bias.

An undue interest of what will interact with our nervous system makes us entertain a very limited view of the world. It limits our view of the world to whatever has the greater chance to encounter our body where our body is, and to come in contact with our body now. This limited view of the world is a self-centered and selfish view. On the other hand, to be temperate is to let our intellect be unconstrained by the limited sphere of our physical existence, by the here and the now of our body.

Temperance is not only the preservation of the body under the control of the mind but the preservation of the proper place of each of the elements of the human body.

Temperance is the force that preserves the integrity of the human body and therefore of the human person, as one single organized and harmonized entity.

Conversely, the lack of temperance is the chief means by which the human body and the human person are going to self-destruct.

Temperance belonging to the nature of man, the more natural way for man to fall apart is by a lack of temperance.

Sex and Food

It is interesting that sex and food and drink are really very important spheres of interest in modern day culture. All those who do not participate in the limitless veneration of these modern gods are basically branded as asocial.

This situation is all the more dangerous in that it leads an important minority of the population to the pure and simple rejection of all sex and food as impure and basically bad. This rejection is one of the most common sources of heresies.

Albigentianism, a heresy rampant in the south of France in the 13th century, drew its principles from the Manichean philosophy. Manicheans saw the universe in black and white: they considered only what belonged to the spirit to be good, what belonged to the flesh to be bad. Existence itself as it represented the entrapment of a good soul in a bad body was essentially evil. Suicide was encouraged as a high form of spiritual exercise.

In opposition to these beliefs, Aristotle and Aquinas consider that chastity is, like all the virtues, a happy mean between a vice by excess and a vice by default. To be oversexed, in other words is a vice, but so is to be "under-sexed." Indeed, lack of sexual interest is considered by these giants as a lack of sensitivity and a defect.

In the Summa Theologicae, IIa, IIae question 142, answers, Aquinas writes: "Wherefore the natural order requires that man should make use of these pleasures, in so far as they are necessary for man's well-being, as regards the preservation either of the individual or of the species. Accordingly, if anyone were to reject pleasure to the extent of omitting things that are necessary for nature's preservation, he would sin, as acting counter to the order of nature."

That may be astonishing to modern minds who tend to equate religion and Puritanism. Aquinas also responds to the objection that could be made which follows: "in the sexual act the abundance of pleasure overwhelms the possibility of spiritual cognition," this is a proof that "there is no act of begetting without sin," and the sexual act is inherently bad. Aquinas replied: "as long as the sexual act itself corresponds to the rational order, the abundance of pleasure does not conflict with the proper mean of virtue..."

Aquinas also states that in Paradise the pleasure of intercourse would have been even stronger than it is today in our Fallen state, because awareness was unclouded and because of the delicacy of human nature and the higher sensitivity of the body.

Thus, when the proper conditions are fulfilled, a couple having intercourse can be as saintly as angels.

Chastity, as part of the virtue of temperance, fulfills the proper conditions.

Chastity and temperance, which are sometimes viewed as the primary subjects of preaching by moralists and reformers, are actually and objectively the least important categories of vice. However, they are important in the sense that they are the most frequent vices. They are likely to be the first steps which one will take turning away from God.

Drunkenness in the pleasures of the flesh is capable of clouding one's clear thinking and resolve, warp all the other qualities and turn them away from their destination of helping the soul in its progression towards God. But let is warn that a "zero-tolerance" for drunkenness is itself a vice: Our Lord did drink wine.

Curiosity

Curiosity is a vice against temperance. It is the pursuit of knowledge that is of no value to the person or group experiencing this curiosity.

The proper virtue that opposes curiosity has really not received a proper name in English. Its Latin name is "Studiositas," the proper attitude towards learning subjects that are of great purpose to the learner.

Objects of learning which are proper are, naturally, first related to the spiritual salvation of the learner. At another level, proper matters of learning are related to the learner's state in life as long as it is not taking precedence over his salvation. A librarian can learn a lot about library sciences and books, provided that does not distract him from having a spiritual life and taking care of his family.

Curiosity may be opposed as a vice that has no real meaning in our age which values entertainment so much. Entertainment is indeed a valid human activity. But, when youngsters and adults are watching so much television, don't we think that they are having a little too much entertainment, that even if they are learning something from TV there is a threshold at which what they are learning is not really relevant nor useful to them?

Curiosity is the vice that indicates that even in intellectual endeavors we can sin against temperance.

The temperate manager

Business managers, when they arrive in a new job, must become familiarized with the policies attached to their job and to their company. These policies are not always described in a book of policy. And even if they are, helpful workmates are most likely to point out gleefully that a specific policy that is written in the book of policies is superseded. In other words, most of policies that have been consigned to paper are often without value as concerns learning how to operate and behave in a given corporation.

Growing in the job, the manager learns these policies, until the day when he would be much surprised to learn that something he is doing almost automatically is really solely the corporate policy of the particular company he is working for and that there are other ways to do the same things.

In addition to these corporate policies, the manager has ideas of his own about his job and his company. One of his objectives will be to promote these ideas. Sometimes, realizing the amount of opposition to his idea, he will understand that he will have to make the decision to push his ideas a little harder that he really intended to. He may be a little unfair pushing this idea but, he will rationalize, this is the only way to give this idea a chance.

Ideas presented by a new manager may be good policy initiatives. Corporations should welcome the introduction of proposals for new policy initiatives. These initiatives need to be evaluated and a decision should be made about them regarding whether they should be retained or not. Often they will not be retained.

Just as it is good to have a plentiful crop of new initiatives, it is good to have a means to select among these initiatives. New managers should, at a certain point, yield to the corporate process that rejects their initiatives. To push too far for their initiatives to be accepted is sometimes an effort that goes against the virtue of temperance as its consequences may lead to a loss of balance for the corporation which would be too active in one area and not enough in another area.

In the other direction, the long-time manager who is quite familiar with all the policies of his firm and who has already fought all his battles about changes of policies within his firm and has become comfortable with the outcomes, may fight new policy initiatives a little too hard. It may be just that he does not want to be bothered with new ideas and likes things just the way they are, thank you. This seasoned manager, by clinging too hard to old ways of doing things, to old policies, may jeopardize the balance of the company. Companies need to adjust their priorities, to shift their balance to keep in touch with the realities of the ever changing business environment.

There are other ways to be temperate or intemperate as a manager. The manager who is in charge of a department, like the mailing room, a team or even a business division may attach more value to this department, this team or this division than to the company as a whole. This organizational problem, known in management as "empire building" is the result of a lack of temperance on the part of such a manager.

The temperate corporation

Corporations are made up of different functional departments such as finance, marketing, manufacturing, personnel, accounting.

These departments have also a tendency to enter in conflicts with each other. The sales department is ready to grant all sorts of discounts to potential customers to get more orders, but the finance department may object to the discounts as they narrow the profit margin.

The engineering department may wish to postpone the decision to put a product in the production phase, because they are quite close to bringing out a new, much improved, product. Marketing which has been promising a new product to its customers does not want to wait and risk that the clients become impatient. Finance would like to see that a product comes out of manufacturing as soon as possible and start paying for the Research and Development expenditures made so far.

The temperate corporation is a corporation where the different functional departments are operating in a condition of equilibrium.

They may compete against each other to a certain degree but they are not out to destroy the company.

Also some corporations, for reasons related to their own history, have a certain degree of bias in their make-up. A glass making corporation may be dominated by chemical engineers. These engineers are not only in manufacturing, but they are also in marketing and in finance and traditionally, the president of the company has always been a chemical engineer.

In principle there is nothing inherently wrong about such bias. Such corporations have unique potentialities in communicating information between individuals sharing the same educational background. Even financial issues can be better communicated between a chemical engineer and another chemical engineer because their patterns of thoughts are similar. However, people who are not chemical engineers are not going to feel very much at ease in such a corporation. A Vice President of Finance who is not a chemical engineer by background is looking hopelessly at the prospect for his possibility of promotion to President of the corporation to be very poor. It is the unwritten law in this corporation that all presidents must be chemical engineers. A marketing man who is not a chemical engineer may resent the fact that other marketing men with a chemical engineering background are somewhat banding together and are just not communicating very well with their other colleagues.

Such intra-corporation bias may thus have drawbacks, as well as advantages. Such bias may become a vice when, in spite of a very dangerous lack of balance, the corporation will not accept shedding this bias.

Many corporations whose roots go back to the XIXth century have a bias in favor of engineering. The new disciplines of finance and especially marketing are often considered newfangled and not deserving of respect on the part of engineers. Many of such engineer-dominated

115

corporations have disappeared because they refused to change their perspective from a production-dominated economy to a consumption-dominated economy. They managed themselves right out of the economy and into bankruptcy.

11. What Kind of Action - The Nature of Work

Christian work is an activity of the human person. This human person is endowed with an intellect and a will which he can exercise and perfect, so that he himself can grow in the virtues and gain eternal salvation.(15)

The four parts of work

a - In work, the human person summons and uses his skills,, talents and virtues that are interior to him and thereby, by each work performed, he increases in these skills, talents and virtues. This part of work is referred to as "labor" in the Church's social teachings. We can also call it: the "psychological" (from "psyche", soul), or individualistic, element of work. In philosophy this first part of work relates to the subject of what human beings "do."

b - In work, the human being applies these skills,, talents and virtues to something exterior to him, whether a piece of wood, a piece of paper, a sheet of music, a stack of brick, a business organization, team or department etc. and transform them, adding value to that something. This "something" is called "capital" in the Church social teachings and is

116

opposed to "labor" which brings this thing into being. In philosophy, this second part of work relates to the subject of what human beings "make."

This element b has been called by the Pope John Paul II: the "transitive" element of work.

Only God can work with something that is not exterior to Him. His work of God is called "creation," not work.

c - Man being a social animal, and an intelligent social animal at that, has soon understood the value of the principle of division of labor. When man works he contributes to society, not only the tangible goods he produces but the attitude and values with which they are produced. This is the communal and "sociological" element of work.

d - By adding value to his work, the human being makes a contribution to the material economy of his environment and is rewarded for it; thus he provides for his own subsistence, he makes a living.

The relative importance of the parts

Parts a and b of the definition of work are irreducible and must be present in all types of work. There cannot be work if the person at work does not utilize his skills,, talents or virtues, and if these are not applied to something exterior to him to transform it.

If the skills,, etc., are utilized not on something exterior, but interior, to the person, this is not work. It can be another activity like a learning process, a growth in virtue or an ascetic exercise. This shows how closely work is related to other important human activities.

Part c, contribution to society, is not absolutely necessary for work to be work, but is most often present. There is no contribution to society for men working in isolation, for example, men stranded on an island. But the exceptions are very rare as most individuals live in some sort of social organization.

Part d - making a living - is the least necessary, at least theoretically in this definition of the nature of work. Indeed volunteer work does not contribute to providing for the worker's subsistence by definition. Although volunteers are an exception, they are not rare. Most people do work some of the time on a voluntary basis. Volunteer work is real work.

Housework is work in the full sense; it also does contain elements c and d. By working for our household we do provide for an segment of society, even if this segment is limited to the members of a household. Housework is also part of making a living, for we are providing services necessary to our living, and which, if not provided by us would have to be bought from outside sources, thus depleting resources that would have to be otherwise made up.

Students are working when they are working on a term paper or an assignment. When they are memorizing a textbook they are not working, they are studying.

The four dimensions of work

	Subjective	Objective
Positive	Worker's growth in Excellence	Production of Products and Services
Negative	Work as toil and Drudgery	Transformation and Destruction of Raw Materials

To apply oneself to a task is always somewhat of a toil – this is the subjective-negative side of work. We can look at work from this subjective-negative point of view. The something exterior to oneself that is modified to produce objective work is often destroyed or is made other than it originally was: this is the objective-negative side of work. By working, one increases in talents, skills and virtue, this is the subjective-positive side of work. By working one is adding value to something: this is the objective-positive side of work.

The above definitions hold true for all work, whether Christian or not. However, it has been developed on the basis of Christian philosophy and teachings. It will not be found in secular management textbooks. It is their loss. However, true Christian work includes important additional considerations.

The Christian aspect of the dimensions of work

	Subjective	Objective
Positive	Workers growth in holiness	Re-creation of the World
Negative	Following Christ on the Cross	The seed dies

Christian considerations to elements a and b or work:

The subjective-negative side of work, or work as drudgery, is given a special meaning according to Christian teaching. By this work, we pay for original sin but also we associate ourselves to Our Lord on the Cross.

The subjective-positive side of work, the increase in skills,, talents and virtues, is sign and consequence that, by our association with Our Lord on the Cross, we also share in His Redemption. We are being rebuilt just as the world is being rebuilt by the objective-positive side of work, the value-adding element.

The objective-negative side of work, the losses or transformation of resources in any given type of work, also has Christian significance from the Biblical story of the Fall and Redemption. They are grains that have to die before a new life can be born.

The subjective side of work cannot be disassociated from the spiritual life of the working Christian, his life of prayer and worship, which influences his work and gives it depth and quality.

Work, Justice and Mercy

The Christian at work also does not forget the charitable part of work. He will always consider the people with whom he is in contact in his work as more than coworkers, suppliers, employees, bosses, competitors or clients. He will see them as individuals who are destined to belong to the same Body of Christ. He will see them as people towards whom he needs to exercise his virtue of justice.

He sees a spiritual solidarity with them that should translate into his performing works of mercy towards them. Many circumstances allow such works of mercy in the work place, especially spiritual works of mercy that are adapted to the type of one's vocational work, but without neglecting performing also general physical works of mercy, when necessary.

Work and Providence

Working as a means of providing for one's subsistence cannot be understood by a Christian without reference to Divine Providence. Indeed it is God's Providence that provides for our subsistence, and God uses our own skills to provide us a job. In turn the job will bring a paycheck or profit that will allow us to provide for our needs.

However, the relationship between God-given skills and talents, the quantity and quality of effort put in a work and the productivity of that work should also be viewed from the perspective of Divine Providence.

Returning to basics, Providence is the means by which God provides for our needs and those of others. However, He always chooses spiritual needs over physical needs as His first priority is to redeem us rather than to make us affluent. Also, He may sometimes provide more, through our work, for the needs of others than for our own.

121

God allows that the correlation between talents, skills and virtues on one hand, quality or quantity of work on another hand and material productivity for our personal sake of that work not always be direct. One conclusion is that to work more just to gain more riches is both morally wrong, but also practically ineffective. Christians at work must always trust in Providence, no matter how Providence shows itself.

The work of the Manager

Beyond the preceding observations common to all workers, Christian considerations to be made specifically about the work of businessmen and managers are related to three types of responsibilities.

1 - The responsibilities related to ownership. Managers act as the proxies of the business owners and as the ownership entails responsibilities. e.g. in reference to the common destination of the earth's riches.

2 - The responsibilities related to the process of money-making as the effective goal of corporations is to make profits and this objective has its own set of responsibilities e.g. the ethics of business operations in particular as relates to the proper prioritization of means and ends.

3 - The responsibilities related to the matter of the authority of one man, the manager, over another man, the employee as management is essentially the exercise of authority, e.g. as relates to the dignity of the person.

PART II

The Busy Village – Work and the Managing of

Organizations and Businesses.

-1. Double Perfection and Sweet Success – The Nature of Business

Business as the Establishment of New Work.

What is a business? It is the institution of a new concrete type of work. The word "institution" is taken here with its two different meanings. The first definition of "institution" (Latin in-stare): putting in place; and the second definition is a comprehensive, wholesome and self-sufficient organization, in such ways that we can refer to an educational institution.

When, before the industrial age or even yesterday, someone opened a shoe shop or a bakery, the essential purpose of the artisan was to create the environment where he could work as a shoemaker or as a baker. To open a new business, for the most part, means to set up a new type of work.

Opening a new business has really seldom the connotation that popular imagery has developed for it: taking the first step to becoming a great tycoon. The shop, as a new business, was thus an extension of the work function and a mandatory requirement for this work function.

The shoemaker may have chosen to work for an established shoemaker, as an employee or as a partner; he would not have founded a new business. If the shoemaker wanted to work in a street or a village where there was no shoemaker, he had no choice but to start a new business. If he wanted to work with radically new methods of shoemaking, or create radically new styles, he had to start a new business.

A business always connotes the idea that a different type of work had been the source of its birth. A new business necessarily denotes novelty in work. Such novelty is evident when it relates to a new product or a new technology. More often than not it refers to a new manner of doing business, new financing methods, new merchandising, or simply a new location for a store. Novelty in a new business does not have to have the glamour of new technology.

Even an established business may go into a new line of business. In one way it may be easier for an established business to branch out. Resources may be stretched a little bit in the established business to accommodate the new business. A secretary, an office can be shared.

In other ways, it is more difficult for an established business to go into a new line of business: this is the whole point, made in the Bible, about "new wine" which should be put into "new skins." Existing companies have a tendency to control too much their own new ventures and especially to be very cautious that the new business does not even appear to take away some of the business of the established organization. However, this is precisely how progress is made: the new eventually replaces the old, by necessity.

But the nature of a business is not simply the putting in place of a new type of work.

Business as Environment for Work

Business is also an institution of work in the sense that it consists in developing around a specific type of work a complete and self-sufficient organization.

In all types of work there is a need to create the business environment for the principal work activity. This business environment is constituted by different services that support the core activity of the business.

It would seem that the shoemaker needs only to know his tools and select his leathers. He needs to control his hammers and anvil and the design of his shoes and the techniques he will utilize to complete his shoes. But if that is all that the shoemaker can do, he cannot operate as a shoemaker.

In addition to making shoes, he must rent or own a shop, deal with the authorities for the proper work permits, hire assistants, order his tools and supplies, attend to customers, investigate what customers would most likely buy, make agreements with banks and other sources of financing, etc.

We note that these support activities take the shoemaker away from his somehow solitary activity of making shoes, to put him in the situation where he has to deal with a large number of groups of people.

Whether he rents or owns his shop, he must know something about the real estate market and realtors. He needs to deal with the different governmental offices and their representatives. He must know about the personnel pool available in his line of work. He needs to have a working knowledge of all providers and suppliers of tools and supplies in his field, as well as in the technical developments in their trades.

He must know about his present customers, as well as his potential customers, their tastes and habits.

He must know about the other shoemakers and how they view their craft, the trends in shoemaking and the new styles that are coming from the big cities, the technologies and new working methods for making shoes, which are being developed.

The support services to the basic craft of shoemaking all have a strong social dimension. They make it impossible for the shoemaker to live and work in isolation of other human beings.

External Cooperation with a Business

The different economic relationships of a new business constitute as many bridges with society in general and, at the same time, are all support functions of the core work of shoemaking for the shoemaker's shop.

However, their support responsibilities are unequal in quality, importance and difficulty.

Once the proper steps are taken and the fees paid, the necessary working permits will be granted for a reasonably long time. It is not too difficult, either, to buy the premises of the shop or to contract a leasing agreement for a shop, when one has the money for it. Similarly, suppliers and providers of other services will be most pleasant to deal with when one has the financing to pay them adequately.

Also, a financial plan, which is sound and includes adequate collateral will find a banker and investors ready to assist in different tight spots where fresh financing may be required. The banker is also a supplier; he supplies money and needs to be friendly to his customers to stay in business.

All these different business functions, these support services that need be established for the business to function, can be developed without too many difficulties. Because their development consists in dealing with individuals who are also in business and whose role is to make the relationship with the new business as smooth as possible.

The Marketing function; a Financial Imperative

This is where the marketing function stands out. Customers need not make it easy for the business to sell them its wares.

Customers may not come to the shop. They may not buy any of the different models proposed. They may not accept the financial conditions offered them. If a new cabinet-maker offers 6 months' credit facilities, the customers may want a longer term for the credit.

Because of this essential independence of choice of the customers - a wild card element in new business ventures – the marketing function is the most difficult and the most important. A business will not survive if it cannot offer a scheme of products and service and prices to its customers that will ensure a reasonable level of stability in the selling function of the business, therefore of income, and therefore of stability to the business as a whole.

As long as the marketing function is not assured a corporation cannot claim to be "in business." The marketing function is the most important part of the puzzle in what constitutes a business.

As long as a business cannot develop properly its marketing function, it cannot sell and it cannot sell at a profit.

Although it has been stated that the fourth part of work – work as a means to make a living - was not a compulsory part of work for an individual person (as in the case of volunteer work), it is important to note that, at the level of the business enterprise, it certainly is compulsory. A business needs be self-supporting, even a non-profit business. To turn out a profit is an essential consequence of the social nature of business.

A business does not have father, uncles, an inheritance, unemployment benefits or other latent sources of income. There is no financial slack in a business. As soon as a business gets at to end of its financial rope, it falls out.

The Marketing Function: Social Imperative

Because of this inherent vulnerability that businesses have towards their customers, businesses need to develop and maintain a very important attitude toward their customers: an attitude of service.

The police keep order inside the nation. The army keeps order at the border. Police and army are justified by their objectives. They are also performing within a system that controls them and monitors how well they meet their objectives: the government which is, in turn, accountable to the nation.

What are, similarly, the justification and control of the private business sector?

Businesses primarily provide us with material goods and services, the material necessities of life. This is their major justification for existing.

Second question: who and what controls them? We do, and we do it automatically through the proper and automatic mechanism of the marketing function. We want to decide directly which material goods and services we want businesses to offer us. We want each of our buying decisions to have a direct impact on the potential of businesses to bring us more of what we want and less of what we do not want.

Such purchasing choices are often too subtle and too intuitive for us to rely on intermediate organizations, whether they are public or private, to act as agents for us. Countries where such public agents exist, like Communist countries where the people are theoretically represented in the decision making for the development of a product policy of manufacturing plans, the adjustment between supply and demand of goods is the worst possible. Styles and sizes are not available. Qualities of goods are far below the acceptable norm, etc.

The private sector, as a component of society, is subjected to the principle of "division of work." Usually, when we mention "division of work," it is done in a narrower perspective, e.g., bakers make and sell bread, candle makers make and sell candles. But, at a broader level, the private business sector supplies material goods. It finds its full justification, its job in society, when it is responsive - this also often means "vulnerable" - to customers' buying decisions.

The marketing function is the activity by which businesses primarily comply with their need to be accepted by society at large.

In the case of people such as Robinson Crusoe, the work of those persons who are not in society is indeed work, even though there is no social dimension in building a cabin on a deserted island. For most of us who are in society, our work has a social dimension that carries with it an array of social responsibilities. These responsibilities of businesses correspond to the third element of work.

The relationship between the "business" and "work" is inescapable. Because businesses are composed of a number of individuals who work, these individuals have social responsibilities - and we are not talking yet of ethical responsibilities - in their work. In addition, because some individuals work in businesses, their responsibility will espouse a specific form, different for example from the responsibilities of military people or civil servants.

Specifically, people in business and businesses themselves must supply material goods to the population in ways that satisfies this population.

The marketing function: source of perfection

The vulnerability of businesses to the different desires, and even whims, of customers, which incorporates the fundamental responsibilities of businesses to society, should not be viewed solely as a weakness inherent to business activities and to which businesses need to accommodate themselves willy-nilly. It is, on the contrary, the source of their strength.

This vulnerability and responsibility are the first source of perfection of businesses. An incessant zeal must exist at the leadership level of a business to respond as quickly, efficiently and correctly as possible to the desires of customers.

Whereas businesses have no souls, there are principles that may lead to their organizational perfection. The first principle is the extent to which they develop this attitude of responsiveness towards customers.

When a business is the first to provide customers something they want, this business is usually generously rewarded in many ways. Financially, new products tend to have bigger profit margins. Commercially, new product companies have faster growth. Companies who are well ahead of their competition need not worry about dirty tricks that rival companies may prepare against them because their competition will not catch up with them.

On the other hand, businesses that are not kept on their toes by a policy of responsiveness to customers, which are not driven to seek and furnish customers with what they want, are very likely to become sluggish in all their other functions.

In a business, the marketing function is a means necessary to energize and give direction to all the other functions of the business. These other functions will obtain their criteria of effectiveness, not from exterior academic or scientific reasons, but to the extent that they can support the marketing function of that particular business. A business that lacks this orientation will tend to witness an attitude of independence on the part of its various functional departments and that will eventually pull the whole business apart.

Developing the Marketing Imperative

How do managers cultivate the proper attitude of primacy for the marketing function, of the zeal to respond to customers' wants in their businesses?

They do so by appealing to both the sense of social responsibilities and the sense of responsibilities towards work of their employees and other managers and by translating, applying and focusing these senses of responsibilities to the benefit of customers.

Managers need to convince their employees that these employees must furnish the best quality of work possible so that customers will be satisfied.

The Second Justification of Business

Since business is a means to institutionalize work in society, another justification for business is to facilitate, for as many people as possible, their finding work and their finding work that is commensurable with their abilities.

It is widely believed - erroneously so - that the purpose of business is primarily to provide jobs. Job creation is a very important responsibility of the private sector; however, it is not its primary responsibility.

The other sectors of the economy - the non-profit sector, the public sector - are also capable of providing jobs. Modern economies have seen a significant development of the non-profit sector and it may be argued that the information revolution will further spur the growth of the non-profit sector. Providing jobs is not a responsibility that can be met by the private sector alone, although in practice it is the private sector that will provide the most jobs by far.

It is also a matter of form and function of businesses. Manpower is a resource for businesses and the selection of a resource must depend on the objectives of an operation. A business needs to know what it is really doing to select the employees that it needs. If the business is unsure of its market, the hiring of new employees who may not be made productive - through no fault of their own - will become a burden which may even lead to the bankruptcy of the business, a counter-productive measure as far as a full employment objective is concerned.

Another reason why the marketing function must be the dominant justification for businesses: putting the marketing function of business before the job-creating function is a correct understanding of social demands on a business.

Although society as a whole, or even society represented by the smaller population of active political groups, may want businesses to view their job creating function as their number one priority, that is not what individual businesses in practice feel is the strongest pressure that is put on them.

The customer base of a business is first interested by the quality, types and prices of products and services offered by the business. Seldom, if ever, will the hiring policies of a business affect consumer behavior in its regard. At the level of a single business the pressure to fulfill its job creating function may be very light. The pressure on individual businesses to fulfill their job-creating responsibility can almost solely be exerted through political and legal means.

The question is how much pressure politicians and lawmakers should put on businesses. We have seen that too much pressure may lead firms to bankruptcy.

Also, many jobs are exported: they disappear from Western countries and reappear in poorer countries. The inhabitants of these poorer countries are God's children too. Is it wise to oppose a natural economic shift in job allocation and what may also be the hand of Divine Providence to provide jobs to these poorer brothers?

Also, politicians and decision-makers in matter of economic policy have another means to develop job creation: encouraging the creation of new businesses, notoriously the most potent source of new jobs. These policy makers can promote new businesses by an array of incentives: fiscal, technological, regulatory, etc.

It is most important for the top man in an organization and his close staff to be personally committed to the issue of job creation and full employment. However, if top management is not committed - and is not motivated by a strong sense of justice - to do its best in that area, it is difficult for society to impose on them the responsibilities that they do not want to take.

But, if it takes a strong sense of justice for top management to be committed to an active policy of job creation, there is another dimension in personnel management in which they can do much good both for the nation's employment scene and for the success of their organizations: it is the matter of employee training and education. Naturally also, it is not to say that management should not be conducting a policy of fair hiring as concerns its own manpower.

The Second Business Perfection

We have seen above that managers need develop in their employees a sense of perfection in their work so that the customers of the business will be best satisfied, thus meeting the challenge of the first source of business perfection.

The best that these employees are capable of is not only their best as professionals or workers, but also their best as human beings, as persons.

The second principle of perfection of a business is for the business to give its employees all means and motivation to better themselves.

Indeed employees, who are often called the "human resources" of a business, are essentially the only true resources. If one entrepreneurial human being can start a chain of businesses, an organization with thousands of entrepreneurial employees must have an incredibly creative potential to develop an existing business and to create new ones.

The development of the work force and its perfection, we have learned in the first part of this book, cannot be done apart from an effort of perfection of the virtuous qualities of employees. Employees need become more virtuous both in general and in the particular applications and the specific conditions of their work.

The development of the work force needs also a direction, a criterion. This criterion is the extent to which the employee is fulfilling his responsibilities to better satisfy the business' customers and society as a whole.

This criterion will also orient and give focus, power and unity, to the development of the employee. When a special job requires courage in carrying out a physically burdensome work, that means that the employee needs to develop this type of courage rather than any other type of courage, e.g., the type of courage required to undertake a dangerous work. If an assistant is asked to perform rapid research work to provide essential data so that a manager can write an important business proposal within a short deadline, the virtues asked of her are not the virtues necessary to conduct an exhaustive research.

Society, and by proxy the customers of a business, thus decide in which direction a worker will concentrate his efforts towards his growth in virtues and his own inner perfection.

In order to fulfill the self-sufficiency imperative of the third part of work, as translated for business institutions, the third part of work, the social part which operates as society places a pressure on business, now becomes the criterion for the shaping and defining the second and first parts of work for business management and ultimately each employee, the (a) part relative to the worker's personal perfection, and (b) on the

135

selection of which products and services these workers will apply their efforts.

Parts of work

a/ Utilization of skills talents and virtues.

b/ Application of skills,, talents and virtues on something exterior.

c/ Interaction with others to work in society.

d/ Make a living in exchange for contributing to the common good.

The prioritization is now:

From a/ to d/, from the most necessary to the least necessary part of the work of an individual, from the viewpoint of the perfection of this individual.

From d/ to a/, from the most significant to the least significant part of the work of an individual, from the viewpoint of its contribution to society and the general economy.

And from d/ to a/ also, from the most sensitive to the least sensitive part of the work of an individual from the viewpoint of the manner by which society will impact on the work of this individual.

Innovation and Change

Intimately connected with the need to keep up with the changing wants of customers, and therefore with the core of what it is to be a business, businesses need to develop a great level of flexibility. Flexibility is required to perceive new patterns in the political, social, technical environment of the business and of its customers.

Flexibility is required to abandon old ways of doing things and to take up new ways.

To provide new products and services to customers, a business also needs to be very innovative. It is not enough to be flexible: a business has to produce a steady stream of new well-thought out and concrete products and services for approval by the market.

To simplify this difficult and expensive function of new products development, new techniques, called in-depth testing, have been developed and experimented. They involve the testing, through questionnaires and other behavioral methods, of initial concepts of potential new products and services that could be developed by the business. But such tests are of limited reliability. After the tests' results are in, prototypes are built or pilot services are developed, incorporating the tested concepts. Often customers do not really like them. That is again the customers' prerogative. Such programs do, however, indicate an effort of flexibility in the methodology of new product development programs, itself a definite effort in flexibility.

Flexibility and innovation are both connected with the principle of change. Businesses have been called "agents of change." Indeed, driven by the need to meet the wants of their customers, businesses become major sources of change, not only for them and the business sector, but also for all of society.

But change of the exterior world is much easier when change of the interior world has been conquered. Change in the exterior world of business is much easier for employees when they are familiar with change in the interior world of their own habits and virtues.

To promote growth in virtues, the slow learning to change from one stable psychological disposition to another, is the best training program for employees to understand the nature of change.

The search for virtuous perfection teaches employees what is genuinely required to change different programs in their business and to change the environment of this business. The virtuous employee has a great advantage in understanding and mastering flexibility, which is associated with temperance, and innovation, which requires courage.

As an added bonus, the virtuous employee is willing to develop new virtues because he is always ready to change and improve himself, prompted to do so by a sense of justice. Any business that employs a number of employees and managers with such familiarity and interest in the virtuous life is comfortably well ahead of its competition.

Therefore Divine Providence has provided that the two areas of perfection for businesses, the imperative to serve their customers and the imperative to develop the human value of their workforce as well as possible, are the surest ways for businesses to be successful.

- 2. - In the Image of Man - The nature and function of organizations.

What is an Organization

When in a business, people, procedures, premises and equipment are structured in an organized manner, this business is an organization.

What is organized is the core activity of the business and the support services that are organized around this core activity so that the business may be as effective as possible in making its mark in the economic sphere of a community.

The objective of the process of organization is for the different parts of the business to be in the proper location and of the proper size for the business and to have the proper degree of importance in affecting the business.

The accounting department must be just right for a business. The accounting system must not be too simplistic nor too detailed and the accounting department must communicate adequately with other departments, e.g., with the sales department in billing matters and the finance department to prepare reports for banks and annual reports for shareholders.

"Organization" connotes a sense of balance and the idea of a body whose different parts are arranged harmoniously to achieve a given business mission; the different parts of the business fit the roles of the organs of a body.

The functional levels

An organization is composed of different functional departments, e.g., production, finance, marketing, accounting, etc. These levels somewhat divide the organization vertically.

A typical organization chart shows first the top level where the president alone appears. Under the president, the different vice presidents are lined up at the second level with the portion of the organization that they supervise underneath them. Thus, going from one end to the other and from one vice president to the other, e.g., finance to marketing, we can describe the organization by mentioning the finance department, the marketing department, etc.

139

President

VP Finance	VP Marketing	VP Sales
Accounting Finance Staff	Dir. Mktg	Regional Dir. Sales.
Bookkpg Fin. Analysts	Mktg Research	Sales team leaders
	Mktg analysts	Salesmen

Vertical divisions and mission

In many organizations, even of moderate size, it is sometimes difficult to point to one person and to state that this person is performing the core work of the organization, and that the rest of the organization is only supporting this work.

However, the notion of core work needs to be kept in an organization, although we may prefer to call it the "mission" of the organization. We will see in strategic planning how important that notion of mission is.

Very often, the mission is clear when the founder is still alive who gave the organization its mission. The founder started the business to manufacture and commercialize his patent of an improved lock system for doors. The production department of the organization is then the premier department where the lock is manufactured after different models have been designed by design engineers, tested by test engineers. The production engineers make sure that production series are produced without flaws and waste. The marketing department strives to sell the locks even before they are produced. The service department keeps previous customers happy by keeping their locks in top shape, etc.

At this company, after the founder's death, the importance of the marketing department has probably grown over the years and superseded the production department in importance, especially after the patent has fallen in the public domain. Engineering still produces an effective product and changes its styles to keep pace with the public's changing tastes. But the mission has remained the same: to satisfy customers with the best engineered locks on the market. If the "engineering of locks" part of the mission has become less important, the "satisfaction of the customers" part of the mission has grown, and the organizational mission is sensibly the same as of the time of the founding of the business.

The proper interaction between the functional departments is what permits the organization to keep its mission alive and meaningful.

The Hierarchical levels

An organization is also divided between hierarchical levels, usually divided between three levels: top management, middle management, employees.

Hierarchical levels may multiply and be found also within functional departments: the plant workers, the foremen and the plant director together represent hierarchical divisions within the production department. (16)

Hierarchical levels are more than a simple division between sergeants, corporals and soldiers. Each level has a different type of function: the top of the organization has a strategic function, the middle of the organization has a "transactional" function (it is at this level that the organization transacts directly with its environment), the lower part of the organization has an operational function; this is the level at which operations are performed.

The operational level

The members of the organization at this level perform the basic work related directly to the production of products and services.

These workers first secure the input of production; they acquire and receive raw materials. Second, they transform inputs into outputs; these outputs may run the gamut between forging steel to educating students, or cutting hair. Third, the workers at the operational level distribute the outputs so that these outputs come out of the organization to society at large. Fourth, the workers provide direct support to the first three functions, including maintenance on machines, inventory of raw materials, or billing a restaurant patron.

The essential work of the organization is performed at this level. All the other levels are in some fashion as many services to support this operational level.

The Strategic level

The strategic part of the organization has the responsibility of ensuring that the organization serves the mission it has been given. This strategic level also verifies that the organization is responsive to the owners of the organization or those who are supposed to have control over it.

It is at the strategic level that the need of the managerial principle of "unity of command" is the most clear, although it is not the single place in the organization where it is required. Each person must receive his order from a single person. Confusion of command (with two or more superiors) usually leads to miscommunication, disorganization, paralysis, loss of motivation, and procrastination.

The Bible states that no one can serve two masters, namely God and Mammon, illustrating the validity of the same principle of unity of command.

The responsibility of the strategic level entails three sets of duties.

One set of duties is supervision that can be further broken down into resource allocator (organizational structure design, people and tasks assignment, issuing of work orders, decisions, authorizations), disturbance handler, monitor, disseminator, and leader. Direct supervision is precisely the role of ensuring that the organization is running smoothly as a single integrated unit.

The second set of duties involves the management of the organization's boundary conditions, its relationship with the environment. The managers at this level spend much of their time as spokespeople for the organization, as liaison with other groups and organizations and as negotiator for their organization.

The third set of duties relates to the development of the organization strategy that we will study separately.

The transactional level

The strategic level is joined to the operational level by middle-line managers. These middle managers have formal "line" authority over the members of the operational level. In addition, the transactional level also includes middle-line managers who have no authority over the operational level but instead supply the strategic level with direct supporting services to facilitate the tasks of the strategic level.

Middle managers of the second type are not part of the "line" function, but of the "staff" function.

Two principles are used for the supervisory tasks of middle-line managers: the principles of "chain of command" and of "span of control." All individuals in the organization should have a supervisor to whom they are directly accountable. They receive their orders from that individual. As the supervisors must in turn follow the orders of their own supervisors, this forms a chain-like structure.

Looking downwards, each supervisor has responsibility over not only one but also several employees. The number of employees under the supervision of a middle-line manager is what is called the "span of control." This span of control varies very much with what type of work the organization is involved and what the employees are specifically doing. On an assembly line for TV sets, a supervisor can control dozens of workers. In a research lab, a supervisor may have a much narrower span of control, as he needs to spend much time with each of the researchers and go over their work.

The Bible gives an illustration of supervision and spans of control:

"At the same time, from the people at large choose capable and God-fearing men, men who are trustworthy and incorruptible, and put them in charge of them as heads of thousands, hundreds, fifties and tens, and make them the people's permanent judges. They will refer all important matters to you, but all minor matters they will decide themselves, so making things easier for you by sharing the burden with you. If you do this - and may God so command you – you will be able to stand the strain, and all these people will go home satisfied"

144

(Exodus 18: 21-23) New Jerusalem Bible.

The soul of the organization

As already mentioned, organizations can be courageous, temperate, prudent and just. That is possible because the organization has something that resembles a human soul.

That soul of the organization, like the soul of a living body, makes the organization function and pre-determines the way according to which this organization will operate.

Organizations are not alive but they have a definite existence that is autonomous from the existence of any individual human being, including the founder and the top manager. When the founders and CEO die or are transferred the organization goes on. Often, founders and CEO themselves have difficulties understanding the autonomous nature of organizations and confuse them with their own private operations.

The soul of the organization exists as long as the organization exists. The souls of all organizations have the same nature.

Because all organizations borrow their existence from human beings, they all have in common characteristics, which belong to human nature.

The fact that organizations have a soul similar to the human soul is neither coincidence nor magical fact. Human beings, consciously or not, project as much as possible their own nature on the organizations they are involved with and this at all the organizational levels.

Now the soul of the organization is like the human soul. The strategic level corresponds to the rational soul, the transactional level corresponds to the animal soul and the operational level corresponds to the vegetative soul.

Strategic level	Rational soul
Transactional level	Animal soul
Operational level	Vegetative soul

The Organizational levels	The Human soul

As it is the case for the vegetative soul, the operational level corresponds to a very rigid structure. Neither the tree nor the operational level of a corporation can move, can maximize their nourishment, growth and reproduction. Supplies, growth and development depend very much on exterior forces.

Production and marketing systems, for example, are fixed at the operational level and cannot be modified autonomously.

Also, the operational level is the location of the maximum level of standardization within the organization: standardization of tasks, standardization of products and services, standardization of job descriptions, standardization of skills.

At the transactional level (the level at which the organization transacts with its environment), middle managers are like fighters in the battlefield. They are in charge of the tactical moves of the corporation. Like the animal soul that uses its mobility and quick reaction, they are called to respond to any new actions in the competition, governmental

146

agencies, the consumer market and the general workforce situation, etc., by a direct and appropriate reaction.

On these mid managers of the transactional level reposes the responsibility to make the organization responsive to the different short-term changes in the needs of society and to do so with the proper timing. The transactional level reflects the fact that the animal soul of the corporation should have what amounts to passions.

Middle managers should possess and display a strong level of motivation and eagerness to succeed at their tasks. They should be "self-starters" and enjoy a strong stamina. They should essentially be sensitive to short-term threats and opportunities to the organization. They should be allowed to withdraw the organization from an area where there are short-term dangers to continue operating.

At the strategic level resides the "brain of the organization." The strategic level develops and implements a rational structure first for the organization itself and second of the manner in which the organization will interact with its environment.

This strategic level needs to develop the long-term schema within which middle managers at the transactional level will be allowed to conduct their tactical maneuvers.

The strategic level should determine the mission of the organization and the business areas in which the motivation of middle managers will be allowed to function freely; and to determine the businesses where these middle managers will be told not to engage themselves.

At the strategic level, top managers should keep in control the aggressiveness of middle managers. The strategic level will make sure that bold new strategic plans will be implemented by middle managers and operational employees even if the latter are very suspicious of the advantage and potential successes of these plans.

147

At the strategic level, top managers should keep control of the fears and apprehensions of middle managers.

The problems of organizations

When there are problems with organizations, it is often because employees and managers do not exercise the virtues which they are called to have and exercise specifically at their organizational levels.

Employees and managers at the operational level create problems when they are opposed to the standardization of their jobs and the consequences of this standardization. We will develop the idea throughout this book that many operational jobs can indeed be enriched.

However, total robotization and automation is not available throughout all industries and service companies. Thus low-level employees still often have to perform tedious tasks. Many tasks at this level will be boring and some will remain physically or emotionally demanding.

There will always be tensions between the possibilities and desires of management to alleviate the boredom of tasks and to improve work safety and the willingness of workers to put up with certain levels of inconvenience.

Employees naturally should insist on the responsibilities of the firm to develop policies and methods, for employees and in coordination with their managers, to improve the working conditions of all, in the long run. However, it is the way employees put up with the tension in that area in the short run that is the test of their virtue and the single factor, as far as their responsibilities are concerned, of the stability of their organizational level.

148

At the transactional level, middle-managers create problems for the whole organization when they are either without enthusiasm, stamina and initiatives (thus lacking courage) or, on the contrary, when they have so much that they refuse to submit to corporate policies and basically operate as "loose cannons" (lacking in loyalty and temperance). For line middle managers, in addition, one not unusual problem arises when they block top management directives to promote the operational workers' Quality of Work Life.

Middle managers often prefer to exercise a tighter control on lower employees because it simplifies their tasks. By so doing they are often lacking in justice and temperance.

Strategic problems with organizational structure

However, the most frequent and enduring problems with organizations comes from the breakdown in the responsibilities of top managers.

In particular, the whole discipline of management that concerns itself with organizations really pivots and has historically been developed around the issue of large organizations that have been allowed to grow in an undisciplined way, as a garden grows to weeds.

It is the responsibility of top management to control the structure of organizations and to trim wild growth to be able always to manage the whole organization.

Defects in these responsibilities are principally defects in the courage to assert leadership and prudence to understand the seriousness of the problem and to develop solutions for it.

Some large organizations, like the federal government agency of

Health and Human Services are so large that they are practically unmanageable. New management at HHS, after spending several months taking its bearings in the bureaucratic jungle begins to understand that it is fighting an uphill battle against bureaucratic inertia, communications problems, problems of lack of loyalty, etc. By the time new management may have had a chance to figure out how to go about it, it is time for a new administration to take over.

The organizational tendency to grow is endemic to all organizations and especially to the organizations where managers cannot achieve professional recognition by making a clear contribution to the bottom line of the organization. By hiring assistants and assistants to their assistants, these managers build themselves up the hierarchical ladder and establish their own status but they have introduced a cancerous growth in the organization.

Top managers of large organizations have often turned to management academics to help them develop methods to structure large organizations. The success of academics in this area also tends to be wanting. The temptation is to see this question of organizational structure purely from a sociological or collective point of view, and to ignore the psychological and individual point of view, especially as concerns the virtues of each single employee who should be greatly concerned with this problem.

The problems of organizational structuring of large businesses will tend to become worse in the future. Large corporations will tend to grow faster to follow the rate of business development, at the same time requirements that organization structures be changed will become more frequent with faster changing business environments.

The two trends will combine into creating more tension in these large corporate structures, therefore a new danger for the economy and instability for society.

The solution resides in developing lighter, temporary structures within the organizations and, at the same time, conducting intense education programs for the employees to understand the need and adopt the policy for ad-hoc teams and departments. Employee education should also include instructions on how to be flexible and temperate and develop the willingness to change teams when necessary.

Strategic problems with long-term planning

The problem with much of modern-day business is that many key decisions in organizations are made for a very short time period, which makes it impossible to develop a strategy. Every time strategists are looking at the short-term view of their organization's operations first, they are not fulfilling their strategic roles. They are glorified captains but not generals.

This short-view of their role has, more often than not, a single source. Essentially, top managers and CEOs are often accused of spending too much time and effort on the quarterly financial results of their corporations that directly impacts on the public price of their corporation stocks.

Indeed, many top managers have an eye riveted to the stock price of their corporation because of greed and fear. Their own compensation includes stock bonuses; how well the stock does appeals to their greed. Furthermore, many top managers think, rightly or not, that their corporation's board of directors evaluates their work primarily on the basis of stock price variations and as they are affected by quarterly earnings; these top managers are consequently afraid for their jobs if prices drop.

A very important remedy to this dangerous shortsightedness of Western top managers and business decision-makers is to encourage business students to take courses in philosophy, as this discipline gives the habit of taking a longer view in human affairs. Japanese management has a much longer view of business than Western management; it is due to their own philosophical bent.

Strategic problems with rational management

The central problem in organizations where the strategic level is not doing its job relates to a misunderstanding by top managers of what it means to act as the brain of the organization.

There is an anti-intellectualist bias with business people because their area of human endeavor is reputed to be the world of hard-knocks and of practicality. Practicality is not opposed to abstract thinking. Software companies are selling much abstract thinking as practical and real products. The zero is a very abstract notion, which we owe to the Arameans: it is abstracted from ... the concept of nothingness. But computers cannot work without zeros.

There is also a pro-behavioral sciences bias in corporations. Consultants, with impeccable credentials academic or otherwise, are often called in to solve a problem in a corporation. Usually, the technical problem as stated to the consultant is not the true problem.

The true problem is a conflict of managerial philosophy or of power between high-level managers on some important decisions concerning operations of the corporation. What is sought from the consultant is a method of conflict reduction whereby the problem will be translated in quantified terms and a hopefully unbiased solution will emerge and settle the dispute.

What is lost in this anti-intellectualism and pro-behavioral sciences bias is the role of hard thinking, using common sense, and addressing most important and general problems affecting the organization, as well

152

as its political, technological, social and cultural environment.

Top managers should address the highest-level questions concerning a business to ensure that the business is sailing in calm waters. When they do not do that, two things happen: 1) the social environment of the business collapses because one of its pillars has been withdrawn and 2) top managers get involved instead with tactical problems of the corporation. By usurping the responsibilities of middle managers, top managers push down one notch the level of thinking responsibilities throughout the whole corporation. That is to say that they will force middle managers not to concern themselves with tactical decisions, although that is their responsibility.

Middle-managers, in turn, will invade the territory of operational level employees who will be asked to shift from their normal responsibilities of thinking about their work as human beings should, to the basement level of the organization, the level of robots.

Manpower problems often come from an incapacity of top managers to fulfill their roles of strategic leaders, and specifically their responsibility to concern themselves with the highest-level questions concerning their businesses.

The remedy is for top managers to learn how to think philosophically. That is to say to select the largest questions open to them concerning their responsibilities and businesses, and to develop a discourse on these questions with the tool of common sense. Top managers should be at ease addressing high level questions and discussing them intelligently without sounding either like wide-eyed adolescents or ignoramuses.

- 3. - A Wheel within a wheel - The social impact of organizations and businesses.

What organizations owe human beings

Because organizations borrow their existence from human beings, they owe something in return to these human beings. In a sense organizations ape human beings. Organizations with their three hierarchical levels, corresponding to the three elements of the human soul, are almost identical to human beings. Their production is done by humans and looks human.

But organizations are not human beings. That fact has to be enshrined somewhere within all organizations and especially translated into programs of action, otherwise it will be forgotten. When organizations are confused with human beings there is confusion and misunderstanding not only about the role and rights of organizations, but especially about the role and rights of the human beings working there.

Essentially, organizations owe human beings their dignity. Organizations do not have an immortal soul. They do not, and will never belong to the supernatural order. The first dignity that human beings have that organizations should respect is the fact that human beings are persons who have immortal souls.

Organizations should be kept in perpetual awe of that fact.

It is not enough, or even really useful, for organizations to salute the special dignity of human beings in a fashion that is purely ritual but empty of real meaning. Organizations should have a position about human beings that should translate into tangible respect for the immortal dimension of human beings.

If organizations do not really make a very special effort to do something to enhance human dignity, the danger is that they will not be able but to treat human beings better than diminutive image of themselves; that is like human beings but without true souls.

Organizations, even as they are led by human CEOs, cannot respect the true dignity of human beings, because they cannot understand the concept.

The top leader within the organization, of his own authority but necessarily not of the authority as defined by his narrow organizational role, must take this responsibility. He will build into the organization different structures that will ensure that due reverence is given to all human beings. This person will have to fight to ensure that these structures stay in place.

He must keep in mind that the normal reaction of all organizations is to strive continually to expel structures that support elements of a different order, the supernatural order, as a body of flesh and bones will keep trying to reject a transplanted organ.

Today, the absence of respect for human beings by organizations is sadly prevalent. All inter-social communications and transfers between people are, in society at large, increasingly performed and codified by organizations, whether private or public. Very few independent human beings really control how they personally conduct their professional interaction with other human beings. They are given a script to communicate with other individuals by the organizations that employ them.

As organizations usually are not respectful of the immortal dimensions of human beings, communication between human beings tends to incorporate very little of that eternal dimension, and society as a whole has become profoundly materialized and secularized.

Promoting human dignity

Peter Drucker, a Catholic and the number one thinker of the management world and an astute observer of society, has agonized over the fact that organizations and businesses will only achieve full legitimacy when they truly offer "status" and "function" to all employees.

"Corporate society" will be truly a social order when it confers status and function upon all its members. "(17)

Status refers to the worth of each human being in society, as recognized by that society. Function refers to the role of each human being in that society as handed down by that society.

There are genuine problems indeed with the corporate community and the corporate phenomenon in society. Top managers are not elected but they influence very much the way life is lived in our society. Further, there are good grounds to suspect co-optation within the ranks of the corporate community, i.e., managers promoting only individuals who share their values and philosophies of life. This is particularly true in the largest corporations. For example, in most news organizations, the average reporter had better share most of his boss's ideology if he is interested in being promoted someday.

What of those who do not belong to the business community, or who have little authority within this community? Are they dropped from the social gameboard? What is their status? Throughout his long experience, Drucker has had many opportunities to observe the Nazis and the Communists pay much lip service to the dignity of human beings, while implementing operations that were directly in contradiction with human dignity. Nazis sent Jews to death because they considered them as not quite human beings, "sub-humans"; only "Aryans" were true "human beings."

Communists send their own people to gulags and death because the dissenters have original ideas about the social contract and are therefore "enemies of the revolution."

156

Naturally, status must not be phony as when it is uniquely based on empty titles, uniforms and epaulets. Likewise, function should be more encompassing than the content of a job description, such as that of director of marketing, chief of bookkeeping, etc., which are limited to the corporate community but have little importance within the broader society.

Employee participation is also an issue related to those of status and function. Very often the discussion of status and function slides into the issue of "participation" of all employees in a business. Participation is an attempt to re-introduce the democratic process in a society mostly concerned by materialistic and economic values and therefore dominated by corporations that, by inner necessity, operate according to a hierarchical order.

The different forms of "participation" include ownership participation, managerial participation, participation in decision- making, etc. Drucker is not satisfied with any of these principles as means to truly convey both "status" and "function" to employees.

First, as we have seen previously, ownership participation by employees is not a pre-requisite for a just society.

Second, direct managerial participation is self-defeating. If employees are as qualified as managers, they should be allowed to be made managers. Furthermore, all employees cannot be made managers at the same time of the same department; the principle of unity of command has to be respected.

Third, employee participation through representation in board rooms is of arguable effectiveness either for the business or for the interests of the employees.

Lastly, participation in the decision-making process contains a certain and valuable degree of "function" imparted to the role of employees but it is totally lacking of status to the extent that it does not

157

enhance the broader social status of employees.

The Christian status of organizational employees

It just happens that organizations can do something about upholding human dignity and giving function and status to each employee.

The true status of human beings is respected when each human being is acknowledged to be more valuable than the organizations themselves. For example, General Motors will confer true status to the GM janitor only when it takes the formal position that it recognizes that the janitor is essentially of greater value than the whole of the GM organization. And that, definitely, in this materialistic world, is status.

The only way that GM can make such a statement and mean it, is when it acknowledges the immortal dimension of the GM janitor. At the material and social levels, naturally, the janitor is but a speck in the GM organization. GM, therefore, to be a truly wholesome organization and to give maximum possible status to its employees, is forced to enter the sphere of religion, or at least of the "philosophy of being." Pretty heady notion for top managers at the strategic level, isn't it?

The Christian function of organizational employees

The Christian function that can also be conferred by corporations on all employees is to formally assign them to assist all the human beings that they encounter and communicate with in the course of their work, to achieve salvation, and to grow as persons in the virtues.

158

Naturally, it will be acknowledged that each employee has first the function to grow himself in the virtues before helping others around him to do the same.

Organizations can indeed help human beings become more meritorious of their heavenly reward. They can help human beings grow as persons by developing their intellect and will. First by developing a strong intellect and a strong will, through better education and inner-discipline development. Also, and what is more important, in developing the intellect and will in a manner compatible with growth in the virtues.

How convenient! The first function that any organizational employee will receive from his Christian organization is totally compatible with the more important function that the employee already has as a private Christian human being: to grow in holiness. How convenient for organizations!

Also, how convenient for employees that, not only does the organization give the employee this function to grow in holiness but it also provides him all the tools and opportunities to do so, since the tasks of management so often require managers and employees to exercise the virtues.

Only status viable for organizations

With Drucker, we agree that it is very important to grant organizational employees an elevated status; otherwise organizations will crush human beings like ants, in addition, a possible backlash against this organizational oppression would be the breakdown of the "corporate society," that is of our modern society where so many large organizations, most of them - but not all -business organizations, operate.

On the other hand, if employees are given status, but this status is defined essentially according to material or physical criteria, that will be of great danger to organizations, and a possible source of other social disturbances.

Some organizations need their employees to exert a high level of initiative because of the specific nature of their business. For example, the apparel retailing industry mandates a high level of flexibility and fast adaptation to the market. Such organizations need to express in their managerial philosophy the position that they highly value their employees' individualities beyond what the employees directly contribute to the organization by a mere fulfillment of their tasks.

Clearly, such organizations cannot program employees to take initiatives.

When employees are valued for themselves in addition to their function, and this valuation is circumscribed in the material sphere, they may logically think that they have an additional claim on the organization beyond their salaries, wages, bonuses, profit- sharing and employee stock-ownership plans. They are likely to want a piece of the soul of the organization. Since there are no possible benchmarks to evaluate how individual employees can be valued beyond their direct contribution, they will tend to want as much control of the organization as possible.

These seem to be the roots of most of labor-management, or labor-capital, disputes.

In sum, organizations whose managerial philosophy is not Christian and which would not adopt the notion that the status of employees comes from its spiritual dimension are left with an uneasy choice. Either they want something extra from their employees without offering them anything of substance in exchange.

Or they offer them material status but are unable to promote or

160

satisfy their appreciation for this status.

Promoting human dignity outside the organization

The status to be given by organizations to individual human beings who are outside the organization is the same as the status to be acknowledged for employees by the organization. Clients, suppliers and all individuals who come in contact with the organization must be valued more than the organization itself because they each have an immortal soul and because the organization does not.

When a Christian business organization then states that it values its customer, this statement has meaning because it is based on concepts that the customers can relate to and find acceptable.

The Christian business acknowledges the true dignity of the customer, that is with both its Christian-defined rights and responsibilities. It puts the customer on a pedestal.

When a non-Christian business organization states that it greatly values its clientele, it is comparatively a shallow statement. It only means, in this case, that the business organization acknowledges that it is very dependent on its customers. There is something one dimensional and servile in this appreciation.

Non-Christian business organizations that express that they value their customers are also merely stating a fact in doing so. They do not really impart status to their customers.

As with the case of employees, organizations which pretend to value customers beyond the status of mere customers but which limit this valuation within the material realm have a problem.

161

Customers may tend to think that if they are so valuable to business organizations, they may be entitled to something more than a good product at a good price from such organizations. In the commercial transaction between them and such organizations, these customers may want something material for nothing. This psychological attitude may even be an important cause of the phenomenon of individuals shoplifting from stores, even when the thieves they are not needy.

Responsibilities of ownership

Private property is justifiable as a means to better develop, distribute and transfer the material goods of this world to the people living on it, as a group.

Private property, as we stated earlier, is limited by the necessity for the owner to abide by social constraints on the manner in which this property is used.

Some large modern organizations have become not only the centers of employment for thousands, even tens and hundreds of thousands of people, but also the owners of property valued at hundreds of millions and even billions of dollars.

Today, capitalist democracy has been generally achieved in the sense that the largest corporations in the country are, largely, owned by the populace.

This technical ownership has been made possible because the man in the street owns pieces of every large corporation, usually through his retirement fund or insurance plan, rather than directly.

This democratic ownership of large corporations has still not made possible a democratic decision-making process relative to the management of their properties. These decisions are still in the hands of top management at the corporations, or in the hands of decision-makers of pension plans, insurance plans, bank trust departments and mutual funds.

Responsibilities of ownership can be divided in two categories:

1/ what is the mission of the organization and

2/ in which manner are we to administer the assets of the organization to attain its mission and objectives.

The mission of the organization must fulfill the public good and the management of the assets must respect imperatives of justice.

Naturally an organization cannot have an agenda that is criminal, but neither can it, for Christian stockholders, have an agenda which, although legal, is perpetuating an objective evil such as the publishing of pornographic material.

All shareholders share not only in the profits and losses of a corporation but also in the responsibilities of ownership. When a corporation gives money to Planned Parenthood, its stockholders are directly responsible for it, under their responsibility as owners.

Questions of asset management also include issues of responsibilities towards communities, such as the social impact of an organization moving out of a company town, or issues bearing on the preservation of the environment.

When a company leaves a town where it is essentially the principal and central provider of jobs, it needs to take many reasonable steps to alleviate the negative effects of its departure, such as early announcement, severance pay and assistance in finding other jobs in the area or assisting employees in relocating.

Beyond the hysteria of narrow-minded ecologists and other worshippers of greenery, it is indubitable that the potential of modern industry and technology to affect the environment negatively has grown to the point that the matter is a real subject of concern. Corporations which may cause massive physical impacts on the environment need to feel responsible. They must not affect the environment so badly that it will never be able to regenerate itself, or produce effects which will significantly disrupt the health of people.

Ethics of organizations vs. business ethics.

Even though most examples given above in this section refer to business organizations, the principles presented are applicable to all organizations, whether business organizations or organizations that are not businesses. The social impact of organizations in general is the subject of "organizational ethics."

Business ethics includes additional issues that relate to business activities, essentially issues relative to money-making, such as justice in product manufacturing and marketing, etc. Most of these issues fall under the principle of commutative justice: there are contracts, explicit or not, between the buyer and the seller. The selling company must abide by the terms of the contract and owes the buyer what it promises him.

Many non-business organizations actually also do sell services and information. They are therefore expected to also follow the principles of commutative justice relative to business contracts. A Catholic school that does not teach true Catholic doctrine can be sued for false advertising, for example. It is not delivering the product it implicitly advertises.

Organizational ethics by itself is applicable to all sorts of organizations, including educational establishments, government agencies, non-profit organizations, etc. The police, the YMCA, the Health and Human Services agency, the Sierra Club, the Ford Foundation, Harvard University all are subject to organizational ethics. They need to treat their employees, professors, volunteers, staff personnel, agents, as human beings with immortal souls. They need be entirely convinced - and translate that conviction in their policies - that each one of them, as a soul-less organization is not worth as much as the most humble human being.

Organizations unethical by design

Some non-profit organizations, for example, are so infatuated with the importance of their mission and self-perceived lofty objectives that they treat not only the opponents they encounter in fighting their causes, but also their own employees, their members and members of the general public as negligible entities.

The National Organization for Women has no patience for the cause of unborn children because NOW's interest is in women threatened by unwanted pregnancies. Some environmental groups have little sensitivity for economic expansion and the fate of the jobless in a region which they want to preserve in its pristine state. What some of these organizations want are tough pro-environmental laws. Period.

Likewise, some policy-advocating groups fight ruthlessly for their causes. They become so callous to general human sensitivities that they cannot accommodate their own volunteer staff to decent working conditions.

The issue of the respect of their employees as human beings, called to be children of God, is also part of the larger issue of authority in organizations. What gives a manager the right to decide to fire an employee, or simply to ask the employee to change his behavior, apart from the fact that the organization has the means to providing the job to the employee?

We will treat the problem of authority in a later section but the central question of the legitimacy of authority can be posed now in the framework of the responsibilities of ownership.

This issue of the legitimacy of organizational authority exists whether the organization is for profit or not.

Some non-profit organizations are perpetuating truly evil acts like abortion. Planned Parenthood which routinely performs abortions is the typical organization which is gravely unethical by design - on a par with the Mafia and drug cartels.

Other organizations, including corporations, support abortion by making donations to Planned Parenthood. They are unethical in respect to the manner in which they administer their assets. If they think making donations to Planned Parenthood is a way for them as corporations to increase their goodwill in the public's eyes, they show very little prudence as relates to either ethics or commercial goodwill.

Organizational ethics more fundamental than business ethics

Issues of organizational ethics are more fundamental than the other issues of business ethics. All matters of purely interpersonal relations eventually belong to organizational ethics. Interpersonal relations are the most important issues in ethics, because persons are among the most important values to preserve in all human activities.

Issues which are purely in the domain of business ethics deal with limited questions: the specific rights to material things and money, people who misappropriate them and those who are robbed. The intrinsic value of human beings is not addressed.

Businesses must naturally conform to all tenets of organizational ethics, but in these responsibilities they are far from being alone. Many organizations that are not businesses are responsible for abiding by principles of organizational ethics. Business ethics proper refers to the specialty of business organizations, which is to be businesses.

The roots of business and organizational ethics.

The specialty of businesses is to provide products and services to human beings so that their material needs can be satisfied.

Businesses are therefore, as a group within society, responsible for the two functions of production and delivery of goods.

"Business ethics" in the limited sense of the concept refers to the ethics of production and the ethics of trade. We need be well aware that the ethical issues specific to businesses - apart from organizational ethics - can all be related to principles of justice.

In this sense, it is most important to have a correct understanding of justice before studying business ethics.

The matter of what is a just business was developed in the first part of this book. It is not useless to repeat that there are three parts to justice. Justice is something that can be objectively determined.

Today, it seems that a civil or criminal case needs only to enter the "justice system" and later come out of it for all involved to be able to say that "justice has been served." This is confusing the "process of law" with justice. It is furthermore less true that "due process of law" renders justice. Laws and judges are increasingly departing from the realm of Christian ethics.

Another problem with matters of justice is that it is important to get to the root of the injustice. It has been stated that the major impetus for the development of a code of ethics in corporations was the Foreign Corrupt Practice Act of 1977 that primarily condemned bribes in international trade. Bribes are condemnable because they go against the spirit of justice... and only as far as they go against the spirit of justice.

In democratic governments where government officials are expected to perform their duties without undue influence on their decisions, any bribe given by parties interested in the decisions of these officials is meant to influence the decisions of these officials in the favor of the payers of the bribes. Bribes in democracies are given to commit an injustice. They are unethical.

However, there are many non-democratic governments where official positions such as judge, minister or policeman, are very poorly paid and the officials are expected to receive money from the parties affected by their decisions. In such governments, judges are paid by both parties; all applicants pay officials granting licenses. The donations look like bribes but they are essentially different from bribes. These payments are not paid to commit injustices in favor of the parties or the solicitors who have given the money. Plaintiffs and defendants pay to have their day in court, not really to be vindicated. These types of bribes are considered supplemental pay for the official. They are "users' fees" of sorts for the justice system of these nations.

These payments are intrinsic elements of the political system of many primitive nations. They are consequences rather than causes of heir type of government. Westerners are not justified to feel smug about them and to condemn them with horror. Instead they should be moved to deal with the root causes of this social behavior and to evangelize these people. Indeed only from Christian teaching can true democracy spring forth.

One matter that complicates the whole issue of payments too officials of developing countries is that many of these non-democratic governments pretend to be democratic - or to be on their way to be democratic - and they officially request to be held to the same standards as democracies. They have to be told that bribes in democracies are unacceptable.

What is important in cases of payments to officials is whether justice is rendered. If a hospital complex in a third world nation is not operating because a minister delays giving the required permits because he feels he has not received the payment he expected from the venture, justice is not rendered. The building of the hospital was a waste of resources if the hospital is not utilized. Patients are not treated.

On the other hand, a lack of ethical and anthropological understanding of prudence as well as ethno-centered complacency has prevented seeing that other activities that are conducted in democratic nations are tantamount to bribes and that they do aim at creating injustices. Lobbyists, who allegedly offer strategic or legal advice at inflated prices, in reality are former government officials who offer access to friends and former colleagues of theirs who are still in government and ask these friends to be influenced in favor of the paying party.

Paying such lobbyists is in many ways tantamount to paying the officials, except that there is a time-lag in the payment and a substitution of recipients. The system of lobbyists has been proven efficient, from the perspective of the participants, even with this time-lag and substitution. Officials in public office who render these services can reasonably expect that they will eventually be paid for them even though they will have to wait to be lobbyist themselves and to receive the payment for other cases and at a later time.

Many organizations - including many organizations that are not

169

businesses but are "single interest groups" - use such lobbyists and influence peddling and can, at least as far as ethical principles are concerned, be indicted for injustice in their activities.

To understand issues of justice, many pre-conceived ideas must be discarded. We seem to be quick to find injustices in unfamiliar systems, such as in developing countries, and to be most understanding of the complexity of our own systems that may appear unjust to others. This type of bias may be found across cultures but also across professional occupations.

Educators and journalists will find many injustices in the business world when they do not see the injustices in their own professions.

There are cases when thorough analysis will objectively show that there was no injustice, in spite of appearances. In other cases, there is definite injustice, in spite also of appearances to the contrary.

The business organization as good citizen

The social responsibilities of business organizations, or their responsibilities as good citizens, are not limited to the most familiar issues that are thoroughly covered in the media such as ecological responsibilities, economic responsibilities towards communities, responsibilities towards job creation or exportation.

The responsibilities of business organizations include all these and more and in a particular perspective that is much broader. They share in the responsibility for supporting society; they are responsible, with others, for making sure that society functions correctly.

The drug problem for a corporation is much larger than an employee's drug problem. The drug problem of society is the drug problem of corporations.

Mediating organizations

The Church has repeatedly asked that the cultural development of society be conducted by using what has been called mediating organizations.

Between the level of families and grass-root citizenship, on one hand, and the level of the government that is in position of authority over all of us, on the other hand, there are too few levels in the social fabric. This scarcity of levels causes a scarcity of means of communication and of institutions to ensure that the nation operates with a culture which possesses consistency and integrity.

The danger is that the individuals at the bottom of the social pyramid operate with one set of values and the government operates with another set because there is no real contact between the two levels. In third world countries this problem is endemic where a large section of political, social and economic activities are conducted outside their formal framework.

Business firms represent another layer in the middle that is attentive to the wants and needs of the individual citizens and does follow the corporate laws that come from on high, i.e., the government.

The Church has encouraged business organizations and other types of organizations to get together at a higher level in associations that would cater to their natural needs as well as helping to develop the social tissue and propagate it more densely upward and connect it with governmental organizations.

"As we consider the whole field of economics, therefore, it becomes clear - as we pointed out in our encyclical Quadragesimo Anno - that the mutual influence of justice and charity can only be brought to bear upon economic and social relations by means of a federation of professional and interprofessional bodies, established on a Christian basis and constituting, under different forms adapted to time and place, what used to be known as corporations."

Pope Pius XI.   Encyclical Divini Redemptoris, Para. 74.

These associations have been called "corporations," but the word does not mean business firms; it means trade associations according to middle ages parlance. They are sometimes referred to as "interprofessional corporations." Another word used for these associations is "guild," another middle-age word which cannot represent the concept that modern associations of businesses would represent today.

Manufacturers' associations and trade unions are, in principle, good things and should be preserved, but here what the Church has in mind are associations that would include both manufacturers' associations and trade unions, management and labor together.

Management of each firm would bring its technical and commercial concerns to the association. The employees of each firm would bring their concerns with living and working conditions to the association, concerns which are broader than the issue of how to get more pay and better working conditions from their employer.

The purpose of these associations is two-fold. At one level it concerns the relationship between similar business firms; at the other level it concerns the relationship between the business community and the rest of society.

Between business firms, the purpose of these super- associations is to foster a better sense of solidarity between business organizations and avoid cut-throat tactics, promote positive agreements such as standardization of products and services, all this while preserving the principle and reality of economic competition between different firms in the same market.

As concerns the relationship with the whole of society, the purpose of the super-associations is to enrich and preserve the social culture of this society. The economic role of businesses is evident in society, but the political and social roles are not always as evident, although just as real. Too often the government decides unilaterally and without genuine contribution on the part of the citizens and of concerned organizations what is good for society and for all. Super-associations would help change this situation.

The manner by which a business firm handles the drug problem within its walls has political and social components.

The manner by which all organizations handle the same problem, corresponds almost entirely to the manner by which the problem is handled in society at large, as most people work in some type of organization.

Such complex social and political problems are better handled by a group of business organizations which have the same problem rather than each of the organization one by one, as the work otherwise would be unnecessarily duplicated and the resources wasted which could otherwise examine the problem in greater depth.

The drug problem is but one issue where management, the labor force and society at large are concerned. The super-associations would be expected to handle all similar issues and do it before they are really perceived as being issues.

It is only when the drug problem became acute that some persons

173

in authority took note and set up ad-hoc committees to handle them. The super-associations would automatically attract the people concerned by a problem of that nature before it became present in the conscience of all and eventually a problem of greater magnitude.

The super-associations would also, because of their global approach to economic, social and political problems consider each problem according to these different dimensions and would therefore hesitate before trying to solve a problem with a single "silver bullet" that may displace the problem towards a different dimension without solving it.

It is difficult to recommend exactly how these super associations should be set up because their models have never existed in modern times. However, had the top management and labor force of many corporations in an industry been strongly influenced by authentic Christian values, they would have already naturally striven to set up such organizations that would now be in place.

The Christian CEO should do his utmost to look for possibilities to set up such inter-professional associations each time he has a chance, while talking with his peers of other firms on the one hand, and to his employees on the other hand. Christian employees should encourage their top manager to do exactly that and give him effective support in conducting such efforts.

- 4. - What is our Agenda? - Strategic planning for organizations.

Strategy and Mission

Businesses which have been established recently have the benefit of having a founder who still has a strong sense of the business's mission. However, some large and older businesses have often lost their sense of mission.

To state "we are in business to make a profit" is not a proper statement for a business mission. If such a statement truly expresses the attitude of top management, the business is in deep trouble.

A sense of mission must be less mercenary and more specific than the pursuit of profit. Further, the pursuit of profit may be a dangerous goal. Which profit are we talking about? Short-term profit or long-term profit? If it is short-term profit, this objective may be reached by slashing Research and Development, cutting the advertising budget, defunding manpower training. This is tantamount to committing organizational suicide in the long run.

If profit is long-term profit, on the contrary, the company could load up in all these expensive budget items. And that would destroy the possibility of any short-term profit.

How is profit to be measured? R.O.I, return on investment, would push towards leveraging the business by taking as much long-term loans and issuing as many bonds as possible.

R.O.E., return on equity? EPS, earnings per share? This financial statistic is closely observed in the financial markets. The last two measures would give the temptation to undervalue assets in the books and therefore set oneself up to become a target for a LBO, leveraged-buy-out, one of the surest ways for top management to seal its own fate.

Other companies are lured by organizational growth as the prime objective of their business. Growth in for-profit companies, as in government bureaucracies, is very tantalizing to management. The larger the hierarchical pyramid grows under a manager, the higher up in the pyramid the manager will find himself. Growth was especially a strategic fad of the sixties when the formation of conglomerates was the trend. However, it was soon discovered that top management, by putting together these huge organizations, was not bringing any added value to the companies. On the contrary, companies had to pay a cost in their stock prices for having more layers of strategic management to them. The value of their new strategic level was negative. In the eighties, a different game appeared which consisted in buying a conglomerate to break it into its components and resell the components, because the sum of the parts of the conglomerate had more value than the whole. Not only is the rationale correct financially but also business-wise as it liberates independent businesses from undue control by managers who cannot help them in any way.

No. The business which is looking for a mission should be considering the solving of a broad problem that human beings have, contributing to a basic need that human beings share. General Motors is in the transportation business; it seeks to resolve ways to put individuals in transportation machines which will best satisfy their transportation needs. If GM does reasonably well at fulfilling this mission, people will be happy to purchase their products and GM will remain in business. People will have supported the mission of GM. On the other hand, nobody is really interested in helping a company turn out a profit - or simply break even (and that is the root of the political problem of government bail-outs of corporations).

As Drucker once stated: to make a profit is not a privilege for a business, it is a constraint. Profit is part of the definition of business, of the requirements of being in business, but it does not explain what a specific business is being set up to accomplish. One does not define one's endeavors by one's constraints.

GM's mission in the transportation industry has also a technical limit. It is not as broad as it could be. The company builds cars, trucks and locomotives. It does not build planes or boats. When a mission is not narrowed down it is very much "pie in the sky", the resources of the company are spread very thin and that is quite dangerous.

176

A company has to know all it can about its products and what affects the way they are used and abused. Thus, GM knows a great deal about roads and mountains and mountain roads and cities and city roads. It knows about gasoline and about rubber tires. But it does not know about oceans and salt water and clouds and wind shear. It does not know about jet fuel and kerosene, airport administrations and the pleasure boat cruising industry. To learn about these things in depth would require that GM expand more of its resources for this purpose. GM's resources may be enormous but they are also limited and it is not wise to mismanage limited resources.

Strategic planning is an activity which helps businesses redefine their missions, establish objectives which embody this mission, establish specific programs of actions which will help attain the objectives and manage resources so that the programs of action can be carried out.

Strategic planning and managerial style

But even with a well-defined mission, different CEOs will lead the same company along different roads to fulfill the mission. The differences are related to what is now called the "managerial style" of the company's president.

Some presidents leave a fair level of autonomy to their lieutenants to develop new initiatives; others do not. Some presidents are very strict in controlling the resources that go to these initiatives; other presidents are not so strict. In most companies, there is a dollar amount that is fixed at each managerial level above which the manager needs his superior's prior approval to make the outlay. It may be $5OO for a salesman or shop manager. It may be $1O,OOO for a R&D director or a Marketing director, and $25,OOO for a vice-president. But from company to company, the range for such sums can be as wide as of a

177

factor from one to ten.

Some top managers are very interested in receiving frequent and detailed reports on everything of consequence that is going on in the company. Other top managers do not want to be swamped by details; they are only interested in being reported results of activities.

These differences in preferences of top managers do significantly affect the lives of their employees and the manner in which they should perform their work.

Similarly, managerial style will be very strongly felt in the strategic plan. The strategic plan is the major opportunity for the top manager to act as a general ("strategos" in Greek).

For these reasons, the strategic plan has been called the "extension of the CEO's personality" over the company, the shadow of the CEO's stature as it is cast over the company.

Strategic plan and the organizational brain

At the strategic level of the company where the CEO formalizes the strategic plan for the whole company, the activities are comparable to those of the brain of a human being.

The techniques of development of a plan should take this requirement in consideration. The development of the strategic plan is the concerted effort to develop an intelligent over-all purpose into the company's activities.

Until a plan is developed, there may be intelligent efforts on the part of individuals or even of departments but not of the company as a whole.

On the other hand, the analogy of the strategic level of the company doing the thinking for the whole company through the medium of the plan should not be pushed too far.

Specifically, the development of the strategic plan should not regard the CEO and his strategic planning staff as the only people with brains in the company. As silly as it may seem such an elitist attitude in the planning methodology is a grave temptation in practice.

On the contrary and ideally, the strategic plan should devise a method to combine the powers of all the brains of all the employees of the organization, to which should be added all stored and secondary knowledge as well as other intellectual resources easily accessible to the business, in order to devise what would amount to a giant brain for the business.

In essence good strategic planning requires that all possible intellectual contributions to the plan be available and put to good use in the activities of the business.

Strategic plan and the organizational will

It is well known that the immediate effect on employees of an elitist attitude on the part of the CEO and on the part of the strategic planning staff vis-à-vis line managers, is lack of cooperation, if not outright sabotage, by these line managers.

This consequence, in fact, was so important to the strategic planning function, that very soon the emphasis on the brilliance, comprehensiveness, or whatever other intellectual qualities a plan might have, has been put aside in favor of the concern for "implementability" of a strategic plan.

179

The question of "implementability" of the plan refers to the problem of ensuring that the company's employees will generally accept the plan, will make a reasonable effort to make it work, will even contribute to its improvement and will make the success of the plan their own responsibility.

Ideally, all the individual wills of the employees of the organization should combine into a giant single will.

In sum, the strategic planning process can be said, from a philosophical perspective, to be the process by which the organization's personhood is developed. The business which, as an organization possesses a human-like soul, receives full human-like intelligence and will, and therefore a type of personhood, through the strategic planning process.

The business organization in which the strategic planning function is ineffective does not drop from a human-like status to an animal-like or a vegetal-like entity, as if it had retained some integrity. The business which has no plan, and shows no will to implement a plan, cannot have any integrity. It is radically flawed. The analogy for such a corporation is more accurately a severely mentally handicapped human being.

Unfortunately, in most cases we do not know how to re-establish the intellectual faculties and volition of a mentally handicapped person. But we do know how to do it for an organization: it is by means of the proper conduct of the strategic planning process.

The Snake-shaped Strategic process

One technique aimed at fulfilling the above-mentioned objectives of combining the different individual brains of the organization into a mega organizational brain, as well as to combine the will of all

180

employees into a steadfast mega organizational will is called the Snake. (18)

The snake starts at the CEO level and at the level of the strategic planning staff. There, an official order, or call, is made to initiate the strategic planning process. The call is sent downwards, first down to the vice-president level and then further down to each level until the last hierarchical level of the organization. The purpose of the call is to request suggestions for new activities and objectives as well as other qualitative and quantitative contributions to the strategic plan that is underway, from all levels of the organization.

Once the snake has arrived at the bottom of the organization - that it has completed its "top down" progression - a bottom up movement is then initiated. The snake moves upwards with the responses to the call: writings and presentations of reports and suggestions by the lower employees to their supervisors. Supervisors include their employee's suggestions into their own reports and suggestions and communicate them to their own supervisors. The process reaches in this fashion the upper levels and the CEO.

The CEO may wish at this time to firm up the strategic plan into a comprehensive and definitive plan. It will be incumbent upon him, and upon his strategic planning staff, to communicate downwards all the objectives for each managerial level down to the lowest level of the company.

On the other hand, the CEO, now enlightened by the great array of potential objectives and programs that his employees are interested in, may decide to reinitiate the process of requesting downwards objectives and programs from his employees. But this time the CEO will have narrowed somewhat the scope and diversity of initiatives to be proposed, and instead is requesting more in-depth development in the reports to be submitted by the hierarchical levels.

When the new reports filter back up the hierarchical ladder, they together bring about an organizational "broader picture" in which the initiatives of each managerial level is made consistent with the contributions of the other hierarchical levels yielding a rich, comprehensive, and solid plan.

More strategic resolve

The Snake is an effective method for increasing employee participation in the rational component of the strategic process. However, it can be a time-consuming process and it does not automatically ensure a strong willful commitment of the employees to the plan.

The word strategy etymologically means the leading of an army (stratos) by a general. There are many military similitudes between a managerial strategic plan and a military strategic plan. In both instances the end objective is to win. In war, the objective is to win over the enemy.

In business the objective is to win over social inertia and business competition. Many managers see strategic planning as uniquely a fight against business competition. They are misled. One can grind the competition to a powder and have lost the business war if the battle has been so fierce and so costly that a victory leaves the company with the destruction of the moneymaking structures and without significant resources to remain in the business. On the other hand, one can win a strategic commercial plan and have had to some extent collaborated with one's competition. The Japanese philosophy of business competition consists in never humiliating another company on the grounds that one may have to collaborate with it in the future. Business is competition but it is not war.

Military strategy

One most important theoretician of military strategy was Carl von Clausewitz who presented his ideas in his major work "On War". Clausewitz was a German military man who conducted a thorough study of Napoleon's military maneuvers to understand why the German troops had been so thoroughly beaten by the armies of the little Corsican at the beginning of the XIXth century. In the Franco-Prussian war of 187O, the Germans, strong with Clausewitz's research, inflicted in turn a radical defeat to the French. "On War" is still required reading in most military academies all over the world. (19)

"On War", interestingly, presents the techniques of military art and science in their relationship with the nature and degree of exercise of the moral virtues, just as this book is presenting the art and techniques of management under the strong light that the virtues cast on them.

Clausewitz writes: "... therefore most of the subjects which we shall go through in this book shall be composed half of physical, half of moral causes and effects, and we might say the physical are almost no more than the wooden handle, whilst the moral are the noble metal, the real bright-polished weapon".

Clausewitz, in particular, insists on the military virtue of "boldness" which is a combination of physical courage and mental resolve. "From the transport-driver and the drummer up to the General, it is the noblest of virtues, the true steel which gives the weapon its edge and brilliancy".

One most interesting insight Clausewitz offers for the military stage whose applicability for business still has to be verified: it has been a frequent observation that troops have greater boldness than generals. "Boldness becomes a rarer occurrence the higher we ascend the scale of rank", he states, granting that this is a paradox.

But he explains: "The great mass is bound to be a higher will by the framework and joints of the order of battle and of the service, and therefore is guided by an intelligent power which is extraneous. Boldness is therefore here only like a spring held down until its action is required".

Boldness of vision

If in the military the troops who may lose their lives have more boldness than generals whose lives are usually protected at a safe distance from the front line, the situation should be even more acute in business management where employees do not run the risk of losing their lives and where top management may deem itself more vulnerable than its troops in relation to strategic boldness.

Indeed, if a strategic plan fails, everyone will look up at the top man as the principal cause of the failure.

Following Clausewitz's insight and the analogy with the military we should find business rank and file employees bolder than top management. In the majority of cases, this is not so. One exception to this rule is worth mentioning: in the Church, lay people often do wish that their leaders show more boldness in their plans of evangelization, and lay organizations are certainly bolder and show more initiatives than the hierarchy.

But in business, could it be that the strategic planning process unduly restrains the vision employees are allowed to develop concerning the future endeavors of their companies? Could it be that top management does not foster a large enough framework for the employees to use for their vision?

Again, Clausewitz: "The more a General is in the habit of demanding from his troops, the surer he will be that his demands will be

184

answered. The soldier is as proud of overcoming toil as he is of surmounting danger."

Are top managers afraid to demand too much from their employees by allowing the development of a great visionary strategic plan for the company?

Idealized planning

Russell Ackoff has introduced the concept of idealized design as a first step in the strategic planning process. His proposal, as we will see, definitively reintroduces boldness in the strategic planning process. (20)

An idealized design is a design which the designers - hopefully all the employees and participants in the organization for which the design is made - would like this organization to enjoy right now.

The reasons for the idealized design, which allows the larger vision which we mentioned, are several: participation in the planning process by the employees, incorporation of aesthetic values of the stake-holders (whoever has something at stake in the business whether an employee of the company or not) in the system, generation of a consensus among the participants, commitment on their part to the realization of the design, and stimulation of creativity focused on individual and organization development.

An idealized design should include realistic requirements. Ackoff requires that idealized design possess three properties: 1) technological feasibility, 2) operational viability and 3) capable of rapid learning and adaptation.

Thus, an idealized design should not be built around a technology which does not exist. The system designed should be capable of

185

surviving if it were brought to existence but there is no requirement that it be capable of being brought into existence. Rapid learning on the part of the system is possible when its participants can modify the design whenever they care to, if it incorporates processes for resolving future design issues, and when controls are provided for the redesign process.

Essentially Ackoff sees idealized design as the activity which fulfills one of the tasks of the strategic function: "ends planning".

The Christian who has a solid understanding as concerns the issues relative to the ends of business and the ends of the managers, questions which have been previously reviewed above in this book, would feel quite capable of developing a vision for a business which will "focus on individual and organizational development".

In practice, boldness is reintroduced in the strategic planning process at the level of the selection of the corporate mission. Ackoff, who is not Christian, writes: "A mission can mobilize an organization into concerted action. It can be to planning what the Holy Grail was to the Crusades: a vision of something strongly desired accompanied by a commitment to its pursuit."

And Ackoff is not a dreamer. When he started as the principal and strategic consultant for the Anhaueser-Busch company, a few decades ago, the St. Louis-based beer company only enjoyed 5% of the beer market in the U.S. Today it can claim 30% of this market. Until a few years ago Ackoff was chairman of an academic department and director of the Busch Center, a research arm in strategic planning, at the Wharton School, a top business school in the country.

Strategic planning as a permanent activity.

The advantages of the strategic process is so obvious to companies,

186

management and employees alike, that the leap has been made by organizations and individuals who have made strategic planning an on-going activity.

Periodically throughout the year, meetings are held for the purpose of developing, revising and augmenting the steps of the planning function.

All year long, meetings are held to develop the business mission. Other meetings are held to revise the objectives to fit the mission; other meetings review the activities and programs to better meet the objectives, etc.

Why should not the strategic planning process be permanent? If the strategic process indeed corresponds to the true operation of the organization's intellect, should not this intellect operate continuously?

Strategy and operations

If the organization really thinks only through its strategic planning function, what is the nature of activities conducted between strategic meetings, is there any thinking done at this level? Response: the business to be done between strategic sessions is to conduct operations.

There is certainly some thinking done during business operations, but the thinking done is the thinking of individual managers, not the thinking of the organization as a whole.

There is quite a chasm between strategy and operations. Strategic and operational work are quite different and even, in a certain manner, opposed to each other. The purpose of strategic sessions is to question the habitual manner of doing business. Strategic sessions in many ways are also like examinations of conscience during which the organization examines how it conducts its operations, its objectives and whether they are good.

The purpose of strategic planning sessions is also the questioning of the established habits of the organization. As the habits of managers and employees are necessarily affected by the habits of the organization, very often the opposition to the planning process can be quite readily linked to an opposition by managers and employees to the changing of their own personal habits. Implementation of plans also directly affect personal habits and is often fiercely opposed by line managers for that precise reason.

In a Christian corporation in which managers have accepted the emphasis of the management policy of supporting their employees to gain personal salvation through their growth in the virtuous life, changes are better accepted and strategy is therefore more easily designed and articulated and also more readily implemented.

- 5. - Checking the course - Controls.

The Black Fords

An organization is a complex entity. Only in organizations that have strong top managers can these top managers say, "The organization is doing well, it can keep going on this course" or, on the contrary, "There is a definite problem, the organization needs to change here and there." But in most organizations the top manager is really only the top employee and these assessments must be arrived at by some sort of analytical and objective procedures. These procedures are the procedures of controls.

Henry Ford, who brilliantly demonstrated the value of the idea of mass manufacturing automobiles to make them affordable to the great majority of people, was a business genius in this respect.

However, his subjectivity eventually worked against him when he insisted on so much standardization for automobiles that "customers can choose any color they wish, provided it is black." His competition grew quickly when consumer demand for more diversity and greater aesthetic appeal in automobile design was recognized and met by the Dodges and some of the different companies now absorbed into GM.

The objectivity of good managerial controls' procedures prevents the risk for wrong subjective evaluations on the part of individual managers. The higher the managers, the more they are at risk to make such costly errors of evaluation because their lifestyles are so different from the lifestyle of the average consumer and because they may see it as a matter of personal prestige that their marketing intuitions be followed by the organization.

Here, Ford had poor controls over the appropriateness of his automobile design programs, in view of the changing market environment and state of the competition.

Controls as navigation system

Usually when we talk about organizational control we have in mind controls over specific programs to ensure that they are correctly implemented. In other words, we think of control mechanisms and procedures that are entirely within the organization as they seek to measure output against standards defined internally by the organization.

Controls, however, have also and first to be considered in a much broader context than simple technical controls. Otherwise there is a great risk that even the most detailed control procedures will not be properly understood.

Controls do start with controlling where the corporate ship goes. Controls can be viewed as an important element of the navigational system of the corporation that steers that corporation around environmental threats and possibilities, the icebergs of business failures and the luxurious islands of business successes.

Controls of corporate structure

The broad scope of the importance of control can again be illustrated by the Ford example. Henry Ford, since he was losing his market to his competition, could have decided immediately to imitate the competition and design cars like theirs. Such a simple imitation would have been a reaction, a piecemeal response to a specific problem. It would not have changed the organization in such manner that this particular type of problem would not reoccur.

Limited corrections steer the organizational ship in a different direction but do not improve the steering mechanism.

A proper reaction to improve the organizational control mechanism that the Ford company used to design its cars was to set up a marketing department to study trends in consumer tastes and evaluate how much customers would pay for improvements in style as well as for additional features.

Such a department could then come to the sophisticated conclusion that it was a better decision to offer customers the option of different engine sizes because there was more demand for a greater range of power than for a greater range of body styles. Such a sophisticated conclusion is usually difficult to accept within an organization if its only basis is the intuition of a single manager.

A well-managed organization requires that clear and strong evidence supporting any important conclusion of that type be collected and developed in an objective manner.

However the intervention of individuals is also very important. Proper controls require the bold and courageous attitude that leads to the questioning of important assumptions underlying existing corporate strategy. Controls are not an automatic activity but one where imagination and courage are also decisive factors of success.

Long-term vs. short term control

Controls also often relate to measurable variables established in financial terms. If the return on investment of a company has not reached the mark that management had planned for the period, a typical reaction to the shortfall is to look at the control procedures to investigate the elements of the problem.

With his nose very close to the columns of figures, a manager may conclude that Research and Development for the period was relatively too high an expenditure, that advertising was out of bounds with its set percentage of the sales level, that sales were too sluggish, etc...

What management could do is then to immediately cut Research & Development or advertising expenditures, fire the marketing director and replace him with someone with better-demonstrated performance. Top management could also hire more salespeople, delay the introduction of new products, etc. All these actions can immediately be justified on the basis of the direct managerial reports of the past business period. But are they the proper measures to take?

Possibly. Cutting some of these expenditures can be useful, but we must realize that they may only be stopgap measures. They respond to the crisis with short-term solutions.

Research and Development on one hand, advertising on the other, are activities that slowly build up their effects. To curtail such activities will also have a delayed and long-lasting effect, which if conducted to extremes will put the whole company in jeopardy.

To implement the Controls of a corporation requires the courage and patience not to take immediate easy solutions to solve a problem when there are good grounds to believe that only long-term solutions are going to work.

Controls and Strategy

It is often difficult to see when corporate strategy ends and where corporate controls begin.

It is indeed part of the function of controls to set the standards and objectives that serve as the guidelines for performance. Controls need to be flexible enough to adapt themselves. However, we have seen above that strategy that does not design programs of action, and programs that do not incorporate clear standards and objectives, is not strategy but a collection of dreams experienced at the strategic level.

Specific Controls

Controls must also respond to specific criteria. They need to be economical, meaningful, appropriate, congruent to the events controlled, timely, simple and operational.

Controls are needed to increase the efficiency of the organization and must be economical. If they cost more to administer than their direct financial contribution, they are not justified.

Controls must be meaningful and correspond to what is going on in the organization. It is more important to control whether the output of a department's work is satisfactory than to measure the periodicity and the duration of visits by the employees of this department to the coffee room.

Controls must be appropriate. It may be more appropriate in a steel making plant to measure the output of ingots per minute than per second when there are many stop and go periods in the production chain.

Controls must be congruent to the events. In the steel mill where the real objective is the number of tons of steel produced, a percentage ratio of I bars against T-bars of steel is not the chief element of the plant effectiveness.

Controls must be timely. If measurement of a production series is not available before the next similar series is completed or well under way, there is no possibility of correcting the parameters with which the second series are produced. The information obtained by controls does not improve anything if received too late.

Controls need not overburden managers with a very heavy load of information, the interpretation of which weighs on their time and resources. The conclusion of controls should be obvious for the manager to rectify immediately the variables under which a program or process has been conducted. Controls need to be simple.

Controls also need to be operational. The evaluation of controls cannot be vague, such as "too much manpower resources": Is it simply that there are too many employees, or is it that they are they putting too many hours in writing reports? Unless the manager can see a direct conclusion to the recommendations of controls, he cannot use them.

Controls as Police

The function of Controls, after setting objectives and standards, is to observe what is going on in the corporation. This is a role of observation.

In principle there is nothing threatening about that. But, in reality, there is always something threatening about having someone watch over your shoulder when you do anything.

This is the section of the responsibilities of Controls that most specifically gives it the reputation of being the corporation's police. In a large company, where the charges of authoritarianism may be the most difficult for management to fight since such large companies do become easily oppressive if care is not taken, such measurements are usually as objective as possible.

Controls is responsible for placing the time-in and time-out puncher at the entrance of the shop and office. Controls makes sample measurement of the mixtures of cookie batter in the food processing assembly line. Controls measures the time it takes for a new engine to be started at the automobile plant, the temperature of ingots at the steel mill.

But Controls also notes by which percentage sales performance has increased. Controls also conducts studies to see if market shares for the company products have increased.

Controls is in charge of measurement and evaluation.

Controls and correction

It is also the function of Controls to formulate a decision on the appropriateness and the extent to which corrections should be taken.

At a high level of corporate policy, Controls decides that a marketing department needs be established at Ford, for example.

It is a function of Controls to formulate whether a stronger effort need be developed to gain further market share, to develop a different incentive program to ensure that salespeople increase their performance, to restudy production systems when new car engines take too long to start, when food admixture contains too much expensive sugar, or the processed food items fall apart because they do not have enough fat.

Usually, again in a company which tries to avoid conveying to its people that they belong to a giant authoritarian army, the procedures of the decision making which arrive at the evaluation of processes and recommendations for correction are developed on a basis which strives to be as impartial and scientific as possible.

But are these scientific processes reasonable? Is this seeming impartiality preferable? Are we not simply shifting for management the danger of managing an oppressive authoritarian organization to the danger of managing an anonymous and uncaring organization?

Controls as re-organization

As with Organization Design, Controls' ultimate objective is to ensure that the activities of the organization are both effective - that what is set out to be done is being done - and efficient, that what is being done is being done with a low level of time and resources wasted.

Controls provides a means to restructure the organization on the basis of observed results of its existing organization structure.

Just as it is a protection of their dignity when employees contribute in the structuring of their tasks and jobs, it is just as important to have them contribute to the design of the controls of their tasks and jobs. When a corporation has acknowledged the importance for their dignity to involve employees in the designing of their work, it cannot take away this dignity by not allowing them to be involved in designing the controls of this work. Naturally, staff specialists should provide employees with all the relevant technical, organizational and economic information necessary for them to establish their own appropriate work standards, evaluation and correction procedures.

In addition, the decision of having employees involved in the design of controls alleviates the problem of their potential and frequent opposition to controls.

Reaction against standards setting

All employees, especially those whose work output can be easily measured, have an instinctive distrust of standards.

They tend to believe that their effort, the rate at which they produce pieces in a piecework arrangement, for example, is measured so that pressure will be put on them to increase this rate and that they will thereby be taken advantage of.

This raw emotion is sensibly the same core feeling that Marxism has captured and exploited by constructing all its analysis of economic forces around the premises that Capital, those people owning the plant, is taking advantage of Labor, the value contributed by the worker, and is

196

not paying the worker his due share; that the situation is structurally inescapable in capitalist economies; that it is unacceptable; and it makes obligatory the advent of the Communist revolution.

Standards, as they are usually measured by figures, incorporate also their cold exactitude, an inhuman image of lack of caring, lack of flexibility, lack of forgiveness.

Employees should have courage and not be affected by these fearful reactions. Managers should use justice to do whatever it takes and ensure that these feelings are not justified.

Reaction against evaluations

Controls are often a cumbersome set of operations and they may often be off-mark in many areas. They may not always fulfill perfectly the above-mentioned criteria of economy, meaningfulness, appropriateness, congruence to events controlled, timeliness, simplicity and operationality.

When controls are not perfect, employees tend to believe that they themselves are necessarily the prime victims of these imperfections; that the controls do not really take a good account of their genuine efforts and contributions to the organization's objectives.

Involving employees in the process of developing controls should help avoid such potential injustices, as the employees will have a responsibility to design controls that will not make them victims of such injustices.

On the other hand, employee collaboration in the design of controls also takes away from employees the argument that the controls are not genuinely measuring what they are intended to measure.

197

Employees will have to face honestly the cases when controls do observe instances of discrepancies between planned standards and observed performances.

Reaction against correction

No one likes to be corrected because in our state of fallen creatures we instinctively oppose change and being told that we need to change.

Controls, eventually, necessarily point out situations that need to be changed. And there are always individuals responsible for these situations; they necessarily need to correct something in their behavior so that the situation will not reoccur.

When employees contribute to the setting of controls, they must have in mind the possibility that these control mechanisms they are defining may later pick up discrepancies between observed performances and standards and that something will have to be done about these discrepancies.

The employees' involvement in the design of controls is a good psychological preparation for them for the correction phase.

The training of employees who develop their own controls system needs to include a teaching on humility and Christian forgiveness. Humility indeed, normally the fertile soil in which all virtues grow and thrive, is a particularly relevant virtue where controls is concerned.

Humility teaches that as imperfect creatures we fall short of meeting standards. However, as long as we pick ourselves up and ask for forgiveness - not really to our supervisors but to God and to ourselves - we are all the stronger to correct our failings and start afresh.

It has been theorized by others that the lack of technical skills and misunderstanding of the need for technical maintenance in non-Christian, especially Moslem, countries come from the conviction that their mechanics cannot fail and neither can their machines. These Moslem mechanics believe they belong to the true faith that translates for them in the confidence that they are immune to human failure and thus have no use for divine forgiveness. Broken parts are ignored until the whole machine is inoperable. Broken machines are put in a corner and forgotten.

The nature of human resources

A certain philosophical background should be in the minds of managers who preside over the development of controls mechanisms, even when their employees contribute directly to setting the standards and designing these controls.

There is tremendous variation in many human activities and skills. It is absolutely inconceivable to expect all employees to contribute at the same level in work situations, even when their work is standardized so well that it can be definitely established that one employee is providing a higher level of effort than another employee.

A corporation that would set its standards so high that it would be looking only for employees with very high standards of work may have a very self-defeating policy, as it would spend an unreasonable high amount of resources looking for such rare individuals in a given working population.

Even positive incentive systems like bonuses, although they should encourage the most productive and effective employees, should not be an institutionalized source of sadness and despair for the more common employees who can never reach the highest standards.

A controls system should be designed with a great quantity of organizational slack to take into account such individual variations.

Work design and Human performance

Often the output of a given production department can be radically improved through a better design of the works and tasks of the employees without requiring an increased effort of this personnel.

Workstations can be subjected to intensive studies to determine the most economical dispositions of instruments and materials around the employee to increase his productivity and quality of work.

A manager should be very conscious of the fact that the output of a department may depend as much on such modifiable structural physical and organizational constraints as on employees' efforts, morale and motivation.

The manager should be dedicated to a constant search for greater improvements on constraints borne by employees. Thereby the manager should feel that the pressure is largely on him to improve the productivity and quality of his people's work. A good and just manager cannot have the attitude that all the productivity and quality of work depend uniquely on the laziness or hard work of his people, lest he adopts the attitude of the slave driver.

Again, the effectiveness of such changes in workstation configurations must be abundantly demonstrated to employees and not imposed on them without adequate explanation so that they can usefully and approvingly adopt these changes.

- 6. - How to Think - Decision Making and the Staff function.

Japanese Decision-Making

One of the most important areas where there is so much difference between Japanese and Western management techniques is the way decision-making is conducted in Japanese companies.

Usual scenario: One team of employees from the MIKITA Japanese company visits the EFG Western company and takes abundant notes. The EFG executives discuss some of the elements of the deal they would like to make with their Japanese counterparts.

Several weeks later, a second team, but this time of junior executives, meet with the representatives of the Western company. They also take abundant notes. They are also willing to discuss everything about the deal again. Although the Western executives thought they had made some progress in negotiating with the first team of Japanese, they realize that the second team does not consider any element of the deal as a given in the discussion. The deal is still wide open.

A third, fourth and, perhaps, fifth Japanese team will also come to discuss the deal without leaving the slightest impression that the negotiations have progressed.

At this point, the Japanese make their definitive decision and return to the Western company with their decision. They typically also expect immediate implementation of the terms of the deal.

The cultural lesson here is that different departments of the Japanese companies were involved in the decision-making. These different departments all saw the deal from their own different perspectives and contributed somewhat to the final decision.

However, eventually the top management of the Japanese company decided which team representing which department of the company would develop the final decision. Naturally this selection pre-conditions in advance the final decision.

In our example the marketing department of the Japanese company is the department selected to make the final decision and it has decided to go ahead and license the Western technology, not only for the technology itself but because it places the Japanese company at a critical point for entering a new class of markets.

The Japanese Research and Development people, still in our story, have opposed the move because one of its consequences is that it makes obsolete some of their study programs being presently conducted within the walls of the Mikita company.

The social impact of decisions

The Japanese technique of group decision-making is designed to achieve several objectives. All-important segments of the company are warned in advance of the important deal that is going to be made. Objections by several of the forces within the company can be expressed before the deal is finalized. The groups insisting on modifications of the deal in order to accommodate some of their claims have a chance to win these modifications from top management. The Japanese R&D people ask for the opportunity to work on the technology and to have cross-licensing agreement possibilities allowed in the contract with the Western company.

In the Japanese company, when the decision is finally made it is presold in the company. The difficulties of its implementation have been examined. The arguments against are known. The opponents to the decision are known. These arguments and opponents have not been ruled out. They simply have been asked to submit to the final decision after having been allowed to make some contribution to it.

In the Western company when the decision has been made by top management - as it is usually the top management which sends its own team for important decisions - the whole job of "selling" the decision to the rest of the company still needs to be done. There are very often great difficulties there because people do not like to be presented with a "fait accompli", a done deal. They may well use their skills and expertise in organizational inertia to sabotage the whole project.

When the Japanese company is ready to deal, the Western company has not completed the most important phase of the organizational decision making process - the acceptance of the decision by the rest of the organization. This is because the Japanese company is very sensitive to the group element in decision-making, whereas the Western company takes it as granted that the rest of the company accepts orders from on high with neither discussion nor opposition, which is often an erroneous assumption.

Society impact on decisions

Important decisions made in organizations have naturally a very significant impact on these organizations as a whole. Everyone in the organization will have to agree with the decisions so that the decisions can be turned from the decisions of top management into the decisions of the whole organization.

Another body of study on decision-making by theorists of management claim that, even apart from the social side of decisions at the implementation level, pure rational decision-making which considers only economic factors does not exist anyway.

They quote Freud, the grand-daddy of modern, man-centered, soul-free and sex-driven psychology to state that decisions taken by individuals are the result of pressures from a mixture of forces including hidden personal emotions as well as the social influences put on the decision-maker.

Similarly, the "Garbage Can" theory of management indicates that organizations are a place where solutions, problems and decision-makers are tossed together in complete random fashion like garbage in a garbage can. What the authors of this latter theory suggest is simply to manage the garbage so that the odds corresponding to the likelihood that the proper problems and the proper solutions will actually meet should increase.

Such theorists actually legitimize organizational chaos with their ludicrous but pretentious intellectual labeling. They terrorize intellectually bent status-conscious managers to accept their confused theories - which are widely promoted in the top business schools. These theories are the prime culprits for the inertia and inefficiencies of the large bureaucracies that are unable to compete in world markets.

Metaphysics and Social Sciences

Herbert Simon, the only theoretician of management who has received a Nobel Prize for this work, proposed his "satisficing model" as an explanation of organizational decision making.

Managers, according to Simon, are not in a perfect world of information and are not capable of devising the most rational and mathematically exact solution to a problem. He said they were subject to "bonded rationality". Managers then have to pick solutions which "will do", that are "good enough". Managers will pick solutions which are both satisfying and that will suffice, hence the word "satisficing".

Theologically, the import of such theories - and there are many other similar theories in the social sciences in general and management in particular - are enormous.

The first movement of such social science researchers is to assume that the world is perfect. It is the "I'm OK, you're OK" attitude taught to them by the school of Selfist Psychology.

Then, as their first observations tell them that the world is less than perfect, they have to change their approach. They then shift to the other extreme and assume that the world is in a irretrievable mess and they set themselves to make do and cooperate with all the evil in the world, in order to come up with solutions to human problems.

These social scientists should instead utilize a proper theology which teaches that Satan's "Non serviam" and Adam's and Eve's disobedience have changed creation by introducing Original Sin. The theorists then would have to build into their theory from the start the consideration that the whole of this vale of tears is not part of paradise. The second theological error of these scientists is to postulate that redemption - or, more modestly and specifically, the correction of managerial problems - can be achieved, on the part of groups of individuals as well as of individuals, by collaborating with evil.

A management theory cannot enshrine the notion that it is imperative to rely on people's fear, anger, intellectual laziness and disdain of challenging ideas in order to somehow improve the process of organizational decision-making.

Also to take the evil in individual human beings as a given is to give little value to human dignity. This insult is further compounded when social scientists take the position that techniques to improve human affairs can effectively be developed without relying on the contribution, and even in spite of, their human subjects.

Human groups are not herds of animals; one cannot develop

programs for them, even for their own good, without their participation in designing these programs (the major error of so-called "scientific" Communism and the misguided "welfare state".)

Improvement of managerial problems has to be related to what is good in people and based on procedures by which these people can become even better. The acknowledgment of personal sins and social imperfections should be included in these programs. But the programs should principally hinge on the proposition that individuals should always be turned away from physical, intellectual and moral shortcomings. Only such theologically correct programs are dynamic and effective. Those programs which take evil for granted and unbeatable are static and ineffective.

Decision-making and mathematics

As concerns decision-making in management, the problem needs also to be addressed positively. It just happens that there are several avenues to study positively the problems of organizational decision-making. (21)

In particular, a whole discipline is emerging called "Decision Sciences". In this discipline, there are unfortunately elements of the psychology and sociology crowds who contribute mostly to undermining what the rest of the researchers are working on.

However, many new techniques are being developed which are very impressive and are a tribute to human ingenuity. Most of these techniques utilize mathematical approaches. They include statistical methods of decision-making, methods developed by a discipline called "operations research", and techniques and approaches that derive from the computer sciences, including systems theories.

206

Many of these techniques are taught in business schools and contribute in no small degree to the prestige of these business schools. However, in truth these techniques are very delicate and very few among the business school graduates really learn how to utilize them in a manner that is both theoretically correct and makes sense business-wise.

Naturally, the solutions found with these methods should also be implemented with a correct understanding of the issue of organizational and human acceptation of change.

Epistemology and decision-making

Once it is postulated and accepted that truth can indeed be arrived at, it is amazing the advances which the human mind can make to come nearer to the truth. Unfortunately the mathematical techniques above cited are most often devoid of a well-developed philosophy which can justify them and properly insert them in the broader field of management.

The effect is that the skills of many junior analysts who do not enjoy the necessary clout to have the value of their studies accepted are under-utilized.

In particular, they lack the supporting presence of a proper epistemology, the philosophy which studies how we know and how we know we know. Such a proper epistemology is absolutely renounced by modern philosophers and social scientists. They believe that ultimate truth cannot be found.

Modern philosophy and the underlying attitude of most social scientists actually are unwilling witnesses to the fact that they are quite conscious that ultimate truth is Our Lord Jesus Christ. They have established barriers around this reality so to remove themselves several times from it. One protection against discovering Christ is for philosophers of science to state that truth cannot be found.

Nevertheless, a discipline which can come close to serving the role of a proper epistemology to the decision sciences is the discipline of "cognitive psychology". This sub-field of psychology studies how the mind works. It does so by having channels of communications open to the work of neuro-physicists who are making many exciting discoveries about brain anatomy and neural connections and who would like to know what these physical realities of the human brain mean relative to the way the human mind functions.

Cognitive psychologists are also researching the mind to respond to questions of computer and information scientists who would like to know how a computer should manage information so as to make it best available to the human mind.

Pressed by these two positive fields of neuro-physics and computer sciences, this discipline of cognitive psychology has thus been lead to take the attitude that truth is something that is normally sought by the mind. The good news is that the more computers are involved in the most delicate tasks of management the more they will bring with them the influence of cognitive psychology in management.

Human Acts and Decision-making

However, mathematical approaches to decision-making and cognitive psychology are not the only positive approaches to studying the process of decision-making. Another process centers on identifying the place and importance of the virtues in the act of decision-making.

But first we need to realize that decision-making is at a very high degree what is called a human act. Because decision-making is a human

208

faculty which is voluntary and utilizes the eminent human faculties of the will, the power to choose among rational alternatives, as well as of the intellect, the power of understanding.

The psychological process of decision-making is divided into different steps, according to St. Thomas Aquinas.

The first step is a movement of the will which has concluded in the goodness in seeking a decision on a particular matter, as opposed to refusing to bother to make such a decision. The will sets itself up to prepare the process of decision-making.

For example the manager, feeling that there is a need, begins to think about a new product to include to his line and to offer consumers.

The will first activates its act of volition which is the act of seeking the good decision. The will indeed believes firmly at this stage that there should be a good decision to be identified and selected even before being reassured by the intellect of the reasons for this hope.

The manager is convinced that a product line with one additional product is better than the present situation.

By volition, the intellect is then consulted to identify the options of the decision as well as the means to attain these options.

The manager looks at possible alternatives: in-house development, buying a smaller company, licensing a new invention, licensing from a foreign manufacturer, etc.

The intellect next presents to the will what it concludes to be the best decision. The will must accept the ranking that the intellect makes between poor, good, better and best decisions.

The manager decides on in-house development.

The will must accept that this decision, presented by the intellect as the best decision, is indeed the best decision. However the will is not forced by the intellect to adopt and run with this selection of a decision. The will can still drop the selection of the best decision made by the intellect, as well as the act of decision-making, altogether.

The manager's mind may tell him that in-house development of the new product is the best rational decision but he may feel uncomfortable with it, in which case he will not pursue the matter.

However, in our example the manager is very comfortable with his intellect's finding that in-house development is the route to take.

The will seeks then to enjoy the best decision. This enjoyment is another act that the will can perform in order to take possession of its objective, here the objective being this best decision that is to be made. Enjoyment is a movement where the will takes the best decision as presented by the intellect and brings it to itself and dwells on it, enjoying it as best selection.

However, the will cannot enjoy the selection perfectly at this time for the process is not completed; the decision has not been made yet. Partial enjoyment at this stage is like trying on a new garment to see if we look good in it before buying it; or test-driving a new car at the dealer's.

The will then proceeds to the act of intention. The will starts committing itself to making this best decision. The manager starts circulating memos to collect reactions to the idea of launching a program of in-house new product development. He advertises the fact that this is the choice he is now contemplating.

Next the will comes to the matter of the choice of means to attain this best selection of a decision. Again, the intellect presents all possible choices of means to attain this end. But only the will is able to pick out the means that the intellect presents to the will as being the best means.

For this, the mind must think over the choice of means and take counsel with itself; it ponders on the suitability of the best means. The intellect will offer this counsel to the will.

The manager has to decide whether to hire a new specialist to conduct the program or give additional training to his people. He must decide whether to rent or acquire new facilities or whether to set aside some place on his present premises, etc.

He eventually decides on hiring a specialist but using part of his present plant.

At this time the will accepts the choice of means proposed by the intellect under counsel. This psychological phase is called "consent".

The manager now is firming up his plan to the last nut and bolt.

It is not over yet. The last step is called "use", that is to say use of will, by which the will applies itself to carry out the decision which has been arrived at by this lengthy process. By "use", the will makes sure that the action decided upon will be carried out so that the expected consequences of this action will occur.

The manager obtains the money for the program, hires the specialist, orders the corner of the plant cleared for the new program's equipment to move in.

Prudence and Decision-Making

As mentioned above these different psychological steps of the process of decision-making can be grouped into three major steps: deliberation, judgment and decision.

Each of these steps requires the involvement of the virtue of

211

prudence.

There are other smaller virtues, which contribute to make the greater virtue of prudence what it is. These smaller virtues are called "parts of prudence".

Of these smaller virtues, five are intellectual virtues: memory, reasoning, understanding, docility and shrewdness.

In addition, three smaller virtues have something to do with applying knowledge to action: foresight, circumspection and caution. At first it seems strange to see memory, reasoning and understanding to be listed as virtues. One is more commonly used to see them as functions of the human intelligence. They are indeed functions but they are also virtues in the sense that they can be cultivated and have all the other characteristics of a virtue.

It is difficult to imagine for a modern person that docility should be part of prudence. However, when we recall that prudence is mostly about making up one's mind about something, it becomes more understandable. Docility is the virtue relative to the ability to keep an open mind, not for the modern purpose of accepting indiscriminately all kinds of opinions and behaviors, but to be able to accept the opinions of people who can really teach us something.

"Lean not on thy own prudence" (Prov. 3:5). but "Stand in the multitude of the ancients, that are wise, and join thyself from thy heart to their wisdom" (Ecclesiasticus 6:35).

Shrewdness is a prudential virtue because: "A solicitous man is one who is shrewd and alert (solers citus)" according to St. Isidore. Solicitude is part of prudence as it is intellectual watchfulness. Shrewdness is a virtue, which allows rapid reasoning on one's own.

Foresight is an interesting and quite useful virtue. It allows a man with foresight to sense the future so that he can know in advance how things are going to turn out. This is not a miraculous gift but an intellectual ability to perceive trends in society and human affairs, to perceive dispositions and bents in the psychological make-up of people. Furthermore the word "foresight" has the same etymology as the word "Providence". The Christian with foresight perceives these trends and dispositions with an acute awareness of the hand of God in all human affairs. It is an ability to sense the purpose of Providence.

Now we can see that prudence is not limited to the narrow modern-day understanding: the virtue of proceeding slowly, looking back to the past. It is also the virtue of proceeding boldly ahead, confident in the future.

Circumspection is the virtue which makes it possible for the decision maker to "look around" and understand well the circumstances of a decision. Sometimes these circumstances may turn a good decision into a bad decision, and only an awareness of and a good assessment of these circumstances prevents the decision maker from making what in the end would be a bad decision.

If foresight allows us to look forward with a sense of confidence in the future, as prudent decision-makers we still need caution, which is the virtue which keeps us on our guard. In particular, when we are cautious we know that good is oftentimes mixed with evil and evil with good. Evil sometimes has the appearance of good. And good is sometimes hindered by evil. Caution allows us to figure out when these situations exist in practical circumstances so that we can indeed do the good and avoid the evil.

Other virtues should be exercised in decision-making which are not strictly part of the virtue of prudence but are connected with it. Among those: the virtue relative to a disposition to take good counsel, the virtue relative to a good general faculty of judging, the virtue relative to a good sense of discrimination in judgment whereby one can effectively judge according to true principles of the morality in cases where the circumstances are very special and ethical analysis is difficult.

The Staff function

In corporations there is a division among managers between staff and line functions. The line functions are functions of authority down the different managerial levels. At a line position, a manager takes orders from his boss and has responsibilities over his employees. They all share in the responsibility of getting things done, of achieving things. The head of production engineering makes decisions which will help shape the products manufactured by the corporation. The head of marketing decides on packaging and rebates which will be made available to the public. Whatever these managers achieve will ultimately produce an effect outside of the corporation and touch the general public.

In staff positions, a manager may or may not have supervision over other employees. The authority of this manager does not reach the operational levels of the company. His authority is only over an assignment. An R&D engineer will present a report to the head of engineering R&D, who will incorporate it in a broader study made by his department. A strategic planning analyst presents to his boss an overall study of future opportunities for the corporation. Eventually, in staff departments the completed work goes back up and is delivered by the head of the staff office to top management.

Typically the responsibility of staff departments is not to produce anything which contributes to the production of the enterprise's products and services. The responsibility of the staff department is only to assist top management on specific decision issues. Top management may even ignore the recommendations of staff; it may decide to inspire itself somewhat with this recommendation while going a definitely different route in its decisions.

Naturally this privilege of the line manager to ignore their advice often does breed resentment in staff employees. A human reaction is for staffers to emotionally protect themselves against marks of possible rejections by pretending to be disinterested in the future of their recommendations.

There is no doubt that staff departments make a real contribution to corporate work as they bring in expertise and develop in-depth studies on issues which top management may have neither the skill nor time to delve into even though the corporation, as a whole, should be concerned with issues studied by staff.

However, there are several modes of corruption of these staff department functions, which not only render their work ineffective but also dangerous for corporations and even society as a whole.

Many members of staff departments often are highly sophisticated academics. Some of these employees may not see or may not want to see the differences between working for a university research department and a corporate research department. They want the same type of "academic freedom" to conduct their research in the manner they see fit without interference from management. Sometimes, corporations themselves encourage such an attitude for they badly want these high level academics even though they know the researchers may not contribute to the work of the corporation. It is felt, at any rate, that they can contribute immediately to the prestige of the corporation's research staff.

Staff departments and employees may refuse to work in the best interest of the corporation. They follow their own agendas, usually with the pretext that they have to follow the demands of their own discipline or science, and have little interest in the agenda of the corporation. Such departments have established their "empire building" program which threatens to pull it apart from the corporation. But a corporation which strives to be temperate cannot afford to have a department, even a non-operational department, go its own way.

Periodically, these departments will submit to top management study reports on fields that are of interest to them without so much as the pretense that their conclusions are relevant to the corporation.

This attitude is usually more predominant in departments doing basic research in the natural sciences. They somehow have the excuse that basic research has a way of turning around, when least expected, and making itself relevant for applied research and then practical work. However other staff departments in large corporations may not have similar excuses.

A marketing research department gone awry may spend some time developing some highly developed research skills,, in order to hone its in-house capabilities, or develop in-depth studies on academically interesting subjects of research which are not cost effective.

What staff departments need to understand is that their primary purpose is to assist the decision-making abilities of top management. In this respect they should take the effort to 1) understand the larger circumstances in which top management will make these decisions and also 2) to facilitate the different steps of the decision making process to be followed by top management.

Reports from the R&D department should be sensitive, for example, to financial and personnel matters in implementing any recommendations that they may provide to top management. It is easy to understand that, by integrating these circumstances in their recommendations, R&D has more chances to influence top management's decisions.

But staff departments also need to be more sensitive to the different steps of the decision-making process undergone by top management as it was described above.

216

The should follow this process step by step. Hence, for example, the marketing research department should be there at the very beginning when the question, "Could this company sell a different line of product to its established customer base?" starts to take root in the mind of the VP marketing.

Marketing research should be there to firm up the VP's marketing will that this is a decision worth pursuing. At this stage the best contribution that staffers can make to the decision-making process is moral support, not analysis and even less conclusions and recommendations. And, similarly, staff departments should be supportive, one after the other at each of the steps of commitment, enjoyment of the selection of a best objective, selection of means, etc, as mentioned above.

There are two possible unhappy alternatives to this ad-hoc, progressive and natural support to the decision making process of top management to be provided by staff.

One alternative is the production of completed reports by staff which correspond to essentially a decision-making process that has been entirely conducted within the staff department. These reports are not the results of decisions by line managers who would have ordered the studies. Such work by staff has a high potential of being ignored; if so ignored, this will breed further resentment within staff.

Conversely, another unhappy alternative is the case of the line manager who has already made his decision, entirely apart from his staff and almost to the most minute details. This manager sets his staff to work on a study only for confirmation or justification of his own decision. In some organizations, the line manager may also feel obliged to order the studies for purposes of an empty organizational ritual. In this mode, the staff must try and guess the assumptions and the conclusions that the boss is already utilizing and has decided upon, not necessarily for the purpose of defending these assumptions

217

and conclusions but maybe simply to make their study relevant to the boss.

The principle of solidarity is highly relevant in this matter of line-staff interaction where closer interactions should prevail and more supportive attitudes should be shared between the two types of organizational managers.

7. The Causes of the Business Organization.

Marcel Clement, a French sociologist who is one of the foremost experts in Church social teachings developed a set of definitions for the business firm or enterprise. (22) He used Aristotle's time-tested system of classification: the four types of causes. Clement showed that the Church has utilized this classification.

Aristotle distinguished between the final cause, the material cause, the formal cause and the efficient cause. Talking about the corporation, the final cause refers to the essential aim of the corporation. Its material cause refers to the members which constitute the corporation. The formal cause is the authority which coordinates these members and elements of the corporation. The efficient cause is the regulating enactments which decide the functions of the corporation.

Pope Pius XII spelled out the final cause of business corporations in a talk of March 7, 1948. "The end to which it aims, by its proper nature, and that individuals must also follow according to the different types of their activities, is to bring about in a stable fashion and for the benefit of all the members of society, the material conditions that are necessary for the development of their cultural and spiritual lives."

218

Business organizations are responsible for more than supplying material goods to the economy. They must supply these goods with a special perspective: the development of the cultural and spiritual lives of all members of society.

The formal cause of the business organization is its legal form. Pope Pius XII in a talk of May 7, 1949: "Whether the business firm is organized as a foundation or an association of all workers as co-owners, or whether it is the private property of an individual who has signed with all his workers work contracts, the business firm depends on private law which regulates economic life... What we just stated is applicable to the legal nature of the business firm."

The efficient cause of the business organization is made up of human acts: it is governed by the free decisions made by human beings that have decided to work together at different levels of authority and responsibility but at the same level of dignity.

Pope Pius XII insists, in a talk of June 6, 1955, about the importance of maintaining this criteria of dignity: "It is only under this condition that it will remain truthful to the principles which We have just recalled, that is, to the precepts of Christian sociology relative to the transcendent value of the human person."

Further defining the place of human acts in the business firm and the special disposition of both the work of manager and worker Pope Pius XII insists, "There are no doubts that both the wage-earner and the employer are subjects, and not objects, of the economy of a nation. There is no questioning this parity...But nothing in the relationships governed by private law, such as the rules of simple work contracts stands in opposition to this fundamental parity." (Talk of June 3, 1951).

The material cause of the business organization are the buildings, the machines, the hardware. The material cause are those elements which are the most obvious to most people about a business enterprise. The components of this material cause constitute, however, factors which are not free from moral consideration. The whole issue concerning the morality of the application of technological advances, both as a support of human work and as a threat to human survival, must be debated at the level of this material cause of the business firm.

Based on the analysis of its causes, Marcel Clement proposes his definition of the business firm "It is the moral and organic union of subjects of rights, bound by the form and the matter freely accepted of working contracts, and cooperating to apply the proper material means in order to produce the goods and services which are necessary or useful for the cultural and spiritual lives of all."

PART III

People at Work - Organizations and the Managing of People.

Within organizations, numerous and various types of inter-human relationships exist and operate at the same time. It is important to possess a basic understanding of these various relationships, their nature and effects to grasp the importance of the impact that individuals have on their organizations.

1. Who is in charge here? - Authority of Managers.

Authority and Similar Concepts

The word "authority" needs be redefined nowadays for it has been blurred in many peoples' minds. Other notions have come to undermine its value as a concept: the notions of power, influence and persuasion.

The issue really is that "authority" is disliked as a concept by many. Authority is the relationship between superior and inferior in a functioning organization. To say that Bill has authority over Jack is to

221

say that Bill is the boss of Jack. It does not refer to whether Bill is the superior in intelligence, knowledge or beauty over Jack. It simply states that Bill has been entrusted by an organization or is somehow in a position to give orders to Jack.

But it appears that in modern society all concepts of superiors and inferiors, of hierarchies are to be fought off.

"Question Authority" is the motto in vogue.

"Authoritarianism" is really the last bastion of evil that can be perceived by liberal journalists, social scientists and their followers in our permissive culture.

But all societies have hierarchies, whether these people like it or not. The only way for a society to function is to have an order in that society and hierarchy provides order toward action. Hierarchies channel the actions and efforts of large numbers of people in a rational and effective way. Thanks to hierarchies, the ends and goals of the different individuals interconnect and support each other and contribute toward the ultimate objectives of the organizations and the common good.

Organizations rely principally on their hierarchical systems to function and meet their objectives. There would be no organizations without hierarchies.

Thus, without conceding the reality of hierarchies, liberals must acknowledge that in organizations some people get others to do what they are told to do, to follow orders. These anti-authority students of society would only admit that Bill has power over Jack.

"Power" is the new concept utilized to analyze how one person can make another person follow his orders; it is a concept void of true understanding of authority because it does not see nor accept the presence of God at the center of men's social contract.

Beyond its divorce from a hierarchical connotation this new understanding of "power" is supposed - by those who favor it over authority - to be a morally neutral concept. There can be good power and bad power. Good power is when good orders are given and bad power is when bad orders are given.

"Influence" is a somewhat weakened, but still often very effective, form of power. A person of influence may be a person of power who does not insist that his orders be followed absolutely. He indicates instead a preference that such or such course of action be taken. A similar utilization of one's power through influence, rather than direct command, usually relies on the possibility for the person in power to drop the softened tone of influence and change it into the giving of direct orders. "If you do not do what I'd like you to do, I'll order you to do it."

A person of influence can also be a person who does not have direct power but only has indirect power. The media have considerable influence on the political process by targeting some individual politicians and destroying them with accusations and innuendos, or by giving no fair recognition and treatment to some political issues.

The media have considerable influence in fashioning the political landscape by default, conserving only the politicians they like and those they cannot touch at a given time, keeping the political discourse within parameters they will accept, and describing their ideological opposition as caricatured straw men.

"Persuasion" is the method we use to try to influence people by resorting to intellectual arguments. Newspaper editorials supposedly concentrate their efforts in order to persuade their readers of the good of their political positions. When, on the other hand, these editorials resort to tactics which are intellectually not valid such as character assassination and utilization of false data, they have abandoned all efforts to persuade and they have instead taken on to influencing their

223

readers by any method that will work.

The nature of Authority

There are in essence several forms of authority: physical authority, intellectual authority, moral authority. (23)

In practice, any type of observable authority is a mix of these essential types. In particular, a boss in any organization should use the three types of authority in a balanced and proper fashion.

With physical authority, the boss uses the authority of his function which is to call security guards to remove someone from a place. Physical authority also refers to control of the paycheck of the employee, particularly by dismissal and fines.

But a boss who has only physical authority over his employees is a poor boss indeed. All bosses should also be able to use, in addition to physical authority, intellectual authority and moral authority.

By intellectual authority, the boss makes a person do something on the basis that it is the rational thing to do. By moral authority the boss makes a person do something on the basis that it is the good or right thing to do.

In any organization which is neither a university nor an intellectual center of learning nor a religious or charitable organization, there will be instances when the inferiors will not accept the intellectual or moral authority of the boss. In those organizations, the boss usually resorts to, or simply implies that he could use, physical authority to have his orders obeyed. He is "pulling rank".

Pure reason and perfect morality are not the operational objectives

224

of business organizations. They function to turn out a product or service. They do possess operational procedures which have been developed in order to make the most logical and ethical decisions most of the time. They further usually also have established procedures, such as questioning specific operations in strategic committees, in order to review their operational procedures systematically.

But they cannot shut down operations and convene an ad-hoc committee each time an employee has a problem with the logic or ethics of an order.

Certainly, on the other hand, these periodical reviews of organizational procedures need be re-evaluated on an on-going basis and to take into account the suggestions of all employees. To automatically insist that orders be followed against the strong opposition of employees is a dangerous source of instability for an organization, as well as being a symptom of ethical problems in its management.

The Christian view of Authority

God, who wants society to function properly, has created natural hierarchies and placed some people in position of power over other people. Some men have more muscle that others, some have more brain, some more diplomas, some more moral sense, some more money, some more social connections and some have a combination of these desirable traits or assets.

Some men are put in position of authority over other men. But God is the source of all good and allows all bad to exist only for us to gain merits towards eternal life. Ultimately all authority comes from God.

Authority is a good thing. It is the best guarantee of social order and rationality in human affairs. It must be accepted as such by Christians. This means that each superior must be viewed as a means that the Divine Will has to make us function better in human society.

The Christian view of authority requires us also to understand that authority is exercised in a context which includes the fact that we are all affected by the Fall and original sin. Our bosses are not necessarily saints, geniuses or supermen. But we still need to accept them as bosses at any given moment.

We are perfectly justified in trying to change bosses, though. We might work hard at getting a degree studying at night. Or we might work on a project which will put us in the limelight for top management to notice us so that we can escape the authority of our present boss. But that is another matter, a matter of long term effort which is totally justifiable but should not weaken our acceptance of the authority of our present boss or of all authority as a matter of principle.

However, authority is not the ultimate good in Christian doctrine. What if a specific authority is flawed? What are the criteria by which this authority needs be corrected?

Authority, Nature and Grace

Authority is necessary to prevent anarchy in society; it is a means for grouping individual human beings living on the earth. Now, in social settings the criteria which pre-dominate rational ordering are the criteria ordering the "level of nature", also called "level of creation". At this level, the good of the group is better than the good of the individual and hierarchical order as well as authority are means of ensuring the good of the many, and bringing about the common interest.

But there is another level in human affairs which has different

226

criteria. It is the "level of grace" which concerns itself with the eternal salvation of individual human beings. At this level, the single human being as person is the focus of analysis.

Authority is justifiable at the level of nature - the level of the many - if it helps the growth of each person, the harmonious development of that person's intellect and will.

We have seen that the ultimate responsibility of organizations is to respect human dignity in its Christian definition. Now we see that the ultimate personal responsibility of each manager is to contribute to the development of the employees who work for him as persons.

The Christian boss must also respect all the principles of justice and morality while exercising his authority and must be aware that there are constraints which protect the dignity of employees. Authority cannot be abused by ordering people to perform unjust and immoral actions.

This personal responsibility of the manager is a response to the fallacious argument that the best expression and protection of human dignity is the abolition of hierarchies, of bosses and inferiors.

The other argument that states that human beings cannot be used nor ordered around because they are great values unto themselves cannot be an argument against the principle of authority in society. The notion of authority pervades the Bible and the Church. It is clear from the order of creation that some people need be bosses and others to follow their bosses' orders.

Further, we may acquire merits through the principle of authority even independently from the responsibilities of our bosses, e.g., when we gracefully put up with a boss who is not particularly likable, has less brains than we do or had more luck than us with his promotions. Such a boss tests, sometimes severely, our will and our docility to accept God's will for us at any given time. When we pass these tests with success we work towards our salvation.

Fundamental issue about authority: God

The concept of authority which should be limited and technical is most often quite far-reaching and emotional.

For many people, "authority" and "father figure" are concepts which go directly to the heart of their attitude toward acceptance in their lives of an all knowing God who has created heaven and earth and has put in place specific laws of behavior for all to follow.

This ultimate dependence on another being, and even more importantly the obligation to follow rules that come from on high is the major problem experienced by many people. Fundamentally, these people want to be free from any exterior constraint.

To these people, the mere concept of the existence of an authoritarian God relates directly to their awareness that they are not conducting their lives according to traditional Christian values, that they have vices, that they sin. As with virtues, vices are established habits which are difficult to dislodge. People tend to identify themselves by their vices just as readily as they also identify themselves by their virtues. By protecting their vices they, in a sense, believe that they are fighting for the integrity of their core personalities and the autonomy of their actions.

They have not yet understood that by their vices they are slaves of their passions. Only by following Christ and obeying His law, they will find the truth that will set them free.

By denying that they are sinning they are protecting, although quite improperly, themselves from the thought of eternal damnation and incorrectly think they are defending their present self-worth. Naturally, such attitude is counter-productive.

Many business organizations would not directly confront people who have such powerful reactions to the concept of authority, and these organizations consequently try their utmost to defuse the issue. These organizations will use softer wordings and an array of precautions to handle these types of personalities.

Again, however, there are hierarchies in organizations and there are centers of authority. That reality cannot be changed and every individual in the organization eventually has to accept that reality or leave the organization.

Fundamental issue about authority: Property

The other fundamental issue about authority is the issue of private property. That issue has somewhat diminished in a country like the United States where public corporations are now defining the business landscape and climate.

This issue was very acute when, a century ago, ownership of a corporation and its management were not usually disassociated as they now are. In practice, employees would easily rebel against authority because "the rich were in command". It was perceived that what gave authority to the business manager was the fact that he owned the company. To the poor, it was adding insult to injury that not only the rich were rich but they could also pretend to give orders to the poor.

Acute sensitivity to these issues has naturally created the political forces and ideologies which are still with us to this day. In particular, Marxism has thrived on these feelings of genuine distress at such realizations of the unfairness of life mixed with raw envy.

What was then the most convenient target, in the guise of an attack against authority, was private property. It has taken decades to prove to the masses that by attacking private property they "were cutting off their nose to spite their face". Societies established according to political principles which either weakened or abrogated private property simply did very poorly economically for their governments and their populations.

As the public form is becoming the rule for major corporations all around the world, the issue of the rich as having direct authority over the poor is lessened and Marxist and even socialist ideologies are on their way out.

It remains that the yoke of authority has to be made acceptable, for many people, rightly or wrongly, have difficulty bearing it. There are several approaches to making this yoke bearable.

One theoretical approach is to pretend that it does not exist. This is not a valid solution and can only lead to difficulties. The attraction of "In Search of Excellence" and its "Management by walking around" includes a false sense that authority can be lessened. This approach to management implies that management and employees consult with one another and that everything will be rosy.

But the only way the yoke of authority can be made to be truly accepted is by making plain to management and employees alike its true divine source and by encouraging them to take on this yoke out of love for God. When they do it, management will fulfill its role of authority with proper responsibility and employees will bear the burden with a proper sense of respect for the place that authority takes in the plans of Divine Providence.

They will understand why Jesus said "My yoke is easy, my burden is light".

The question of authority is one of the three central questions of genuine business ethics, along with the preservation of justice as relates to ownership of property, and the preservation of justice as relates to

230

money-making operations.

2. Variety of Persons - Personality and Management

Personality in Management

We all have an operative understanding of what personalities are. People are different not only in their bodily characteristics but also in their mental characteristics. These different mental characteristics constitute a distinctively different and recognizable mental profile for each person, which we usually call this person's personality.

We also have a general understanding that personalities are important in management. Personalities shape the manner by which a person understands information and behaves on the basis of this information.

Then, when we give the same information - orders, general information or any other type of information - to different persons with different personalities, we know that these different persons will very probably understand this information differently and take quite different actions as a consequence.

But as managers or supervisors we need to have a handle on this situation. We want some specific and somewhat normalized response from employees. We do not want to be surprised by the different possible reactions different employees may have to our instructing or ordering them. As employees, we cannot afford to be at the mercy of personalities. We do not want to be surprised by our boss reacting to us in a fashion completely different from what we expected. A better understanding of the nature of personalities will allow us, we hope, gain a better control of our inter-personal relationships.

An understanding of personalities also helps us better formulate the information and orders we give employees and information we give our bosses.

Personalities and Psychology

But what do we know about what constitute different personalities? The problem here is that the discipline which governs the study of personalities, psychology, is, as we know, heavily burdened by a strong anti-Christian bias which necessarily impedes it to attain the truth that we seek.

Professor Paul Vitz has analyzed the different assumptions underlying the type of psychology that is taught in universities and how these assumptions shape understanding of the concept of personality.. (24)

It is important to present Professor Vitz's findings. These assumptions are to be found in most textbooks of management, even the textbooks which present themselves as the most practical, as well as in the common variety of How-To books of management which simply take their cues from the mainstream secular ideology in these matters.

It is to counter the anti-Christian bias so pervasive in Management textbooks, that the present book has adopted such a confrontational tone. Most people prefer to avoid conflicts but there some conflicts that are unavoidable. Conflicts should be properly made explicit and the proper solution to the conflict should be presented without confusion. Oftentimes, when the general population has adopted a position on the issue that is erroneous to point it out may make the representative of a divergent minority opinion sound as a trouble maker. This is sadly unavoidable and necessary. What is important is that Truth prevails.

The Assumptions of Secular Psychology

Atheism: All the major theories of personality are based on atheism. Freud is well known for his attack on religious beliefs as illusions, insists Professor Vitz. According to Freudian analysis the personality of a religious person must be clouded by a disorder, that is: it is under the claws of an illusion.

But the personality of a religious person is the prototype of a healthy personality and all personality traits can be best analyzed in the person of a religiously motivated mind.

Naturalism: For secular psychologist, the mind is an organ which can be studied in abstraction of any other reality. Abraham Maslow, who is wrongly considered by some as a friend of Christianity, views religious experiences as "peak" experiences which have really nothing to do with anything outside the mind, especially not a transcendent reality. For Maslow the mind is capable of generating its own "peak" experiences.

Therefore, a religious personality does not have to process information from spiritual readings or spiritual exercises or communal worship to have spiritual experiences, according to someone like Maslow, which is to say that this spiritual information is void of any meaning for him. He cannot appreciate the information content of the rites, the activities performed and sentences pronounced at these occasions.

Reductionism: There are no "higher" things for secular psychologists. Every seemingly "higher" experiences can be explained by lower functions. For Freud, religious experiences are really sublimated "sex". Even love is a kind of peculiar offshoot of sex. Family ties, friendship, will be analyzed according to sexual motivations.

This reductionism in science is ironically (since science pretends to be independent from philosophy), the stepchild of Bentham's philosophy of Utilitarianism, itself an offshoot of Kantian philosophy. Kant wanted a "categorical imperative" in his philosophy that would make it universal, something that would logically constrain everybody to be ethical, without that something being God.

Bentham decided that in his philosophy this universal imperative would be the greatest good for the greatest number of people (does not that sound familiar and modern!), or the "greatest utility". As this utility was the highest principle it could not be defined by a higher principle and in particular by a principle which would differentiate between spiritual goods, intellectual goods and material goods. In practice, these utilitarian goods were all at the same level, and that level would be necessarily the lowest level, the level of material goods.

Individualism: this principle considers human beings as self-existent. It negates the value of God, families, even communities as forces which make economic, social and psychological claims on each one of us.

It is at this level that Psychology, as a science, is in direct collision course with Sociology as a science. Modern Social Sciences cannot really integrate these the two disciplines of Psychology and Sociology in view of the definitions they give of themselves, because these are co-destructive. "A House divided against itself cannot survive ...."

234

Relativism: No value is more important than others. Everything changes according to time, context, circumstances. Accordingly, to even attempt to look at principles is fruitless.

This metaphysical and ethical relativism interestingly translates into an ideology of false tolerance: everything is acceptable. First, this tolerance is false because one can be said to be tolerant when one has some flexibility in applying one's principles. When one has no principles, flexibility in the application of these principles is meaningless. Secondly, this ideological tolerance is false because it is intolerant. The ideology of tolerance only tolerates the ideas of those who do not threaten its proponents directly nor immediately. Accordingly, eastern philosophies, witchcraft, and new age philosophies are acceptable to the atheistic mind.

It cannot tolerate any other philosophies which are structured and have strict principles, such as any interpretations of Christian dogmas, vestiges of which can still be found in remote corners like dusty law books, the minds of some antiquated judges, legislators and policemen. These Christian principles still have teeth - some Christian laws can be revived, some Christian judges or policemen can be motivated to apply Christian justice - when the more exotic philosophies do not yet have any teeth.

Subjectivism: Today's psychology considers moral, psychological and spiritual truth as essentially subjective and non-rational. This attitude ranges from complete rejection of anything other than data of direct observation, to amused benevolence and even respect of the moral and subjective only inasmuch as they are conceived in line with artistic preferences experienced by other people and for which it is suitable to have a proper degree of tolerance.

Interestingly, John Henry Cardinal Newman found in the middle of last century that the major British universities placed their theology departments under the control of the art departments. According to theoretical Protestant views, Newman concluded, religion is personal and subjective and therefore there is no use in discussing one's faith rationally other than to witness for it. Today's psychology may not know that it is heir of that Protestant attitude.

"To get in touch with one's feelings" is a proper approach in psychotherapy, it is believed today. In touchy feely sessions the patient liberates himself of his feelings in front of a group. These sessions can be very destructive and have little relationship with Christian charity.

Gnosticism: There is, it is believed by today's psychology, a truly better state for each person to be in, a sort of "salvation" which comes by greater awareness, by self-realization or self-actualization. Therefore individual personalities are not viewed as unblemished but wounded entities.

Psychology recognizes a drive in human beings to become whole again, to regain the power we believe is entitled to us. However this drive, as defined by today's psychology, is not the proper vehicle to use in order to gain true salvation. This drive, out of a Christian context, is the drive of our pride, the drive which is the root of all sins. To follow this drive can only lead to difficulties in life and is no warranty for a sound mind.

Personality and Charity

The issue of Personality is somewhat like the issue of the poor, of poverty, or better said, of the inequality in the distribution of material resources.

In the same manner in which some individuals have more money than others, or are born in better families than others, or have more professional luck than others, people have different personalities with different levels of enviable traits. These differences force us to think: How can a just God allows it to happen that John is more than well off when Bill is a homeless person?

In matters of personality differences, the first question is a question which does not belong to science but which is concerned with the issue of injustice and the problem of evil in this world. This unscientific reaction to reality is a very good moral and humane reaction.

Indeed inequalities abound in personalities. Just as it is preferable to be handsome than to be plain in one's body, there are personality characteristics for one's mind which are preferable to others.

Intelligence is a virtue but also a function of the mind. The virtue really relates to how much we do with what we have, than in what we do with our intellectual faculties. Some people are more intelligent than others by birth.

Self-esteem is a good quality to have because it allows us to make the most of our mental faculties.

Shyness is a quality that is not preferable to possess. Imagination is very useful when it is well controlled. It is necessary to have some imagination to understand things, so that we can rediscover what others are trying to tell us that they have discovered. Unbridled imagination however, makes people live in worlds of fantasy and is a very disruptive personality trait.

The observation in others at different levels of wealth, as at different levels of personality traits, tests our tolerance and understanding for our fellow human beings. These differences are little barriers which give us excuse to put our fellow human beings in little compartments and therefore fraction the Body of Christ in many pieces.

These differences are great impediments for us to love one another and to follow the first commandment, the commandment of love. Personality differences may be a hindrance to Charity.

However, when these personality differences put our charity to the test, they by the same process allow us to gain merits when we manage to overcome our difficulties. They give us a chance to reach towards others when it is not easy to do so. These merits and efforts allow us to grow in Charity. We should consequently be very grateful for them.

Overcoming Personality Differences

The Body of Christ as a whole is a beautiful thing. It is harmonious. As individuals, we need to be different in order to make the body harmonious. A body with ten heads and one leg is not harmonious. Not everyone can be a head.

Harmony is also a matter of plus or minus in some characteristics. To have a beautiful sculpture, there must be some masses of matter at some places in the sculpture and holes at other places. Not everyone in the body of Christ can be a mass of matter. In a musical piece there are notes and there are silences. The silences are necessary to appreciate the notes, and the whole musical piece.

Similarly, handicapped people or people with less preferable psychological traits are intrinsically parts of the Body of Christ. They contribute to the Body of Christ as they are along with their physical or mental handicaps, not in spite of them. They contribute to the harmony of this Body by their differences.

238

There is another positive view of our individual uniqueness. Each one of us, members of the Body of Christ, is unique. That is to say that we have some positive characteristics which cannot be found in any other individual. These characteristics are good and come from God; they reflect God in a unique way.

Therefore, to know God requires that we aggressively seek out these good unique characteristics in all human beings so that we may be able to put together a better and more complete picture of God in our minds and hearts and gain a better understanding and a better love of God. In turn we will express this greater love of God in a greater respect for each individual human being. This is precisely the road followed by many saints in their spiritual quest, especially St. Catherine of Siena.

We have to be very attentive to find the unfamiliar and the different in others. We usually think by analogies, going from one familiar pattern to another. Conversely, when we listen to and care for others we need to try and break that habit and be ready to discover patterns in those persons' personalities; personality traits with which we are not familiar at all.

To rely only on the analogical search for familiar psychological patterns result in complacency towards the objects of our understanding: we tend to undervalue these other people.

When, on the other hand, we have found unique good qualities in an individual, we are much more capable of appreciating the preciousness of this individual. We are well on our way to be loving this person with Christian charity, because we love that person as a creature and reflection of God.

Managing different personalities

As managers we should enjoy having to deal with different personalities in our employees and superiors, clients and suppliers. As much as it is understandable to seek better communications with other human beings and to be able to control these communications, it is part of the human condition that we should work at communicating with each unique individual being. Our ultimate purpose in being managers is not the maximization of profits but gaining personal salvation and saving souls.

To perfectly control our communications with other human beings is impossible for the most part. It is only possible to control the way which very small and fragmented messages will be received. And indeed, there seems to be a new temptation in modern society and, possibly because of the influence of corporate communications techniques, to communicate only simple ideas in a very bland and simplistic manner.

Mass marketing has started this trend. USP, the Unique Selling Proposition principle posits that a product should be promoted for a single advantage: either the toothpaste protects teeth or it freshens breath but not both. Because target audiences cannot handle a double message, it is assumed.

Successively hit by numerous simplistic messages, people finish by concluding that they should use the same techniques in their own inter-personal techniques of communication. Even conversations between friends which traditionally covered many important subjects - although structure and conclusions in these discussions were very much neglected - are being replaced by exchanges of clichés.

A manager needs to be aware of these issues of personality and communications. Although buzz-words are quite handy to speed up communications in the quick-paced work environment of every day, managers need to have made a real effort to reach out and communicate with each one of their employees at a given time. To achieve this a manager may invite the employee for a dinner out and spend the time trying to establish a real human and Christian rapport with this employee.

In trying to understand the personality of his employee, the manager will study this personality in the context of the faith of the employee, including his spiritual characteristics, in opposition to the atheistic and naturalist biases of today's psychology.

The manager will try to appeal to the higher faculties, especially his mental and spiritual faculties, of his employees when discussing even mundane questions, in opposition to the reductionist bias. He will ask the employee to describe the human context in which this employee operates, including his family, parental, community, national and ethnic contexts, in opposition to the individualistic bias.

The manager will endeavor to identify the principles and codes of conduct that the employee has made his own. The employer will also verify the extent to which the employee fits the code of behavior that the employer subscribes to. Thus limits in attitudinal differences are reviewed and identified in a spirit of countering the relativist bias in personality evaluation.

The manager will ask the employee to rationalize several attitudes he possesses in pertinent matters, relative to life in general as well as to the job, so as to counter the sentiment that it is all right to let people do their own thing provided "it works for them", the bias of subjectivity.

The manager will try and probe whether the employee has an inclination towards changing the conditions of his life and whether this inclination comes from Gnosticism or from true Christian beliefs. Businesses must avoid people who seek to become "moral athletes" with some virtues and completely ignore other virtues, which may be well the case with self-actualizing non-Christians employees who may seriously jeopardize the balance of a business.

By trying to understand and help various types of personalities, managers learn about another aspect of the riches of creation which are not available to many. They will learn about the different faces of God and learn to help their neighbors where it truly makes a difference.

3. What is going on here - Perception and Management

Flawed Perception

Today's psychology, which has an innate distrust of any affirmation of knowledge of reality emphasizes the fact that our perception is often flawed or inaccurate. We see a white substance, we think it is sugar when it is salt.

At times, it seems that the whole inner justification of psychology as a science, inasmuch as it applies to persons who are sane, is to understand bias of perception among human beings.

We have already seen that Personality Theories are one avenue to understand variances in perception. Another avenue is to analyze reasons and degrees in the distortion of the information on the part of average human beings.

Sensation and Perception

We need first to understand what is perception, especially as it is opposed to sensation.

Sensation refers to the function of perceiving information through the senses. Perception refers to the interpretation of that information. Looking up we see a blue expanse over us; we perceive that it is the sky.

Sensation then refers to the manner the world around us affects us. Perception refers to our understanding of the reality around us.

Species

The schoolmen with Aquinas developed the notion of "species", meaning those images that the objects of perception leave on our intellectual senses. Our mind abstracts the information provided by our senses and gains an impression of the object perceived in itself, like a piece of wax receives the impression of an object.

This method of understanding perception does not correspond to the habit of most modern scientists and has been attacked for this reason. However, a branch of modern psychology concentrates on one area of studies called "object relations theory". In particular it examines how babies start to make sense of the universe around them.

One interesting finding of this discipline is that the most interesting and soon familiar object known to a child is the face of a human being with the unchangeable configuration: two eyes, a nose, a mouth, hair, ears. This configuration contains some of the most important descriptive elements of the first species known by a child.

Perceptual Selectivity

Because we are constantly bombarded with information, we have learned to screen this information according to certain valid criteria.

Some of these criteria depend entirely on the message sent to us. Intensity, size, contrast, repetition, motion, novelty or familiarity are criteria recognized as positively affecting our perception of a message.

Other criteria which affect our perception are within us. They include learning automatisms which rely on what we really know about the world and the manner in which we use this knowledge. These automatisms sometimes work against us. For example, when we read a series of words such as M-A-C-K-I-N-T-O-S-H, M-A-C-B-R-I-D-E, M-A-C-D-O-N-A-L-D we go through a learning process. When the next word is M-A-C-H-I-N-E, our predisposition is to read it as "MacHine", when it is simply "machine".

Crass advertising and propaganda utilize mostly external factors in order to modify perception. Propaganda does it because it does not want to rely on factors internal to the person. These factors may be too rational. Crass advertising does it in order to reach, through mass marketing, the least educated layers of a population, the section of the population which can be best reached by exterior factors.

Colors and noise are essential techniques of crass advertising. Brainwashing through propaganda was conducted in Korean and North Vietnamese prisoners of war camps with loud speakers repeating the same slogans all day long at a very high volume.

Perceptual Organization

The factors which affect our perception and which are internal to us consist essentially in our ability to organize information for our purpose.

This organization of information may be purely technical. Hence visually we tend to see a closure in an open design. We see a series when items are almost placed in a series. We lump up together items of perception which are physically at proximity to each other. We do the same lumping together of items which appear similar to each other.

Another reason for our organizing information may be more subtly based on our understanding and expectations of the world. We know that the world is basically constant, so we will not see a slight change in a familiar setting. We also see things in their context; we therefore have a bias against incongruity in other familiar settings.

At a third, and still more subtle, level of perception, the skills of perception are directly influenced by our likes and dislikes. We do not want to see things we dislike.

Usually it is not essentially because we dislike them in themselves but mostly for what they mean to us.

In this sense, gory pictures of aborted babies are not perceived for what they are by pro-abortion people. The exterior intensity factor of such scene of an aborted child is less strong than the defense mechanism which prevents the observer from registering the image. The more pro-abortion an individual, the more he would see the bloody picture not for what it is objectively but clothed with its own interpretation of the picture such as an unfair and hideous tool of pro-lifers.

We may drive along an avenue with many colorful and vulgar signs and our attention is stopped by a very tastefully done shop and its artistic sign. Our motivation for good taste may help us screen out all the loud and vulgar and seek the discreet and subdued.

In the realms of affective motivation as a factor of perception, three subjects are known by advertisers as being effective in attracting attention: scantily clad women, babies and pets.

245

The ethics of advertising

Common wisdom in advertising states that we are now being assaulted with so many claims on our attention, on the part of so many products and services, that the first thing that advertising should do is to have the product or service noticed by all possible means.

This priority justifies the crudest methods for reaching the attention of target audiences. These crude methods of advertising include utilizing factors of perception which are external to the observer, like bright colors and huge sizes. They also include the utilization of factors of perception which are internal to the observer and which are crude, this time, because of their low or negative moral value.

In this category can be filed the exploitation of human, usually female, bodies to excite the prurient interest of on-lookers, the exploitation of easy emotionalism with the depiction of cute babies or friendly pets.

But the job of advertising is not simply to attract the attention but also to spur on the viewer to a positive feeling towards the object advertised. This is really where the morality of advertising resides: is advertising simply a method to elicit sinful temptations?

The dilemma of advertising

It is valid for advertisers to try and portray the object advertised in the best possible light; it is also justified to trigger a broad positive feeling towards that object. After all we do not really buy an object for what it is, but for the services that this object will render us. It is therefore helpful to visualize ourselves having this service rendered to us, even if it means for the advertiser to propound a general mood and or broad feeling which help us imagine how the service will be performed for us.

However, it is with these moods and feelings that advertising often goes astray morally. With beer, advertising intends to sell - if even in jest - the atmosphere of unbridled stupidity pervading single bars or the recklessness of partying youth. With luxury cars, advertising intends to sell the feeling of superiority that too often goes with wealth. With clothing, advertising intends to sell self-pride but also immodesty and sexual fantasy.

Although many people in the advertising field may find a profound personal delight in changing the values of the world towards less moral and Christian values, we are really all responsible for the moral level of the advertising industry.

First, if all advertising stopped abruptly, many products would not sell and the economy would crash. Many jobs would be lost. Many honest producers of legitimate products would also disappear. There is an economic solidarity of all citizens with the function of advertising in a society.

We all need advertising to be performed in an economically sophisticated society; therefore we must be aware that we are all responsible for the quality of advertising.

Second, the function of advertising is to stay very close to customers and to communicate well with the immediate level of interest of buyers. This is called "relating with the consumer". Advertisers are obliged to utilize symbols and ideas which are familiar to us. We view the rich as arrogant. We view pieces of clothing as primary tools to elicit sexual attraction, etc.

Advertising as a field of business may precede society in general

247

down the crooked paths of bad taste, obscene images and stupid thinking, but if Christian consumers, as a block, took the initiative to change that state of affairs, advertisers would have to change their approach of advertising very fast.

"If you should boast, boast in the Lord" may be the foundation of a Christian attitude towards advertising.

Perception and Managers

Managers and employees may have different perceptual views of a situation. The manager may think, for example, that the danger areas in his plant are well indicated because of the large DANGER signs posted everywhere. However, he may have forgotten that most of his workers are fresh immigrants who do not know the language or, worse, who are illiterate.

Status and role give a very strong flavor to what a person says. A manager may make what he believes to be a harmless joke which may be perceived by an employee as a stinging criticism. A manager may make what he believes to be a polite compliment to a female employee who, because of feelings of vulnerability, may interpret it as sexual harassment.

One has a tendency to be apprehensive of what a person with a serious-looking, even severe, face may say. We have the tendency to be more willing to find agreeable statements from people with agreeable facial expressions. The reality may sometimes be very counter-intuitive, for the persons with sad faces may have encountered difficult situations in their lives and are more prone to be tolerant, whereas the young and beautiful may have tendency to be more harsh and drastic in their judgments.

Perception Vs. Awareness

All the preceding views of perception are really relating to our perception of things when our mind is on automatic pilot. We can and should train ourselves to catch information even when our perceptual mechanisms work overtime to avoid such information.

The virtue which we need to develop is that of "studiositas", knowing things that are necessary for our salvation, as opposed to the two vices which are on both opposites of this golden mean: 1/ curiosity which is an interest in too many things that cannot help us in any way gain spiritual merits for ourselves or others, and 2/ indifference which is the lack of interest in information coming to us, whether useful to our salvation or not.

All information which can help us make an honest living or wisely manage our budget and raise our family are naturally included in the sphere of information which help us attain our spiritual goal.

A person with a "studious" mind will not be affected by external factors if he does not want to be affected by them. This studious-minded person will have developed his own perceptual screening system by which he would make himself pre-disposed to perceive information on products or other matters which may bear on his salvation.

People who are attentive in particular will be sensible to elements under their observation which are incongruous, out of context, out of order or have changed since the last observation.

It is perfectly feasible to keep out propaganda from one's mind when we have a rich interior life and a life of faith. Experiences of the Gulag as well as of POWs in Vietnam show that prisoners who have a faith to hang on to do not allow themselves to be mentally broken, do not yield to propaganda and even survive more easily than prisoners who do not have a religious faith.

A life of faith is a life of prayer. A life of constant prayer is not necessarily a life in which one recites prayers all day, nor even converses with God ceaselessly, although recitations of prayers and constant communication with Our Lord are indeed important in a life of prayer.

To be always ready to do God's will also corresponds to a prayerful attitude. This last possibility and mode of conducting a prayerful life is very important for those who work intellectually and need to concentrate intellectually on the practical things they do while having committed forever their will to God's pleasure.

Naturally by seeking to do God's will we are attentive to what other people are saying which are really important to them and which are important relative to the work at hand. To be ready at all times to do God's will is the proper attitude which compensates for problems of perception on the job. Managers need to cultivate this prayerful attitude for themselves, as well as to encourage Christian employees to develop the same attitude.

4. Loving what we do - Motivation and Management

Theory X and theory Y

The current wisdom that business schools teach on motivation starts with Douglas McGregor's Theory X and Theory Y. In truth, we must state that this theory was really presented by Peter Drucker first, but McGregor knew how to really sell it, first to academics and then to the business world. (25)

Theory X would be the traditional approach to management. It assumes that people do not like to work, they are lazy. Therefore they have to receive both positive and negative incentives for working, the proverbial carrot and stick.

Theory Y, on the other hand, considers that people love to work and that only bad structures and managerial policies prevent them for working the best they can and want to.

Most management experts are partisans of Theory Y, even though they pretend that there is perfect theoretical balance between the two theories.

The Pluses and Minuses of theory X.

Theory X assumes that it is difficult for people to work. This difficulty is not really dependent on something exterior to the worker but on the contrary it is intrinsic to the worker.

Theory X acknowledges the existence of laziness. Laziness is indeed a barrier which needs be taken down or at least considered in any program designed to increase workers' performance. As previously stated, the opposite of laziness is courage because laziness is a vice opposed to hard work, and the ability of working hard is a part of the virtue of courage. The lazy person is afraid of getting tired; this is a mild form of fear. The pure form of courage opposes the pure form of the fear of being wounded or even killed.

Theory X acknowledges the fact of the existence of virtues and vices. Laziness is a manifestation of evil and sin in the world. Theory X also makes possible, or at least is culturally compatible, at a superficial level, with a view of the world based also on damnation and redemption, that is with a view of the world congruent with the mystery of the Incarnation.

However, theory X does not acknowledge that work is natural to human beings. It implies that when the lazy worker is lazy, the work does not get done and that is the end of that.

The fact that work is natural to human beings tells us that when the worker is lazy and the work does not get done that is not the end of that. What also happens is that the worker does not "get done". For work is a natural process by which human beings improve themselves. If work does not get done the worker does not get to improve as a human being.

That work is natural to human beings also signifies that work is essentially its own reward. The whole approach of incentives of theory X is therefore basically flawed. The incentives for the worker to work are primarily internal to himself. Neither carrots nor sticks can be the prime incentives for people to work.

As we said on the nature of work, people work also in order to gain compensation for their work and to make a living. This element is not the center of the definition of work, although it is for many people so important that they tend to think of it as the major reason for which they work. Work can exist when there is no compensation but work cannot exist where the worker will not apply his talents and skills on something exterior to himself and grow in the process.

If, in a given work setting, the worker is not encouraged to apply his talents and skills and to grow in the process, this work setting is basically undermining the worker's fundamental motivation to work.

The Pluses and Minuses of theory Y.

Theory Y seems to imply that work is its own reward, that workers and employees do find a definite satisfaction in working and especially in doing good work.

Proponents of theory Y have been those who popularized the notion of "significance" in work. Significant work is interesting work which is derived from the fact that it has an intellectual content but also from the fact that it is likely to make a significant difference in society as a whole or at least in the organization where the work is done. Many "policy" jobs are very much sought, even when the scope under which the policy will be exercised is very limited, such as deciding the manner by which stocks are arranged on a warehouse's shelves.

One quick simplification - which is utilized by many - of theory X and theory Y is that theory Y assumes that workers are mature about their work and theory X assumes that workers are immature. As we have seen theory Y ignores the possibility of the moral flaw of laziness.

Mature people may appear to be more moral than children or immature adults. Mature people will go to work when children refuse to go to school because they just would rather play. But, other than appearances, maturity is no remedy for virtue. Mature workers may do poor quality jobs or have the same low productivity as immature workers. Maturity only helps a person recognize that the world is made in such a fashion that we cannot plainly escape work, therefore it is immature to oppose the very notion of working.

Maturity by itself does not provide an incentive for people to work in instances where it is possible for them to shun work and not be penalized for it. Mature people can be lazy, even if they can exercise their laziness in more subtle and hidden fashions than immature people.

In particular, mature workers may hide their laziness under the

253

pretext that a job is not "significant" enough. Managers and their academic advisors who want so much to believe in theory Y - therefore in "significant work" and the impossibility of laziness - are easily duped by this type of argument.

First conclusions

Studies show that, in general, organizations which are utilizing theory X - and they are very few of those in this end of the twentieth century - do not motivate their workers as well as those who practice theory Y.

Studies on positive incentives - such as prizes and bonuses - as well as negative incentives, have shown that these incentives have very limited values of themselves.

Tom Peters, who has made himself known for giving a new life to theory Y, has shown, in his book "In Search of Excellence" the advantages of his MBWA - Management By Walking Around - or consulting one's employees in all things. (26)

Does that mean to say that laziness is irrelevant in modern industrial and office work settings ?

Absolutely not. What it means is that theory Y, which ignores laziness, has a better understanding of the nature of work than theory X. That theory Y ignores laziness is not enough to put the two theories on par. It is important to understand better the fundamental make-up of human beings, and the place of work in this make-up (both things which Theory Y does better than theory X) even when the winning theory still has important flaws. It also underlines the extreme importance of presenting thoroughly, as we did above in this book, the nature of work.

What is of central importance is to recognize that work involves the whole human being in his soul, that is to say in its intelligence and freedom of will.

Theory Y acknowledges intelligence because it recognizes the value of tasks which are intellectually stimulating. Theory Y also recognizes freedom of will because it promotes flexibility for workers to act on their preferences in work settings.

However theory Y does not recognize the full significance, potentials and limits of what it is to have intelligent beings as workers, to have free beings as workers. Theory Y does not recognize what it means that each individual who works has a life to live and to act by using both his intelligence and his will in an harmonious fashion and in a fashion which follows the Will of God.

Qualifiers of theory Y

Peter Drucker insists that when he marked his own preference for something akin to theory Y, he insisted that this was not a "permissive" view of management philosophy.

"On the contrary, I said that to manage worker and working by putting responsibility on the worker and by aiming at achievement made exceedingly high demands on both worker and manager". Peter Drucker in Management, p. 232.

Abraham H. Maslow who was a great proponent of the underlying philosophy of theory Y was, however very concerned about modalities in its implementation. He considered that the demands of theory Y were too great on many people. Maslow criticized both McGregor and Drucker for "'inhumanity to the weak, the vulnerable, the damaged which are unable to take on the responsibility and self-discipline which

Theory Y demands".

Maslow suggested that theory Y has to go far beyond theory X. Drucker concludes that theory Y cannot be permissive as many believe. It cannot be a theory that leads to the pampering of the worker. He writes that theory Y is a stern master, "sterner in many ways than theory X which it replaces".

Now that theory Y is no longer viewed as a license for happy-go-lucky management, unbridled brain-storming and initiatives by employees and workers, it is to be feared that theory Y will drift towards new horizons where Christian virtues are still not recognized.

Peter Drucker is a Catholic and even taught religion before his management career. All his writings clearly reflect this reality and his success is in large part due to the many valid understanding which he owes to his religious upbringing. However, as he seldom brings out Christian doctrine in his management theories, these theories are all the poorer for it.

What are these responsibilities and self-discipline that the new Theory Y seems to demand from the person at work? They seem to be that people at work are now asked to bring their own structure to their tasks and to their work habits.

1) Employees have to make some sense of their personal work initiatives and ideas to put these ideas and initiatives in neat order so that the firm at large can handle them.

2) The new workers also have to be "super-mature" and exhibit patterns of work which would appear to be very strangely like hard work. But would it be hard work?

The brave new manager-less worker

The revised theory Y seems to say that the New Workers will not need any managers since they would be so self-sufficient. But managers' function is not really to be a corporation's slave drivers. What managers do is not to crack whips or the intellectual equivalent.

Managers must ensure that their employees not only act but also interact between themselves. Employees will always have to work with others. They cannot make up independently, each on his own, how they are going to interact with their fellow workers. Somebody needs to coordinate the efforts of many individuals.

Managers also need to direct the whole team of employees towards some objective that is usually far from the immediate scope of these employees.

Should the employees seek a means to help themselves interact and discover objectives worthy of their effort, they would designate a representative from among them for guidance and therefore come to a point where in effect they would have re-invented their manager.

The brave new moral athlete worker

The new improved Theory Y worker would be a self-starter and hard working person. But that is not quite the same as a Christian worker who has vanquished the bad habit of laziness.

The brave new worker would work hard not to improve himself, as a Christian, it would seem, but in order to be more productive. He would not view himself as the first object of work, as a Christian would. but as a mere instrument for the task to be achieved... or at least it is what the experts seem to expect of this new worker. This objective seems to be somewhat unlikely to be met, to put it mildly.

This is where the dilemma lies in this un-Christian theory of worker motivation. If the worker is self-motivated, he will find in himself the reason to work. This inner reason cannot be determined by the work that has to be done or anything else outside the worker. It may be that the self-motivating reasons of the worker in many instances corresponds with the needs of the task to be done. But what happens when it doesn't? If management has to motivate the worker in these instances, then the worker is not self-motivated.

Motivation and ESOPs

Employees Stock Ownership Plans are hailed by many as the silver bullet of employee motivation. These plans make it possible for employees to become part owners of the firm in which they work, the rationale being that if the employee is owner of the means of production he will strive to make the company as successful as possible.

However, the true success of ESOPs is quite mixed. In some firms the plans do help motivate employees, in others they do not. Eastern Airlines had an ESOP plan when it filed for bankruptcy. This is because the existence of ESOPs is not the key element of success of the plans in the companies where they are available.

The management style of a corporate leader may be creating a climate in the corporation where employees are eager to contribute to its success and the existence of ESOPs is only icing on the cake. It may also be that the industrial environment of the company is so positive that the company is growing by leaps and bounds and the stock is appreciating greatly and the employees like that. In this case ESOPs are definitely a good thing.

But ESOPs also means that when the company has a bad year, there is no profit and therefore no profit "bonus" for the employees. Employees do not like that. In a stagnant or even retrenching industry, corporate losses may be frequent and employees may feel that ESOPs are a disguised manner of lowering their salaries as well as making them responsible for business failures. And very often ESOPs indeed are ploys of management to lower employees' incomes.

Workers and employees participation may have different forms: ownership participation, as in ESOPs, participation in top management decision with employees on boards of directors, participation in middle management and work setting responsibilities.

Only the participation of employees in deciding the details and configuration of their work place is really effective as a motivator. Employees on boards and employees making mid-managerial decisions is not effective as a motivator nor as a means to direct a corporation.

The findings about employee motivation show that what is really important for the employee is to have personal control and free use of his intelligence and power to choose and shape the manner in which he will conduct his everyday work.

Not surprisingly, ESOPs may be most effective with the highest level employees whose tools in the workplace happen to be the such of budgets and corporate financial instruments. Therefore the direct work setting of these highest level employees includes instruments of ownership in the corporation.

On the subject of ESOPs, there is also an ideological undercurrent with these plans which is not clear to many, including some supporters of the plans. The Marxist ideology demands that the ownership of the means of production be taken away from private hands and given to the State.

Some counter ideological proposition may consist in presenting

ESOPs as an ideological response to the Marxist's criticism: "OK! let's take the means of production out of the boss's hands and let's put them in the hands of the employees." Well! This is a different demand from asking that they be put in the hands of the State but it does not really condemn the Marxist position that the private ownership of these means by an entrepreneur or a limited number of financial partners is reprehensible.

In other words, promoting, with ESOP plans, the private ownership by employees and workers of the means of production may be a weapon against the principle of the private ownership of the corporation by an entrepreneur or a team of partners; it may be therefore a disguised weapon against the absolute right, by legal means, of acceding to private ownership. The Church unequivocally supports this right; it is the absolute right of USE of this property as the owner wishes that the Church does not support.

When ESOPs may appear as an effort to "democratize capitalism", they may in fact still - in principle and in many practical instances - undermine capitalism.

The basis of workers motivation

How should a Christian manager approach the function of employee motivation? Well, as we have seen, it is first important to decide which anthropological model will be used.

First the proper model is to be selected: the Christian model. It is then important to make this selection of the model and the model itself known to the employees, not simply to educate them, not really to indoctrinate them in this model but more immediately to let them know what to expect. Subsequently, any motivational and incentive program should respect the model.

260

Christian managers need to express that it is their view that the people they are called to manage have an intellect, a freedom of will, a responsibility and a right to exercise both and to exercise them with the view of gaining eternal salvation. As persons who are called to be in the state of grace these employees may be the most precious entities on earth. They must be treated with dignity in all things, including their working conditions and salaries.

Their managers will respect these different elements of their realities, and try to help them, if possible, in their different objectives, whether work-related or not.

Education

First of all, employees should be educated in the life and activities of their firm not only for their general information but also to help them see how their own personal work connects with the objectives and working environment of the firm as a whole.

This seems simple but it is rarely done correctly. It means the information should be accurate, on-going, fairly detailed and unbiased. Corporations tend to provide information especially when they expect something special from their employees. This quickly tends to decrease credibility and interest in the information.

Also, each manager should be able to adapt the information that is put out by the firm as a whole in his own words so that his subordinates can put in focus this general information from the point of view of their own personal manager and therefore in terms of what will be practically expected of them.

Unfortunately, many employees pretend they do not have the time for any information on the firm in general. This entails another responsibility to managers. Managers are responsible to ensure that the information is easy to assimilate and attractive. But managers are also responsible to ensure that this information is indeed absorbed by their employees; they will make it an obligation to the employees to absorb the information. Education should not be optional in this matter.

The second step of establishing a good basis for employees' motivation is to educate employees in all sorts of information concerning their individual tasks and jobs. The information must include all the different techniques for performing the tasks as well as the value of the tasks to the firm as a whole. The latter point is extremely important to encourage employees to gain additional training and pursue an on-going education lest their function becomes obsolete.

Decentralization

We need not come back to this point in detail here.

Decentralization is essentially letting employees have as much responsibility as possible in the structuring of their own work, as we have seen above.

The education and instruction on the firm and their jobs that is given employees are also for the purpose of providing them with the alternative choices to implement this job structuring.

Beyond the basic conditions of workers' motivation

After the basic conditions for workers' and employees' motivation have been set in place, the manager must energize the employees into doing their best at whatever it is they apply themselves to.

It is also precisely the place where the task of the manager ceases to be a pure task of motivator of his employees and starts becoming the true task of a leader. We will treat this subject later.

Motivation and Love

However, it belongs here to present a treatment of the golden side of motivation.

Motivation can be hampered by many obstacles and this requires patient and thoughtful care on the part of management to create the conditions for motivation to blossom in their employees.

But this patient and thoughtful work has somewhat a grayish aspect compared to the golden shine of the employee who exudes motivation.

Studying the motivated employee - which can really be observed as well among knowledge workers as among physical workers, we cannot fail to witness a level of unbridled enthusiasm of the employee for his work.

The motivated person lives and breathes his work. He cannot have enough of the essence of this work. His mind is continuously attuned to finding greater efficiency and novel ways to improve his effectiveness at work. The motivated person eats, relaxes and sleeps with his work.

The motivated person is in love with his work. He is inescapably attracted by and to the subject of his love. He is ecstatic, in the literal sense of the word: he his beside himself. He seeks to lose himself in this love.

In view of this understanding of true motivation, it is impossible -

and would be morally very reprehensible should it be feasible - to seek to artificially motivate one's employees. However, without a good understanding of true motivation in employees - understanding which can hardly be better achieved than by meeting genuinely motivated employees - managers will fail poorly when searching to design and implement the best means to elicit from their employees a strong motivation for their work.

5. Corporate Solomons - Conflict Resolution and Management

Professor Ross Webber of the Wharton School writes:

"Conflict is inevitable, often legitimate, and perhaps even desirable. It does not necessarily indicate organizational breakdown or management failure, as was implied in older management theory and human relations philosophy." (27)

He goes on:

"Three assumptions underlie recent thinking about conflict.

"1. Conflicts are common in organizations because everyone does not agree about their own authority and responsibilities, and are not equally committed to the same organizational objectives".

2. Some types of conflicts are detrimental and others beneficial for both individual and organizational objectives.

3. The principle of minimizing conflict subscribed to by some managers and social scientists may have some validity for crisis organizations (such as armies), but it may not be valid for knowledge- and technology-producing organizations, such as

those engaged in research and development."

Whoever has to manage people and organizations will experience the fact that conflicts are prevalent aspects of organizational life.

However, conflicts are in opposition to the development of an organization. This is why we will defend the position that there is no such thing as a good conflict. There may be conflicts which are happily resolved. But conflicts do not contain "positive" elements.

"Conflicts within" and "conflicts between"

Conflicts can be classified as either "between" different groups and individuals or "within" them.

Two organizations may be in conflict over increases in their market share. Two departments of the same organization, i.e. "sales" and "customers' credit" may be in conflict on how to treat customers, "sales" wishing that much leniency be granted to customers in paying the organization and "customers' credit" being much more hard-nosed about it.

The latest conflict is both within and between, depending on how we look at it. It is within the same organization and it is between two departments of that same organization.

We can also apply the concepts of "conflicts within" and "conflicts between" to individuals instead of organizations. Conflicts can be between two individuals as would be the case between two vice presidents vying to put themselves in better position to be promoted to the post of president.

Conflicts can also be within a single individual who is torn between spending more time at the office and work longer in order to be better appreciated for his contribution to the organization, and spending more time with his family.

Conflicts over what?

We must analyze what the sales department and customers' credit are in conflict over. Indeed what they are conflicting over may appear obvious at first glance but, as we will see, it is not necessarily so.

On one hand they could be conflicting over measures of personal organizational achievements: the sales department wants to increase the volume of sales and wants customers to be granted lenient terms of payment in order to accommodate the greatest number of possible customers. Similarly, customer's credit wants to improve the ratio of payments over sales. Customers' credit is judged according to the good paying habits of customers and if the corresponding measure deteriorates they are showing poor levels of achievement.

But, on the other hand, the two departments may be really conflicting over two different elements which both correspond to necessary goods for the organization at large. The Sales department wants the organization to achieve the highest levels of sales. Customers' credit wants the organization to be as financially sound as possible.

In the first instance - with conflicts over organizational achievements - the two departments are really isolated from each other. The conflicts are seen in a zero-sum game where what one department wins the other department loses.

In the second instance - with conflicts over different views of the organizational good - the two departments are really competing at advancing what they view as the higher good for the organization as a whole. These departments are not isolated when their attitude is to consider themselves as departments of a common organization. Their conflict is not a "conflict between" different departments but a "conflict within" the same organization.

Therefore, it is very important to analyze what the conflict is over. If it is for selfish goals, it will be a conflict between; if it is for the greater good of an entity higher than both parties to the conflict, it will be a conflict within that higher entity, the business firm as a whole.

Types of organizational conflicts

We need to open up the nature of conflicts to the different apparent pretexts of conflicts. Conflicts are usually recognized to be over goals, activities or resources.

Conflicts can be over goals such as our sales department and customers' credit department. What they are technically fighting over are the firm's policy on how to handle certain customers' accounts in respect to how much credit - and the terms of this credit - is granted customers.

Conflicts can be over broader issues as organizational activities. Two vice presidents of a technical firm may fight over what they view should be the mission of the firm. The vice president for engineering thinks the firm should concentrate on high quality engineered products in order to occupy a niche where it will attain high technical recognition within the industry and high image recognition in the market. The vice president of sales believes the firm should have a product line of high quality engineered products but should rely more heavily on a much broader line of lower engineered products at a more reasonable price which will keep the business well-established over a broader market base.

Conflicts may be over resources when Research and Development presents its inter-departmental budget which will have to fight for scarce dollars with Engineering's decision to upgrade some production machinery. The sales department may thus have inner conflicts when Marketing Research is demanding more funding for important studies which will make selling more effective when Distribution is begging for more salespeople to be hired and put on the road and immediately bring in more revenues which will justify several times over the expenses of these salespeople.

Conflicts over goals.

As we can readily see now, all types of conflicts can also be classified, in more philosophical terms, between conflicts over goals and conflicts over means.

Those two types of conflicts are essentially very different.

Conflicts over goals are possible only when two different individuals or departments compete over the setting of goals. When two vice presidents can each decide whether the business organization will become in the future more of a high technology- high quality - high prices - low market share business or rather a lower technology - lower quality - lower prices - greater market share business, conflict results.

Both options and organizational scenarios may be quite valid but someone has to decide which option will be selected. This someone is the person above the two vice-presidents. The president or the board of directors must decide which of the possible options will be selected. The president's or the board of directors' decision should end any further discussion and settle the apparent conflict.

But the conflict may continue when the president or board does not have the moral courage to make a decision and present it as final to all parties. The conflict will continue when the president or the board depends too much on the vice-presidents - as they recognize that they need their full agreement to achieve implementation of the decision - and therefore leave each vice-president to conduct his own personal agenda without consideration of what the other vice-president will do and what is the good of the firm as a whole.

Conflicts over goals can therefore be reduced to a matter of authority and responsibility in a firm. In firms where authority and responsibility issues are effectively settled such conflicts should not exist or should not persist.

Conflicts over means.

Returning to the example of the conflict between the Sales department and Customers' credit first there may seem to be also, in a sense, a conflict of goals because all conflicts over means tend to disguise themselves into conflicts over goals which are usually viewed as more prestigious.

At the level of Sales and of Customers' credit, the issue may be formulated by both parties to appear to be a conflict of policies, therefore both departments may conduct their campaign of persuasion as if their common manager should decide whether the company will have a policy of easy credit or a policy of stringent financial accountability.

This is not a conflict over goals nor of policies because the choices between easy or tight credit is not really a choice between two widely different business organizational scenarios. These are rather low-level choices that, to a large extent, are imposed by the nature of the business and of its competition.

Even if these conflicts were in a very limited way conflicts of goals, their resolution would be much easier than full-fledged conflicts over goals, as the effort to impose the authority of the president over these lower level services would be much less than the effort required from him to impose his authority over more formidable organizational characters such as his own vice-presidents.

As we mentioned, the conflict over easy or tight credit to customers is in many respect imposed by the business environment. In a very large sense, it is a technical question. Technical questions can be easily resolved with all the proper information and when an adequate decision-making process is in place to properly treat the information and arrive at the required decision.

Conflicts over means are therefore on one hand managerial problems: the different departments must have in place the policy and procedures to take the appropriate technical decisions. If those decisions can be made at the same rate as their need arises, conflicts of means should never appear.

However, in the practical world, full information is not always available to make a completely informed decision. In the case of the credit to be granted to customers, the information on the state of the business environment may not be available with 100% certainty. This only means that the person who will have to make the decision has to act as a true manager - that is, that he will have to make a decision based on his personal experience, his intuition and the limited information available.

Should, all the information be available, this person would not be a manager but a technician or even a computer algorithm.

Managing conflicts.

In conclusion, conflicts should never arise when proper authority and responsibilities are assumed in the organization and when proper decision-making processes are in place which are supervised by competent managers.

However, conflicts are sometimes more a matter of the subjective attitude of individuals than the objective existence and effectiveness of processes and procedures. Therefore managers who do not educate their people to acquire the proper Christian attitude in matters which could appear to become sources of conflicts will not be able to avoid conflicts.

In the matter of conflicts over goals, that is to say of conflicts over policy matters which will be settled by people in higher authority, the parties to the potential conflicts should understand that it is indeed their role and responsibility to present their case for their own policy options as forcefully and in the best articulated manner as possible.

However, they should not forget in the process that they are playing this role in a larger context to which they must submit their final consent, display courtesy to other human beings, and that they will respect the God-ordained authority of their superiors when the policy decision is formulated.

Participants in a situation where a conflict over means may arise must acquire the proper attitude and spirit of solidarity with which they will certainly promote their own views, but will also gather all relevant information for their managers to seek a genuine resolution of the situation where the common good of the organization will be best attained.

6. Picking the Best and the Brightest - Selection and Appraisal of Personnel

Recruitment of personnel is a very taxing affair both for the job seeker and for the company doing the hiring. This is also a function of management where intuition, subjectivity, fear and hope are the most central elements of the process and can be suppressed only with difficulty.

The textbook approach of hiring is as follows: a department sends a request to the personnel management department for an employee with a specific set of characteristics. The personnel department organizes the information and publicizes the availability of the position and the characteristics requested from the applicants.

The personnel department uses for this purpose either advertisements in major city papers, business papers or trade association publications or online. It may also pass along the request to a consulting firm specializing in personnel selection with which it has a standing contract.

The prospects are qualified, maybe first with a telephone conversation and usually on the basis of a quick reading of their resume. They are then invited to meet with the personnel manager, interviewed and possibly tested in his office. The best prospects are then recommended to the department which originated the hiring process.

What needs to be remembered about this textbook approach is that it is seldom the process that is effectively utilized, even in organizations where the structures for this process are firmly in place. These structures are in fact a smoke-screen for what actually takes place.

Personnel departments seldom have a dominant role in the hiring process. 80% of new employees are hired directly, that is to say they are

272

known by the people in the department where they are going to work. They are usually known because they are business acquaintances.

Also the prospects may be personal acquaintances and friends of employees who bring them in and make them known to the different department heads until confidence is built in these decision-makers who will then hire the employees' friends or relatives.

As a rule, personnel managers receive a steady stream of unsolicited requests for jobs and positions for which they have nothing immediately available to offer. The usual reply given states that their inquiry will be kept on file until a need for someone with their talent and experience develops. In reality, only the most recent inquiries have a genuine chance to be considered because they will be on the top of the pile when a position becomes available.

In practice, the major role of personnel managers in matters of hiring is to send prospects a negative reply or a reply which appears to offer some hope to the applicant but really does not.

We should not forget that many personnel managers chose their line of work because they feel themselves to be people-oriented. Therefore to send such letters and with such great frequency is really for them a heavy emotional burden which they dread. Personnel managers may even come to resent applicants for causing them to experience such negative feelings.

Subjectivity

Personnel managers are not the only ones to experience strong feelings during the hiring process. The very managers who will be the bosses of the new recruits are even more prone to inject their own subjectivity in this process. The often mentioned fact that first impressions are the most lasting is true. During the first five minutes of the interview, the interviewer has the time to evaluate both the language delivery, the general attitude and the body language of the applicant. He does not have time to go any deeper and verify whether the applicant is wise, is a thoughtful thinker or, conversely, whether he is really a fool and a shallow person.

Further, how applicants will be judged by interviewers does not really lend itself to objective analysis and therefore to effective countermeasures and strategic preparation on the part of applicants; they are very much a matter of personal taste and expectations on the part of interviewers. Even good personal appearance and neatness of dress which are indeed imperative and the best advice to give applicants in the great majority of cases may be an handicap in some professions which value the creativity and originality of its people.

Affability, seriousness, self-confidence, eagerness are all traits which may or may not please in a specific individual as communicated to a would-be supervisor. In a given individual exhibiting such traits, they may be perceived as adequate by an interviewer and excessive by another or lacking in a third; they may sound genuine and refreshing to one interviewing manager and phony and repellent to another.

The search for objectivity

The reality of this subjectivity is doubted by no one. Thus, important efforts are expended with the objective of diminishing this subjectivity.

In particular, different techniques are utilized to try and confer a quasi-scientific approach to the process. Instead of a single interview, it is now recommended that a series of interviews be conducted with several people in the firm. Instead of unstructured discussions during the interview, evaluation sheets are handed out to interviewers with pre-established questions the interviewer should seek to respond to in order to better frame his evaluation of the applicant. In addition, applicants are often subjected to aptitude and psychological tests of different sorts.

Tests and more tests

One differentiation is between aptitude tests and achievement tests. The first class of tests measures personality characteristics which tend to indicate that the respondents possess the required ability to face up to the circumstances in which they would be called to operate in the most professional manner. The other class of test - achievement tests - measure actual performance, they may measure how respondents are doing at responding at a simple mathematical quiz - which may not require much mathematical background but an agile mind - or how much the respondent knows about anything, say marketing, which requires some previous studies in, or experience with, the subject matter.

Another classification of tests distinguishes between Intelligence tests, Personality Tests and Interest Tests. It is difficult to assess how much intelligence and what type of intelligence is really required for a specific job.

As far as Personality Tests are concerned the reader is invited to refer to the chapter on psychologists' understanding of the concept of personality.. But here, as related specifically to Personality tests, is a caveat presented by an industrial psychologist, Fred Luthans (28) (p.584):

"There is little agreement on a practical or analytical definition and almost no agreement on an operational definition of personality".

What Personality Tests measure is as valid as the ancient Roman augurs' assessment of the future on the basis of their examination of a sacrificed chicken's entrails.

Interest tests are usually utilized for vocational training and orientation. They do have some value as they force the respondent to think about what interests him most about major components of different types of jobs and professions. For example, one such test evaluates whether the respondent is 1) people-oriented, 2) interested in figures, 3) interested in things, 4) interested in ideas or any combination of these elements.

On the basis of the fact that there will be individual differences between respondents and that the answers do match the preferences of persons occupying jobs where these elements are prevalent, such tests are somewhat valid for counseling.

However, for hiring purposes it is obvious that respondents will be greatly tempted to try and second guess the examiner in order to display whatever interests are required in order to be offered the job they are applying for.

Emotions and Making a Living

The underlying reason for so much emotion in the personnel selection process is two-fold.

Everyone agrees that the hiring process is very important as it affects the lives of individuals. This is directly related to that element of work which makes work one of the most common means for people to make a living. A good job is a very important element of the life of people and to have the power to grant a job or to deny it is awesome and possibly overwhelming for some managers.

Human beings are very uptight with anything which relates to the acquisition, accumulation and preservation of economic resources, whether these resources are money or physical objects or a job. It is certainly difficult to obtain any one of these categories of resources but few of us sinners easily let ourselves, as we should, rely on Divine Providence as the surest way to secure these resources.

Christ offered a specific and clear teaching directly aimed at addressing this concern: the birds in the sky, and the lilies in the field have their needs taken care of by God.

We are certainly different from the birds and the flowers in the sense that we are persons with intelligence and power of choice. But these human characteristics are no impediment to God's generosity and Providence. They are also God-given and God will utilize our intelligence and our good sense to make us find a remunerated occupation.

We need to learn that when we are expected to utilize our own intelligence and discernment that does not mean that we are on our own, abandoned, that we are fending for ourselves. We need to cultivate the habit of perpetual prayer to the point that we can sense the presence of God all day long whatever we do. A prayerful mind predisposes to do God's will at all times. A perpetual attitude of prayer gives the conviction that each time we understand something and chose something we do not do it by ourselves, but follow the inspiration of the Spirit. God will be with us in our lives, as soon as we commit ourselves to be with God.

Concerning our acts and decisions, whether they are charitable or relative to a profession or job, the person who is in the constant presence of God will not panic that any particular decision or action may mean the loss of revenues, or of a job. Familiarity with God confers confidence in His Providence.

The attitude which makes one set aside, for a time, involvement in the spiritual life in order to cater to economic necessities has limits. Ignoring the spiritual for the purpose of being more efficient in procuring for one's necessities of life may be counter-productive and certainly not a sure method of decreasing the anguish associated with the task of making a living.

In view of the preceding, we can expect organizations where God is the most absent to be the most emotional in the process of personnel selection. The emotion may be translated in either emotionalism or, conversely and more frequently, in an hardened attitude (developed as a protection against these negative feelings) towards the plight of job applicants.

The Right to Subjectivity

The second reason for so much emotionalism is that the process of personnel selection is very subjective. Popular wisdom as well as modern thinking requires that such subjectivity be eliminated. But managers do not want to let go of their subjectivity - and we will show that they are right to have this attitude. They are then caught between two obligations and they feel very uncomfortable with the dilemma.

One advice given to job applicants is to make their interviewers more comfortable by turning the table on them. Job applicants are advised to become the interviewers and to ask the manager to tell them more about the company and the job. It seldom fails, the manager feels much more at ease with that situation and throws himself into a detailed description of the company and the job offered. The manager feels well satisfied with himself and his presentation and, as a result, tends to be quite positive in assessing the applicant on whom he has gathered but little information during the interview.

But to diffuse an otherwise tense situation is no real solution. The artificial glow that the manager will give that applicant who has thus tricked him will soon fade. And the applicant may be hired for a position for which he is not suited.

Subjectivity cannot be eliminated. It cannot be eliminated with interviewer's question sheets. It cannot be eliminated by strings of interviews (the new job holder will report eventually to only one person). It cannot be eliminated by tests which are more or less valid.

It cannot be eliminated because a manager needs to rely on the people that work with him. He must be convinced first that these people understand him. Understanding is not always a matter of intellect but also of psychological compatibility. One word may have a world of meaning for those who share the values connected with the word, whereas it may mean next to nothing to another person.

Naturally, the manager has also to be convinced that the new employee is going to be capable of handling his tasks and assuming his responsibilities. This assessment must be made objectively. But this requirement can only come in second position to compatibility with the future supervisor. The manager must trust the whole person first before he needs to examine the person's capabilities.

When the objectivity in the selection process is over-emphasized - as it normally is, especially with large companies - the background and capabilities of applicants are also over-emphasized, with the result that the quest for employees with experience and excellence in achievements is self-defeated.

Only applicants having demonstrated that they can fill a position will be hired, because past experience is the only objective measure of capability. Only former security analysts will be hired as security analysts, only former assistant directors of marketing will be hired as assistant director of marketing. It is much less important whether that person's achievement is somewhat lackluster, that he was a mediocre security analyst or a mediocre assistant director of marketing.

It is only when the hiring manager has confidence in the individual that he can relax the strict requirements of objectivity and start considering up-and-coming candidates who, given a chance, would be able to grow in the new position.

Thirdly, the manager needs to be convinced that the new employee will react in a crisis situation in a manner comparable to the reaction of the manager. Human beings are indeed the most important resources of any organization, and managers need to be certain that these resources act positively and as an extension of their own efforts. They need to know whether these human resources are going to be assets or liabilities to them.

Eventually, the art of management, of placing different individuals together to accomplish given organizational objectives, is more closely related to the issue of how to make the whole managerial team interact, rather than to the issue of how a single member of this team could act all on his own. The hiring manager has to stretch his powers of imagination to envision this person he is talking to as a member of his present team whom the manager has already formed - at least to his liking if not to perfection - and with which he is already comfortable working with.

Hiring and the Christian Manager

For a Christian manager, all other things being equal, the natural desire is to hire a Christian employee. This desire is totally legitimate and should be satisfied.

Two Christians may have different views on technical points and a manager and his employee may not agree on how to solve a problem on the job. However, there are other reasons why the Christian manager wants to surround himself with Christian employees.

First he wants to feel comfortable exhibiting in front of them his Christian faith and Christian values in whatever he is doing. A religious faith is the most important element that gives orientation to a personality. It is very helpful to have the same faith in order to be psychologically compatible. Not that the manager may be ashamed of his faith but he will not feel that it is appropriate to display his values in front of a group which is mostly Christian when a person in this group is not Christian.

Second, even when he may not agree with the decision a Christian employee will make, provided that the decision is professionally valid, he will be assured that the employee made the decision in a Christian spirit.

Further, this Christian spirit encompasses many values which are very diverse, complex and important. They include technically, managerially and organizationally correct values as well as values which take into account the social teachings of the Church, including the subtleties of these teachings and avoiding the pitfalls resulting from their improper understanding. To take all these elements into account when making a decision cannot be properly be taught, on a purely technical ground, by a boss or on the job.

A proper Christian understanding on work issues has to come from within the Christian employee. They also have to come from years of personal meditation and studies on the Christian significance of his job, as well as from the fruit of many prayers said for the purpose of self-improvement, in that area.

The Christian manager also wants the work done in a Christian fashion because that is the best way he knows how to do the job.

Christian managers should also be courageous.

They should also be open to new applicants and ready to give a chance to a candidate who would be the best qualified except for a characteristic which may be frightening to the hiring manager. A candidate may come out strong from the list of candidates but may be too young, or too old, or not a native of the country. Basically, the reason to turn down this candidate would then be: "you are too young, or you are too old, or you are a woman or you are a minority, or you have an accent". These characteristics may be liabilities and there are reasons to be nervous, but these potential liabilities may never become actual liabilities with the employees in the course of their future employment.

The Christian manager should control this fear. He should control the opposite fear, because of public pressure, of hiring a mediocre candidate over better qualified candidates, exactly because he is too young, or too old or a woman or a minority.

Business Ethics and Employee evaluation.

As concerns on-going evaluation of one's employees, the criteria should be similar to the criteria utilized for hiring purposes, with the addition of the evaluation of recent on the job achievements.

But, although familiarity with existing employees might dictate that the desire to gain confidence in their reactions and behaviors should have lessened, it is most interesting to note that managers still want to re-enforce the confidence they have in their present employees.

Corporate managers nowadays are really interested in having their employees follow courses of business ethics as part of their continuing formation program. The reason for that is not to transform their employees into philosophers, or more well-rounded persons, or even saints.

The reason they promote these courses is that top managers do not want any surprises in the behavior of their employees. They do not want to learn from the press that one of their division has been stealing money from government contracts or that a division has developed, behind their back, a whole scheme to manufacture shoddy products.

Top managers need very much to have confidence in the behavior of their employees. Very practically, they have learned that the alternative can cost them great losses of corporate goodwill, expensive legal fees and penalties for their companies and even sometimes prison sentences for themselves.

However, interested as they are in putting in place a process that would have their employees behave properly, top managers are afraid -- like vampires are afraid of daylight -- to have such business ethics courses presented from a Christian perspective. We know. We have contacted scores of Fortune 5OO CEOs with a similar proposal.

Even when suggested that employees should be free to choose from an array of Catholic, Protestant, Jewish, Moslem or whatever orientation these courses may have, top managers still decline the offer. This is silly and hopefully will change.

One cannot teach a secularized course of business ethics to someone with religious values, because only the love of God really binds consciences. Enlightened interest does not help learn about ethics but teaches hypocrisy.

Further, these so-called business ethics courses do not present the issues as a self-respecting religious approach would, but often present them with a directly opposite perspective, a permissive, faddish, materialistic, New Age, socially divisive (e.g. feminist, pro-homosexual etc.) approach that can only elicit contempt on the part of the employee, who happens to have solid religious values, towards the corporation which obliges him to follow what he perceives to be a nonsensical and repulsive set of values.

When top managers promote these courses as the new philosophy of their corporation they are acting very effectively to dispel from their ranks all religiously minded employees as well as their best employees. They are working hard at building a core of employees consisting of hypocrites, rogues and secular humanists who will accelerate the exodus of decent employees and achieve a corporate culture which will shape the company with values which are also very alien to the values of the general population, their market.

Japanese management is not afraid to teach values in management which incorporate all of Japanese tradition and religious values. They use Shintoist prayers and Buddhist spiritual exercises on the job site. When western managers not only do not teach western values, but teach values which are in opposition to western values, they contribute greatly to the demise of the western economic and managerial system.

PART IV

The Dynamics of Management - Integrating the People In the Organization

In part II we have learned something about the nature of business organizations and how they are supposed to operate. In part III, we have been looking more closely at the matter of individual human beings in these organizations and how they are to interact between themselves.

Now however, we need to look at organizations and human beings together. We also need to put a dynamic spin to the relationship between business organizations and the human beings that make them function.

What really happens in the relationship between the organization and the people who live and work in its midst? What happens when things change? Specifically we will look at the special types of changes, changes which need to be controlled. What is the role of that relationship between human beings and organizations as related to these changes? What is the role of that relationship concerning the good types of change which need to be initiated?

1. Rainbow - Individual Value Systems and Corporate Value Systems.

In discussions of the integration of individuals in organizations, the concepts most often referred to are the concepts of the "values system" of organizations and the value system of individuals. (29)

The values of the corporation may also be expressed in other terms. For example, the management literature mentions the corporate "climate" and the "culture" of a corporation. These terms, just like the terms of "values", also refer to the set of elements which influence how it feels to work in a given corporation. What are the symbolism and the attitudes which are prevalent in that corporation? Further and more specifically, this part of corporate culture which is directly the consequence of the idiosyncrasies of a CEO is called his "managerial style".

When corporate culture is being transmitted to employees, the process that is taking place is also called the function of "corporate communications".

As concerns individuals, the values of an individual may also be referred to as the ethics and the morality of that individual.

All these terms are very fuzzy in the modern culture and one may rightfully ask what could the relationship be between corporate culture and the ethics of an individual if both can be expressed in these same terms of "values", i.e., corporate values and individual values.

286

The nature of values

A full definition of "values", a modern term, has never been really made explicit and especially not in its full significance. We will try here to bring it out.

Values are, first of all, things that we value. Philosophers will say that they are goods. Secondly, what we also mean about values is not only that there are things that we value in themselves but also that there are things that we value more or less compared to other things.

When we say that we value "honesty", it is not so much to say that we value "honesty" as such. Everybody values honesty in a way, even thieves value the honesty of the people they rob who do not have fake jewelry masquerading as true jewelry. What we mean when we say that we value honesty is that we are ready to pay the price for honesty.

If we are salespeople and we want to be honest we will not say that our products have qualities that they do not have, even if we know that by not lying we will be at risk of losing sales. We value "honesty" more than "as many sales as possible"; that is to say we place the value "honesty" above the value "maximum sales".

We may even say that people value honesty all the more when they are ready to pay a high price for it. We may value honesty a little bit if we won't say outrageous lies about the quality of our products but would say little lies. We certainly value honesty a lot if we are ready to die for the sake of honesty.

When we say that people have different values about honesty this only means that they are ready to pay more or less in order to be honest and they place honesty in a more or less elevated position in their order of values.

Let us compare two scales of values:

High on the scale of values

My Life	Honesty
Big sales	My Life
Honesty	Big Sales
Maximum sales	Maximum Sales

Low on the scale of values

Person A	Person B

Person A is ready to compromise his honesty for the sake of achieving big sales. He will not say outrageous lies in order to achieve the maximum possible sales, though.

Person B, on the other hand, values honesty more than his own life.

Then what are values in themselves? Well, they are anything we can value. And people value their wristwatch, their children, their God, their health, their job, their hamburger or even the ketchup on this hamburger. Basically anything that we can perceive separately from something else has a value to us.

288

Everything we have at home has a value from the life and integrity of ourselves and family to the lowest paper clip and pin, including our car, our pension plan, our bed, etc... Similarly at work everything has a value.

In effect there are material values like a bed or a desk, intellectual and moral values, like honesty and wealth, people and God.

The exchangeability of values

Values are "goods". We always strive to attain or obtain what we perceive as good. This is why goods are often "ends," or objectives of our actions. Indeed the object of love is the good.

But values may also be the "means" of our actions. Even though they are good and desirable we are giving to give up these values in a particular occasion. For we are willing in our actions to exchange the values-means, as a method to attain the more desirable goods, the values-ends, the higher values.

Lower values can be either exchanged, traded, utilized, destroyed, transformed in order to attain higher values. One's life may be given up so that we keep our honesty. A hammer can be utilized for the purpose of building a house. Paint and brushes are utilized in order to create a piece of art. The whole purpose of industry is to exchange one set of values for another set, raw materials to which is added human work and the utilization of tools into finished products.

Material values can be exchanged for spiritual values. Alms to the poor and donations to charitable causes help us gain graces and come closer to God, not because we buy sanctity but because we give in a spirit of sacrifice. We are in a spirit of sacrifice when we bear our pains and difficulties with a prayerful attitude but also when we give up precious resources, and that spirit transforms us.

Conversely, spiritual values can also technically be exchanged for material values but that is not a virtuous behavior. Judas received 30 pieces of silver for betraying Jesus.

Systems of values

If we value all things and we value these things differently, we automatically have a system of values. A system is an arrangement of different parts in which each part plays a unique and important role in the system as a whole.

Everything we perceive we value differently from something else we also perceive. Therefore there should be a way of comparing these two values and setting them within a broader context. This broader context is a complete system of values.

All systems of value possess the characteristic of being much wider at the bottom and thinner toward the top, like a pyramid or a Christmas tree.

The reason for this is that higher values actually represent agglomerations or "chunks" of lower values. Therefore the higher in the value system, the fewer the values.

The solar system represents a chunk which includes the sun and the nine planets, therefore this one value, the value "solar system" is above the nine values represented by its planets.

Wealth for some people may mean x number of dollars, but it may also be represented by a large mansion, 3 luxury cars in the garage, etc. a number of finite possessions which are each lower than but implicitly contained in the value "wealth".

The highest value is necessarily God because He is the source of all good, of all values. When a saint was asked by God what he desired for his saintly behavior, the saint, showing that he was also a well-advised negotiator replied, "You, my Lord and nothing else but You".

Ethics, attitudes and behavior

We already have a glimpse of the relationship between value systems as a predicator of behavior. The person who places "hammer" underneath "house" may be expected to agree that a hammer may be used for the purpose of building a house. If the value "pretty backyard" is greater than "idle time" in a person's value system, this tends to indicate that that person will likely devote a good part of his idle time working in his backyard.

We already have also a glimpse of the ethics of an individual based on his value system. If one values material success more than honesty, loyalty and other good qualities, it is reasonable to assume that that person will set those qualities aside when trying to be successful. He will be dishonest.

System of values and worldview

A system of values is an indicator of future behavior but it is not that behavior as such. A system of values is rather how someone sees the world. Philosophers would call it a metaphysics. The Germans have a word for it, Weltanschauung, worldview.

A system of value is intellectual, it is in our minds. We cannot set ourselves to do what we do not know.

Conversely, the advantage of the concept of systems of values is that it shows that if we can be convinced to change, our values we will be most likely to change our attitudes.

A salesman may be shown that if lying to customers will bring quick sales for the short range, disappointed customers will not be repeat customers and that is a major impediment against establishing a stable and large sales base for the long range. This salesman may therefore be persuaded to stop lying when making his sales pitch.

Given values and desired values.

In a person's system of values are included those which he possesses and those which he does not possess. Among the values which we do not possess, some of them are higher values. Further, most of us do not possess most of the highest values. Some of these highest values cannot be secured forever. History and political analysts have taught us that liberty, for example, needs be defended unceasingly. Personal integrity must be strived for until the day we die; we cannot ever assume that we have reached a level of personal sanctity.

On the other hand, some values can reasonably be considered as secured, and from the starting point of these secured values we are looking up towards values which are close at hand but which we do not possess.

We may possess the value of a stable, moderately paid but safe job. However, we may look at the possibility of starting a new company with high earnings potentials. We may be comfortable bachelors but yearn for the married life.

292

These higher values attract us. This attraction is the attraction of love. We seek to attain the object of our love and absorb it entirely.

As long as we are alive we are constantly challenged to swap our given values for better values. This process of trading values is the definition of change and the basic characteristic of life. The intention of pursuing this process of value trading is a normal psychological thing. It is normal to want to reach for the other side of the fence when we perceive that the grass is greener there.

The process of value-trading can become unbalanced when the pattern of transformation of values is biased, for example if we always seem to be seeking only one set of higher values: material values, things to possess, and at the same time that we do not seem particularly picky on what we will do to possess them: we are greedy.

We need to have a balanced and realistic search for higher values; we should not be greedy or overly ambitious.

It is also normal to seek higher intellectual values, like more knowledge, more science, more educational degrees. It is normal to seek higher spiritual values: a feeling of closer relationship with Our Lord and Our Mother. The most realistic and efficient of all people are contemplative monks and nuns who seek God, short-circuiting all other avenues and short-term trades in values and put all their energies to seek the highest value, God, which they exchange for the low values of their prayer time and humble tasks.

To judge people and find them greedy is usually not fair when we do not know their value systems, what they have to deal with in life. It always seems shocking for some people to see the rich want more things. But riches are also a relative concept. Third world inhabitants are often horrified when they see that we are trading a perfectly good car just to parade ourselves in a newer model. What we see as greed in others is quite often a projection of our own envy.

Values System and Action Plans

The distinction between given values/and desired values allows us to establish specific plans of action or even a general life plan diagram. For this purpose we pivot our value system, which is in the form of a pyramid, and put it on the side so that it is now an arrow, pointing, we will chose arbitrarily, to the right symbolizing the future.

On the left, then, are the lower values which are at our disposal. On the right the values we are seeking. The lower values are possible means and the higher values are ends for us to choose.

We have the perfect design for drawing plans and strategies of action, to go from state one to state two, drawing the different steps of a project to attain the final objective, the highest value that we seek.

The principle for drawing a plan is to start from the ultimate objective of the plan on the right part of the arrow, and backtrack towards the left side of the arrow to seek the means.

We follow a line of possible value trades: let us say that the final objective is to build a car, a lower value is to have the production facility to build that car; to achieve that we need to have a production facility, to do that we need either the backing or the cooperation of a group which disposes of such facility; to do that we have to show them that they would benefit from doing what we are proposing; to do that we have to put together a well-developed business plan.

Now to put together a well-developed business plan is something we can readily do since we have the skill. The value "business plan" can easily become a given value. Then it can be traded with higher values, e.g. "convincing a financial consortium", which in turn can be traded to the higher value "having control of a production facility", etc.

Naturally, this path we are giving in example depends pretty much on what our circumstances of operations are, to the values we have access to. If we are General Motors, or a big New York bank or a large food marketing company the circumstances are quite different and we would have to deal with the opportunities, i.e. given values, we would already enjoy in that higher position.

Value Systems and Life Plans

In a overall plan of life, furthermore, it is normal to follow the same process and to start from the highest value we can seek and design our programs of action according to this objective and our particular circumstances of life. It is most efficient then to see that the highest value we can seek is God himself, that salvation is how we attain this value, grace and a virtuous life is how we attain salvation; prayers, good works and the sacraments are how we attain grace and virtues. Now we have to establish a plan of prayer, a plan of reception of the sacraments and look at what we do every day in order to start doing them in a more virtuous manner.

Difference in Value Systems

We have mentioned that some types of values rather belong to one end of a good value system whereas other types should belong to another end.

Material values belong indeed to the bottom of most value systems, whereas intellectual and spiritual values belong to the higher levels of these systems.

However, there can be some flexibility between value systems, depending on personal living circumstances. Not all people are required to have exactly identical value systems. Value systems depend on differences of life experiences and life specializations.

If I am ready to spend $89.95 of my hard earned money for a pair of brown everyday shoes it is because I value the shoes more than this particular sum of money. If I had perfect information I probably would buy another pair of everyday shoes which I would prefer to this pair of shoes, but I do not have the time to keep shopping for shoes. My preference is also related to what I know about shoes, about differences in shoes - I may be a lousy buyer of shoes - and the information I have about available types of shoes. My experience is limited.

My preference between the values is further related to the fact that I am not in the shoe business but that I do need shoes. The shoe shop evidently values my $89.95 more than the pair of shoes since it is selling it to me for that price. My professional specialization is not in the shoe business.

Differences in value systems are therefore quite acceptable in principle. These differences have a social quality. They allow for trade of the values between people, including monetary values, physical values, psychological values.

We may be interested to note that the science of marketing has redefined itself as: "the science of the transfer of values". Marketers sell a bundle of values, the physical aspect and quality of fabrication of a product, the psychological satisfaction of a service, or the psychological message attached to an advertising campaign, against the monetary value which we will pay to obtain this product or service.

Differences of values also allow for social communications. We find interesting that people have different values. We do find that also a little upsetting. The whole course of social communication is to try and find out why people have different values, what is the experience that led them to have these different values and how they justify having these different values based on their experience.

This is the way we learn about people: we study their values, how different or similar they are from ours. Since values predict future behavior and if we can understand the values of people we have them "figured out", we are confident that we can deal with them.

Domains of Reference.

Each individual has different value systems. They are not compromising their values when it is expedient, but they need to adapt not only to different sets of circumstances, but also and especially to a context or "domain of reference".

For example, an employee in a corporation has different value systems when he is looking at the same values in three different contexts: the world as a whole, the corporation as a whole, his job within the corporation.

When he looks at the world as a whole, his corporation is not particularly very high a value in the general scheme of things, even if this corporation is a huge corporation like General Motors.

When, on the other hand, he looks at his corporation as the domain of reference, many elements of reality are quite changed around: at General Motors, extraterrestrial space is not very important at this time. At MacDonald's the Russian population is quite a negligible value.

When the employee of General Motors looks at his company from the single perspective of his own job which happens to be, say, assembling car seats, the value of car dealerships in Japan is not crucial to him.

Understanding and Interest

An individual can have different types of systems of values according to the perspective from which he places himself. In particular, the members of a business organization, will have the following perspectives: the world as a whole, my company, my job.

But the number of possible different systems of values the same individual may harbor are again twice as numerous when we take another criterion to distinguish between different types of personal systems of values: the criterion of importance and the criterion of personal interest.

Worldviews which are systems of values according to the criterion of importance are emotionless. Everyone can see that a big city is more important than a small town. The value "big city" will be higher for descriptive reasons: there are more people, more important things are being done in big cities than small towns, etc.

However, we also have systems of values where the whole system is based on our particular likes and dislikes. And we may prefer small cities to big towns, which is fine. It may be an artistic preference and limited to the domain of reference of my own life, the system of values which I will use to select a place to live.

Also I may believe that traditional values are better preserved in small towns or any other reason of the sort. However, there are cases when the discrepancy of values systems based on understanding (power of the intellect), the criterion of importance, and those based on liking (power of the will), the criterion of interest, cannot be acceptable. If I am head of a government agency, preference for small towns over big cities in establishing government programs will most likely result in great injustices.

A commercial artist cannot disdain totally the marketing people in the company in which he works even under the pretense that there are pushy, materialistic and vulgar people. Inasmuch as they are important to the company, everyone in the company should be interested in everyone else as being members of the same body and the good of the body cannot be without the good of all the members.

Individual values and Organizational values

Now we have most of the elements in place. Value systems of individuals and companies can easily be compared.

The values we are talking about are things which are valued more or less by the different individuals in the company. Each individual values these values differently. The precise valuation can actually be measured on a scale, say from 1 to 100.

Now the values of the organization will be composed of the things valued by all the individuals in the company with the grade which will result from computing the average grade given by all individuals in the company for that value.

When we have this values system of the company as a whole we can compare the values of any one individual. We will see discrepancies. Some of these discrepancies will be understandable after researching their origin. Others can help pinpoint a specific problem with this individual.

The Organizational Values Information System

We strongly recommend that all companies do establish a method for projecting the values of all their employees, an Organizational Values Information System (OVIS), so as to obtain an agglomerate value system which will be the value system of the company.

It is quite shocking that when CEO's have, in the best managed firms, a clear and almost up-to-the-minute view of the finances of the company, they usually do not have any similar tool to give them a view of their employees' thinking and feeling. As far as the human side of their management capabilities is concerned, CEO's are basically flying without instruments and with a very short view outside their cockpit's window, what they really see is within the cockpit, usually limited to their direct staff. Still they claim that their people are their greatest asset!

But a value system, and a OVIS, is also of great interest when it is available to all, and not only to the CEO. Each employee should be able to witness the introduction of new values as new pieces of reality in the corporate culture and new resources in the company. They can compare their own value system to the corporate value system and perform a self-diagnosis of how their own views stand in the context of the company's views.

Corporate value systems must be updated quite often, preferably every day. Employees should be able to work on their own values system at all times with easy access to a computer, preferably with a password protection, and the general up-dating program would take these changes into account after working hours.

The process for elaborating a corporate value system may be made anonymous since people in general are very concerned about the privacy of their minds and souls. However, general discrepancy studies can be performed to see whether a particular employee has a normal level of discrepancy and in which general area of knowledge and interest. New applicants for a job can be evaluated to see how compatible they are with the corporation's value system.

300

A corporate value system should include job and non-job related values because that is the way people are: they do not make a clear distinction between their interest at work and their interest off the job. Psychological problems will most likely overlap the two areas anyway; it is important to be able to trap them wherever they appear.

However, all employees do not need to have ready access to all the corporate values, both for reasons of corporate security and for a greater simplicity of communications. Marketing people do need to know all the values of engineering, and vice-versa, but can be satisfied with "chunks" or "black boxes", like the value "R&D" (Research and Development) or the value "market research".

When we would have put in place a OVIS or program of elaboration of a corporate value systems with a complete array of values and their rankings, we will be ready to move to a stage when we can really talk about a Value Theory of Management. All the themes in this book can be restated in the context of an OVIS.

We would now be able to relate many issues of management, either theoretical or applied, by pointing to specific values and their precise ranking in a corporation's value system.

2. Following the flow - Change: The Development of Human Resources and the Development of Organizations.

Change and human beings

When we look at the negative of a non-digital movie by holding it in front of a source of light we clearly see that it is made of a succession of images, similar to each other and which change imperceptibly from one take to the next. But when these many images are run quite quickly one after the other during the projection of the movie, what we see on the screen is movement.

Change is also a succession of similar stages. The difference between these stages may be great or not. Then the movement, or rate of change, will be fast or not.

One type of change is essential in any biological process and affects therefore also human beings. Biological change affects from within. We are born, we grow, we become mature, we become old and we die. Animals and plants also change in a similar pre-arranged and immutable sequence.

Non-living things like mountains can also change but not according to a pre-arranged sequence, they change according only to exterior influences: underground forces of magma that pushes the mountain up, a forest that grows on top of them, or men who chop off one side to build houses with the stone. Living things, naturally, can also be affected by changes which originate from outside. Plants receive the water from rain. Animals kill each other. Men socialize and learn from one another.

Change is also part of the development of the soul. The intellect changes in that it learns more information. Some of this information may be incorrect. The intellect may forget other information. The will becomes stronger or weaker over time. Our skills may become more sharp, or, on the contrary they may become blunt. Some skills,, like riding a bicycle do not really ever disappear because they are not intellectual skills but reflexes.

Our habits also change. The good habits or virtues can become better virtues or they can be lost. The bad habits or vices can become worse vices or they can be corrected.

There is a built-in tendency for habits to stay as they are. That is because it is the nature of habits to be stable. Habits by definition are stable dispositions of the human soul.

On the other hand, there is contrary tendency for habits to become worse because this is the consequence of the introduction of evil in the world, the Fall.

If we do not do anything about our habits, they will slowly but surely become worse. To combat the negative trend towards a worsening of habits, we have to want to keep good habits, we want to exercise our habits and skills like athletes exercise their bodies.

We need to pray in order to enjoy the grace of keeping the most precious good habits, such as the virtues of Faith, Hope and Charity which are also gifts from God. They are readily available for the asking from God but they are not given once and for all. We have to keep asking for them constantly for that is what we were meant to be. If we do not ask for graces constantly, we effectively reject these free gifts of grace.

Unfortunately, in the long run the trend towards a worsening of habits is stronger than the trend towards a maintenance of habits levels. Therefore we do have to be vigilant about the changing of our habits, even if we do not need to be too worried about their deteriorating tendency in the short run.

Change in organizations.

Organizations also change. They are not living things. They are not non-living things, like mountains, either. Organizations have an existence which they borrow from the people who inhabit them, manage them, use them.

Organizations may be affected by change like mountains, that is

303

from the exterior. We say they react to change. A whole theory of management is based on this view of change in organizations. it is called the Contingency Theory of Management. This theory believes that managing a company consists essentially in reacting to changes forced from the outside. This is a very limited view of companies, of strategic planning and even of the human intellectual abilities of managers.

Organizations may be affected by change from within like living things. This is the case when human beings are making these changes in organizations. But organizations are not living things, therefore when they are changed from within, they do not have to change according to any biological sequence. They do not have to grow old and die. They can renew themselves and they can postpone their termination indefinitely.

Therefore the principle of change in organizations is the same as the principle of change as relative to human virtues. Actually, it is really the changes in virtues transmitted by the management and the employees which is reflected in the changes in the organization as a whole.

Personal changes and value systems

We can see the issue of personal change with the approach of value systems.

One thing that happens when people change is that their value systems have more elements; some elements may have dropped out which are forgotten or do not belong any longer to the person's living circumstances. Another thing that happens is that values change places; they can be higher or lower in the value system. That may be good or that may be bad.

One interesting study of change is an increase of faith. The first step in the acquisition of faith is to place God at the top of the value system when He had not previously been put there. But this is only the first step. The second step is actually a very long process of many steps, and the fruit of much meditation; it is the linkage between that highest value, God, and all the other values in the system. It is the understanding of the importance of God in our life, in our understanding of the world.

When we see these linkages better, we become more capable of acting on these new insights, in ways that are both more effective, since we have found new resources for desired objectives and more in concordance with the faith.

Change, Virtues and value systems

Working with an expressed value system (either written out or printed out from a computer data base) allows us to take stock of our virtues, as we exercise them either on or off the workplace.

Courage is the virtue of "actualization of potential good". That is to say that after we have 1) perceived a worthwhile objective and 2) found the manner or resource to achieve this objective, something is still missing : the will to get started and utilize this resource so that the good objective may be attained.

We can mark in our value system that we have drawn out on paper a linkage between all resources and objectives that we see are connectable. Periodically we can go back and see if we have actually acted upon these premises of as many plans of action, if we have been courageous.

Temperance requires that we do not always utilize the same

intermediate values either as objectives or as instruments. We should not always try to do things the same way but try different approaches which may be more effective. We should not always try to promote the interests of a single department of the organization, nor of a single employee, nor of a single corporate function. A system of values put on paper may allow us to see what we have been up to in these areas.

Justice requires that we take into account the whole cloud of values which surround both the objective-value and the instrument-value at the moment of making a decision. We may then realize that some values better deserve to be our objective-values because they are higher, or need to be revised and placed higher in our system of values. Some other values deserve to be our instrument or means values because they are lower, or should have been placed lower in our value system, and therefore are more efficient to attain our objective.

The whole issue of the validity of a system of values is whether values are at their proper level. This difficulty is basically an issue of justice as relates to the action by which two values are exchanged which are not in their proper place. It is also an issue of prudence even when there is no actual exchange of the two values, because our value system, our view of the world, as far as these two values are concerned, is flawed.

We cannot use people as things, for example, since the value "people" is a lot higher than the value "things". If we never use people as things but still view people as things (the whole point in Jean-Paul Sartre philosophy's "regard chosifiant", also the core evil in pornography) we are still guilty of lack of prudence.

Even if we do not technically exchange the places of the two values, the objective value and the instrument value, we often take an objective value which is too low compared to the instrument value and to other available objective values, or an instrument value which is too high compared to the objective value, or to other instrument values: this is the classic case of killing a fly with a ten-ton press. The "killing of a fly" is too low an objective value. The use of a "ten-ton press" is too high as an instrument value.

It is imprudent in the sense that it shows a bad appreciation of selection of values, objectives and instruments. It may be unjust in the sense that we may have better things to do than kill a fly. We also are using a very important instrument, the ten ton press, when someone else could be using a simpler tool.

We need therefore to periodically assess whether our value system is prudent and whether our past actions have been just and prudent.

It is not necessary for managers to look specifically over the shoulders of their employees in order to be involved with any assessment of changes and the virtues of their employees, as supported with the technique of expressed value systems. It would be very helpful, on the other hand, that they train their employees in this technique and that they verify that these assessments are regularly conducted by the employees.

Change management in individuals - the "scientific view"

Let us look at what "experts" think of the whole proposition that an employee should confront change and learn to deal with it in a positive manner and learn to control change in his life and work setting.

First a patronizing statement on traditional approaches to encouraging employees to be responsible:

"In the past, whenever discussions of self-management were brought up, the importance of positive thinking, will power, or perhaps self-motivation were brought out. This approach to self-management certainly didn't do any harm, and may have done some people some good."

Then the arrogance: "However, as a systematic approach to more effective management, a behavioral approach to self-management is required." Luthans p. 641-642. (3O)

Oh! Oh! Soooo... self-management is not quite valid until it is scientific and it is not scientific until it is behavioral. So what makes it "behavioral"?

"Modern behaviorism marks its beginning with the work of B.F. Skinner. Skinner is generally recognized as the most influential recently living psychologist. He felt that the early behaviorists helped to explain respondent behaviors (those behaviors elicited by stimuli) but not the more complex operant behaviors (those behaviors not elicited by stimuli, which simply occur: operant behaviors are emitted by the organism.)"

Please note that the word "organism" here refers to that man who is made in the image of God.

"... it is important to understand that the behavioristic approach is environmentally based. It implies that cognitive processes such as thinking, expectancies and perception do not play a role in behavior." Luthans. p.62

Thus behavioral psychology is only interested in the behavior of people. It is not interested in what they think. It does not really believe that people think. It believes that people act almost automatically for the consequences of their act of which they learn in their growing process. If people are placed in circumstances in which they can obtain certain pleasant consequences they will always act to attain these consequences but this human effort, behaviorists believe, uses only slightly more intellectual power than the reflex following the tapping of a knee.

308

Behaviorists basically consider human beings not very differently from rats. Rats will learn to go through a maze to get food at the end of the maze. The rats have to act first before the reward. This is exactly this behaviorist principle of "Response before Stimulus".

B.F. Skinner, who, as Luthans mentioned, is the darling of psychologists, has contributed to the promotion of human dignity about as much as Hitler and Stalin. In his 1971 book "Beyond Freedom and Dignity", Skinner also argues that "we can no longer afford freedom" to solve today's most pressing problems and he proposed a "detailed stunning plan for change that challenges many of Western man's most sacred ideals and personal freedoms". Having done away with the human intellect, he was going after the human will. (31)

We must rejoice that he did not manage to gather powers quite as extensive as the German and Russian tyrants he was so obviously jealous of.

On the other hand, we must realize that many organizations have management policies and busy little management experts who are committed followers of Skinner's behaviorism.

These people are creating havoc on the lives of employees in many organizations, especially the largest corporations who can afford them. These behaviorists are destroying organizations while pretending to contribute to building them up. And they are destroying whole modern societies which, as described in "Organizational America" (32), are increasingly becoming societies where only large organizations are recognized as valid social entities. Individuals have no identity of their own if they are not connected with any of these organizations.

These societies, it is charged are becoming increasingly limited to being agglomerations of organizations and of other institutions similar to business organizations. The individuals who do not fit any of these organizations and institutions have no status and fall between the cracks of that organizational society.

Managing change in organizations - Organization Development

Business schools have chosen the term of Organization Development to put together all their efforts as related to the management of change in organizations.

Warren Bennis defined OD, as it is affectionately called by people in the know:

".. a response to change, a complex educational strategy intended to change the beliefs, attitudes, values and structure of organizations so that they can better adapt to new technologies, markets, and challenges, and the dizzying rate of change itself." (32)

For those who would prefer a newer definition of OD:

"Organization development is a long-range effort to improve an organization's problem-solving and renewal processes, particularly through a more effective and collaborative management or organization culture - with special emphasis on the culture of formal work teams - with the assistance of a change agent, or catalyst, and the use of the theory and technology of applied behavior science, including action research". (34)

Others have identified the following elements to be the essential components of OD:

1) Planned change. OD initiates change.

2) Comprehensive change. OD is supposed to affect the total organization.

3) Emphasis upon work groups. OD prefers to work with groups rather than individuals one by one.

4) Long-range change. OD is supposed to take a long time to be implemented.

5. Participation of a change agent. An expert needs be there. Do-it-yourself programs are discouraged.

6. Emphasis upon intervention and action research. Basically it means the OD people have always something cooking to keep the rest of the organization on their toes.

"Sensitivity Training"

The major instrument of OD is Sensitivity Training or Training Group (T-group) approach which originated first in England then at the US branch of the National Training Laboratories in Maine.

Sensitivity training has many purposes, but really the main purpose is to have people go through a very special process, which will definitely leave them different from what they were upon entering it, which includes:

"1. To make participants increasingly aware of, and sensitive to, the emotional reactions and expressions in themselves and others.

"2. To increase the ability of participants to perceive, and to learn from, the consequences of their actions through attention to their own and other's feelings.

"3. To stimulate the clarification and development of personal values and goals consonant with a democratic and scientific approach to problems of social and personal decision and action.

"4. To develop concepts and theoretical insights which will serve as tools in linking personal values, goals, and intentions to actions consistent with these inner factors and with the requirements of the situation.

"5. To foster the achievement of behavioral effectiveness in transactions with the participant's environments. (35)

Sensitivity training is possibly the key achievement and most symbolical activity of the '60s and the hippy generation. It is the number one source of the "touchy feely" school of philosophy.

Items one and two above correspond to the principle of "letting it all hang out", and "keeping in touch with one's feelings". Sensitivity training encourages people to cry, to scream, to insult each other in order to express their feelings. They lead to very violent and emotionally charged sessions in which all negative feelings are encouraged to be expressed in the most destructive fashion if necessary.

Silly and illicit attractions between participants are also encouraged and allowed to express themselves beyond all bonds of decency. More than one individual has had his sanity shattered during these sessions.

Items two and three are the introduction of values alien to Western culture, and especially opposed to religious doctrine and teachings, according to the principle, "Do your own thing, man". A more modern version of these 2 items is now called "values clarification" which, in opposition to our OVIS method of systems of values, considers that all value systems are all right and that there are no principles which make one set of values better than another.

"Value clarification" is really not compatible with system of values because it is a program which opposes the concept of an hierarchy of values. But since values take signification from the overall system, "value clarification" is fundamentally against values and therefore ethics.

Sensitivity training as Business Evil

Essentially, we must say that all programs in Organization Development, as far as they incorporate the above techniques and assumptions of sensitivity training, whether explicitly or not, are extremely evil in themselves and the main potential source of evil behavior in corporations, because they make light of any decency and truth in the business scene. They also institutionalize within the corporation errors in the employees' minds and justify any wrongful behavior.

Business managers often complain that the number one cause of unethical activity in their corporation is the dissolution of values in society at large, but many such managers have strongly worked hand in hand with the institutional forces which helped this dissolution, such as the media and the major part of the social sciences.

No training in secular "business ethics" can correct the attitude that has been acquired by business students and employees who have received an OD program formation. Nor does business ethics make any sense, when the sensitivity training philosophy has been assimilated by students.

However, this is exactly what happens: most business school curriculums that offer courses in business ethics also list courses in this destructive nonsense.

The inconsistency does not seem to embarrass many of the faculty members of the business ethics courses who come from the Organization Development side of management and consider "business ethics" courses as just another approach to teach the same sets of unprincipled, amoral and anti-religious ideas.

Not surprisingly, in practice, these business ethics courses would include issues on the protection of homosexuals in the work place and "women's' issues", that is, most often than not, easy access to abortion, etc.

For those professors of business ethics who, on the other hand, do not come from management but from philosophy or theology, they are either ignorant of these teachings of "management" or are intimidated by the "scientific" air that these social scientists use to silence their opponents.

One should not be surprised that it is in this issue of "change" that secular business management will have to clash with religious values because the right change of attitudes and behavior means increased virtue. That is unacceptable with many of our opinion leaders.

Secular opinion is very tolerant of religion as long as religion does not make any difference in the lives of people and in society at large. But when change is concerned, the issue is precisely which change and how to elicit this change or which differences are going to appear in individuals and social groups between what they are and what they will become. The tolerance of the world is tested on this basic issue concerning "change", which is essentially in its view a political issue, and is found much wanting.

In ancient Rome, Christians were initially tolerated to believe whatever they wanted. But when they refused to bow to the emperor-God and when they tried to tell the rest of society that this society lived in sinful ways, it was no longer time for tolerance. They became on the contrary the targets of the most violent persecutions.

314

Sensitivity Training and Society

The whole evil of Sensitivity Training courses was initiated within the walls of corporations because that is where the money was to finance these dangerous experiences. But, very quickly the activists "scientists" were looking at the rest of the world as their potential victims as soon as their techniques were well honed.

This training is targeted at six major populations, in the words of their promoters:

"1. Professional helpers with educational and consultative responsibilities (workers in religion, wives of corporation presidents, school superintendents, classroom teachers, juvenile court judges, and youth workers)

"2. Middle and top management

"3. Total membership of a given organization (Red Cross executives, a family, or a business organization)

"4. Laymen and/or professionals in a heterogeneous occupational group

"5. Children, youth and college students

"6. Persons with different cultural and/or national backgrounds. (36)

In particular some seminaries and religious schools offer their students as the most willing prey for these techniques. Such seminaries and schools turn out ministers, priests and nuns who seem to be much more convinced of the validity of these techniques than of any tenet of the faith, as they are more impressed by the varnish of science rather than the love of Truth Himself.

Their students, in turn, educate the laity, under the cover of courses of religion, and make them believe that they have received some religious education when in fact in they will lack the most basic rudiments of the faith.

Religious experts formed by sensitivity training produce manuals for religion courses which are full of "lovy dovy" nonsense where sin is excused on the basis that we need be "tolerant" and of the emphasis for each student to state whatever silliness is his own view of theology and religion. These confused people, whether religious or lay, are likely to fight the true faith with great eagerness because they are incapable of recognizing the eternal truth.

The prime responsibility of this state of affairs rests squarely with bishops who are responsible because of their leadership position in the teaching of the faith. Some bishops are doing a superb job at dealing with a situation which they have by and large inherited. Other bishops are not correcting the situation and are definitely more part of the problem than of the solution.

Sensitivity training in particular and OD in general, as expressions of a period of moral collapse, the '6Os, and as the most potent instruments of this expression are some of the most important causes of the de-christianization in our modern world.

Anyone with an interest in evangelization should therefore be concerned with this type of activity which takes place in business organizations.

Organizational change - A true Value approach

Let us go back to what OD is really supposed to achieve:

1) Planned change.

2) Comprehensive change.

3) Emphasis upon work groups.

4) Long-range change.

5) Participation of a change agent.

6) Emphasis upon intervention and action research.

Basically all that is worthwhile here can be achieved with our organization value systems-supported OVIS method without trauma, without inefficiency and without imperiling anyone's soul.

We have seen how given values and desirable values can be isolated in a value system in order to work towards "planned change". So can they be in an organization value system.

"Comprehensive change" is ensured first by a frequent revision of the organizational value system, then by organizational efforts to select the best objectives and the most appropriate means to attain them in well-designed programs.

We agree that, in addition to the individual work of employees on the organizational value system and their own personal value system, additional work should be performed by teams of employees to define objectives and work plans by the team as a whole.

As stated, all changes that can be affected either on individuals or on organizations are the "virtue" type of change, and always need to be followed closely and never abandoned. This take care of "long range change".

As far as feather-bedding the position of a change agent in the organization, we do not believe in it. We believe that the organization should be designed for all individuals to acquire the ability to be their own, and the organization's, change agents, for the sake of a better efficiency in the organization as well as of greater human dignity of its employees. Specialists can be resources in this effort but not ring leaders.

Neither do we believe in the need for "action research" or any activity of the sort which may be interesting niceties for professional social scientists but are really cluttering the work place of others. The only action should be an action which is related to the business of the organization. The only research on this action should be the monitoring by anyone, whatever his position in the chain of command, that that action has a virtuous component which he will be able to utilize for his own growth in the virtues for improving the business of the organization.

3. Each age has its problems - Managing the growing organization.

There is a type of change to which the organization is subjected and which is related to the difficulties of its own process of growth.

This type of change is not really a biological change because it relates only to growth and not to maturity and death. It is not a "virtue" type of change because it is dependent on material structures, in particular the number of managers in key positions, the number of employees, the size of markets.

It is also not a non-living-thing, like a mountain, type of change

318

because it is principally exerted from within the organization and not imposed from the outside.

Growth and Development

First we need to feel at ease with the two words "growth" and "development". When these two words are utilized at the same time, there is usually a moral connotation given to these words.

Growth often implies growth for growth sake, like what motivated CEOs in the '6Os who put together conglomerates by piling companies on top of other companies, without concern whether they were creating a monster as long as the consolidated balance sheet yielded the biggest possible figures.

"Development" would be growth with a heart. It usually implies that a company is going bigger, that it has more people, more assets, more premises, more money but that it grew in a way that was rational and harmonious.

Actually these descriptions have some value as extreme representations of the reality. Most companies grow according to a mode which is somewhere between these two extremes.

The Five phases of Growth

The description of the issues associated with corporate growth which makes great sense has been offered by Larry E. Greiner. (37)

What he calls "evolution" are periods of more or less stable development for the organization. What he calls revolution are really periods of crisis.

Phase 1 - Creativity

The company is very entrepreneurial. It is busy establishing both a product and a market. The top manager is entrepreneurial, does not like formal management procedures and manages to keep communications informal and frequent.

Employees put in long hours of work. Top managers are working for low salaries but the hope of sharing in the equity bonanza once the corporation's value start moving up.

The company is very close to the market and adjusts quickly to satisfy this market.

The crisis which follows this phase is a crisis of leadership.

The company has grown; more people are involved and processes and procedures are becoming a little more complex. The new people, who are more professional, are more dedicated to their craft than to the company.

There is a strong need to formalize communications and processes. This formalization is not very much to the taste of the founding manager. The company needs an experienced manager at the top.

Would the manager-founder acquire the necessary skills,, or step aside and let in a professional manager, or dig in, insist on his ways and stunt the growth of the operation?

Phase 2 - Direction

The company at this stage has a strong and able leader which gives it direction.

The functional departments of the companies are separated; individuals have their responsibilities made more clear. Incentives, budgets and work standards are adopted.

Communications, inventory and personnel systems are put in place. Only the top people are really policy-makers; middle-level managers become specialists.

The crisis that follows is a crisis of autonomy. Some of the managerial systems are too formal. Top management is losing contact with the market and cannot adapt as well to market demands. Middle-management is not equipped to make decisions in order to promote these adaptations.

Phase 3 - Delegation.

The system has put in place the possibility for top managers to delegate to able middle managers.

Greater responsibilities are given to plant managers, territorial market managers etc. Profit centers appear.

Top executives come into the habit of handling only crises and not micro-managing the company. These top managers often redirect their energies at looking for corporate acquisitions which can make good additions to the present array of decentralized divisions.

Communication from top managers with the lower levels of the company is infrequent. But decentralized line managers are pretty well equipped to handle their operation in a manner which is responsive to markets' and other demands and still be of an impressive size.

The Crisis following this phase is a crisis of control. Freedom is a heady wine and many general managers or profit center managers want greater independence, without caring how their projects would mesh with the best interests of the overall corporation. Top management may try to re-centralize which is often not possible nor desirable because the company has grown so much. A balanced solution must be found.

Phase 4 - Coordination.

This is the stage of the large corporations which have put in place whole sets of committees and coordinating links between departments and across departments.

Product groups are arranged under one roof. "Business units" is another principle of organization in these companies.

Coordination is taken very seriously and intensely monitored. Standards, especially financial standards, are selected on which basis the different groups are evaluated and they are expected to satisfy company-wide norms.

Some services are centralized, like data processing and accounting. Company-wide profit-sharing programs are put in place to develop a sense of identity with the company as a whole.

The crisis which ensues is a crisis of red-tape. The control and communications systems lose their freshness and supervisors tend to do things because "that is how they have been doing them in the past". Innovation is the great victim.

Phase 5 : Collaboration.

The company is too large to be managed by any formal system

which tends to dominate and stifle other activities.

The solution is the building of ad-hoc committees and action teams. Experts are reduced in numbers. Matrix systems are adopted. More conferences between line managers take place.

Educational programs are held to train managers for this new emphasis on collaboration. Innovation is encouraged especially on a team basis.

The Crisis of this phase is: ? Greiner believes that we do not have the information to decide which crisis is lurking at this stage. However, as he states that many more US corporations are at this stage the problem is pressing.

His hunch is that the crisis will be a crisis of "psychological saturation" of employees who grow emotionally and physically exhausted by the pressure of teamwork and the demand for innovative solutions.

The solution would be a program to help employees to "revitalize themselves".

Pattern not Immutable.

What the author does not mention is that this pattern of growth does not need to really happen in that sequence, even under his own logic.

For example the '80s have shown that a number of Leverage buy outs (LBOs) ended in a large conglomerate being dismantled and the parts sold separately which did pretty well on their own.

Large companies have spinned off businesses, especially of divisions whose activities where too far from the "mission" of the company as a whole.

Large companies can revert easily to stage three where executives have to learn to delegate.

Furthermore, most of the crises of management at these different phases are either crisis of virtues and/or crisis of information. We will look below at the crises of virtues. The crisis of information can be greatly reduced even in very large organizations with the help of modern technology such as closed-circuit TV corporation-wide communications programs and better software integration including the corporate value based information system OVIS which we advocate.

With modern telecommunication techniques and a good understanding and implementation of the virtues in management, multi-billion dollar companies can be managed by an approach which is essentially a Phase One approach, with a CEO really trying to manage his thousands of employees as if he were the personal friend of each employee.

That is possible if both CEO and employees understand that the CEO is genuinely interested in what is truly best for the employee, that this truly best is the employee's moral and spiritual dimensions. On the other hand the CEO cannot reasonably be asked to be involved in each employee's personal material interests and work set-up beyond ensuring that personnel management programs are sound and well designed.

In large corporations there can be a "phase one" approach to management, by establishing that the relationship between the CEO and each employee is a soul-to-soul relationship. Unfortunately an entire-human-being to entire-human-being relationship is impossible because it would take much too much time with so many people involved.

The issue of small corporations.

Another important problem that the business world has to solve, however, is with the first stages and the first crises. There are many more small business organizations than there are large organizations. Tens of thousands of mid-size companies; even hundreds of thousands of Mom-and-Pop operations against a few hundred large corporations.

To improve the economic development of a country it simply makes more sense to concentrate on making these large number of small organizations advance one stage up rather than concentrate on making more efficient the very large business organizations. The large corporations often operate with older products and older markets and their efficiency can only be marginally improved.

The key issues regarding the development of small organizations are first focused on the habits of top management, if not of the top executive him- or her self.

The companies in Phase One will be successful if their top exceutives are not only innovative and entrepreneurial but if they also have a knack for informal management.

Some very innovative scientists who could design very useful products for society are completely asocial and would never start a company for that reason. Some entrepreneurs are real sharks who cannot build a team as their preference is to motivate principally by fear, and fear is hardly a promoter of managerial flexibility.

Should top managers be capable of building not only a product and a market but also good managerial teams, they have to learn to go to the next step. They have to be more flexible when the company evolves to the point when managerial teams themselves are insufficient to handle the company's business because the organization is becoming too complex.

Virtues

In the first phases of development of a business organization, the issue is really whether the top executive, or the top team is virtuous enough to let the organization develop.

The top executive, in addition to other essential qualities, must have a strong sense of authority and responsibility, that is of justice, but also of trust, that is another aspect of justice joined with Hope.

When the company grows, it is the virtues of the middle management which become crucial. Whether plant directors, product managers, etc. are capable of impartial and competent government over their center of responsibility is of prime concern. At the same time, they should be temperate enough to be able to control their desire for total independence from the company as a whole but be most willing to collaborate in putting in place the different information and managerial systems necessary to improve the coordination and management of the overall company.

Last, in the largest companies, the virtues of the lower employees are the key issues. Are these employees who are the final motor of the success of the corporation going to live up to the challenge? Will they be able to manufacture a quality product, or will their poor work habits be tantamount to economic sabotage? If employees of a service company, would they be eager to serve the public or would they concentrate their efforts mostly in promoting their own rights and benefits? Do they appreciate all that it signifies to be at work and to fulfill their God-given mission in life?

Theology of work and Management

The XIXth century was mostly preoccupied with the virtues of the "entrepreneur". Economics, which, as a discipline, really spends most of its time analyzing the last economic war, is satisfied to ruminate the problems of yesterday, still is strongly shaped by the assumptions it makes on the virtues of entrepreneurs.

Business management has gone one step further than economics and is presently looking very closely at the different issues which constitutes the virtues of middle-managers.

But one of the most important sets of issues in the economic development of today is related to the virtues of simple employees.

On one hand the attitude of the employee who does not see his professional activities seriously, "it's only a job" attitude, must be dealt with.

On the other hand, the attitude of managers who want to make line employees better wheels in the managerial mechanism of large corporations is also totally unacceptable.

Employees, at the ground floor of large corporations, must be treated both fairly and with great concern for their contribution to the larger corporations. This can be only achieved when employees are treated systematically and consistently by the managerial philosophy or style of the CEO, as well as by the managerial structure, as children of God who have different sets of responsibilities.

In particular, the managerial philosophy of each corporation needs to recognize the fact that employees have sets of responsibilities which are outside and often superior to their responsibilities at work.

Management, with the proper sense of dedication as well as with humility towards the spiritual vocation of their people, can help them considerably, in the work setting itself, fulfill partly these larger responsibilities.

4. The Sky is the Limit - Innovative Management.

The Cortisone story

To understand innovative management, it greatly helps to understand the matters of invention, of innovation and of the management of innovation.

Nazi pilots, during WWII, were rumored to use drugs, including cortisone and other hormones, manufactured from the adrenal glands of animals, which allegedly allowed them to function much more efficiently in combat. The Germans were buying huge quantities of glands from Argentina's livestock industry.

The US government wanted that drug. It ordered research on extracts. That program came to a dead end when they realized that there were not enough animals in the country to obtain such extracts and satisfy all the needs for the drug.

Then the government turned to a pharmaceutical firm, Merck, to make synthetic cortisone. After months of research and much expense a scientist came up with a 36-steps method to produce synthetic cortisone which was very expensive and yielded minute amounts of the drug.

However, some tests on patients brought astonishing results as victims of paralyzing arthritis were able to dance after one treatment. These tests made headlines in the newspapers. All major drug companies were then interested in finding a method to produce cortisone more cheaply. At Upjohn, the president's word was: "Don't spare the horses. We want cortisone". The company set up six different approaches for research with a team of researchers per approach and more than 150 scientists altogether.

Team six was following the "bug approach" using micro-organisms to do molecular restructuring, rather than chemicals.

This approach was considered the dark horse of the six approaches. They were really "groping in the dark". However, one of the team members remembered that in his school years a mold had changed a hormone solution into something else. Team six picked their mold on their windowsill; a very common strain of a mold. They had no basis to believe it would work.

It did work. It led them to a breakthrough that allowed to manufacture synthetic cortisone easily and cheaply. (38)

This story is interesting as it is a rare example of institutional invention. That is to say that the parties involved through the different stages of the process of invention were institutions rather than individuals.

The process of invention

Most inventions, however, even those developed in corporate laboratories are really not the product of whole institutions, but the product of a single researcher.

But, let us first analyze the cortisone story. The US government believed strongly that adrenalin glands could be used and believed that the result would be most useful. It really had no real basis to believe that drug story and could very well have been the victim of Nazi propaganda, which it in fact apparently was.

The single inventor often starts with such fuzzy goals: either a strong conviction that a human need is not properly met, or a strong intuitive feeling that a method has to be tried which should be very worthwhile, or the strong desire to bring to life a machine or apparatus or even a process which can be imagined to work even though the inventor does yet have a precise understanding of its mechanisms.

That is a little bit like Jules Verne's or Da Vinci's fantastic machines, including the rocket or the submarine, which they could imagine but which had to be invented by others in earnest years later after these authors described what the machines would be able to do.

Then the inventor, and UpJohn with its different research teams, starts looking for anything and everything that can help him fulfill his inventing goal. He needs to find new means to attain his objectives.

The important psychological attitude of the inventor at this time is to really look with fresh eyes at a problem. The inventor knows that the solution has not been found to that problem by using known means. He stands ready to look at all approaches, bar none, and including those which are most likely going to feel strange, silly, ludicrous, stupid.

He then acquires the sense that one of these strange approaches is the good one.

The next step of the invention process requires that the inventor keeps working on that approach which he has selected, - either by intuition, or at random or by default - and which remains very strange and silly throughout a dry period when he has no certainty the approach is valid but he has to devote his efforts to tedious tasks such as building a complicated prototype of running elaborate testing procedures.

The inventor in a sense will go through an extended research period where he will be entirely exposed as having selected this strange avenue of research and will be at risk of being ridiculed, as well as at risk of wasting time and money.

The triple pressure ridicule/time/money is tremendous in having him stop this research. Even worse is that the inventor does not know how long the research is going to last, whether the solution is just around the corner or whether it will take many more months and even years.

When the US government had Merck study methods to synthesize cortisone, it was an expensive, lengthy process with no sure outcome. When the president of Upjohn said "Don't spare the horses", he had no guarantee that he would obtain anything from this determination.

Virtues and Invention

The inventor wants to invent because he has a very special appreciation of a very special type of good. He feels more strongly than others that a human need must be met that is not properly met. He is more willing than others to see if a known means can be applied to a different problem that large segments of humanity share.

The inventor has a strong sense of the good. He is attracted by this good. Very often inventors are people who are enthusiastic about everything - many things besides inventing - and are of a very eager attitude towards life in general. This attraction for the good in inventors is a special and strong ability to love which is part of their psychological profile.

Inventors have the virtue of hope, that is that the good they are striving for will come about.

Inventors further often show all the telling signs of a strong will, often associated with a strong sense of justice. They do not let the fact that experts told them not to investigate a specific route of research to discourage them. Also, they tend to believe that special areas of inquiry are really not investigated by these experts because there are vested interests to prevent such investigations.

Most General Motors engineers are mechanical engineers; they know very little about aeronautics; they are not about to investigate the technology of cars that might fly in the air.

The inventor is also willing to try new means and apply them to known objectives. He is therefore, by definition, courageous. He is willing to reach a difficult good.

When the inventor is looking at all possible methods to arrive at his end, he must exhibit the virtue of temperance. We have seen that a broader definition of temperance is the ability to detach oneself from any particular good, both materially and intellectually and therefore includes intellectual flexibility.

He knows he must not feel bound by known laws or principles of industry or of nature because these laws and principles may very well be poorly understood.

However, as soon as he attains partial success, the inventor must be able to rationalize this success, to analyze what went right so that he can build on it. An inventor must have a strong quality of prudence to be successful in the end.

Thanks to the virtue of prudence the inventor assimilates the new evidence that he has attained and place this evidence to fit his understanding of the situation in a correct perspective in relation to the other matters. Prudence will help him recognize intuitively that he has achieved a small success, even when it is not quite the result he was looking for in an experiment, and when others will not see the success of the apparently flawed experiment.

When Fleming found out one morning that there was a mold in his laboratory culture, he did not throw it away but examined what he had. What he had was Penicillin.

Serendipity, or unexpected invention, is really in great extent due to the virtue of prudence of the inventor.

The inventor must be willing to keep working on his odd project even when the pressure on him is very strong. In addition to the general virtue of courage, the inventor exhibits the virtues of patience - for his ability to withstand the pressure of time - and humility for his ability to withstand the pressure of ridicule; patience is a part of the general virtue of courage and humility is a part of temperance.

The inventor may be motivated by the profit motive but not for long. Very rare are the inventors who actually make a lot of money from their inventions. Most "professional" inventors realize those facts sooner or later.

Inventors have to be able to shift from one of the phases of the invention process to the next. First they are absorbed in the problem which they have given to themselves. Then they look at all possible solutions. They have to leave the fascination of the problem in order to look at the different solutions in a calm manner.

Next, they must study closely one of the approaches. They have to stop looking for different solutions while they study that one solution they selected for closer study. This application at following the different phases of the invention process is quite demanding in self-control and therefore in courage.

Inventing and thinking.

The process of invention is basically not very different from the process of thinking. This process was described in the above section on decision-making as described by St. Thomas Aquinas. We refer our readers to the more elaborate stages of the thinking process and the virtues attached to it to complement the description of the psychological parts of the invention process.

The difference between the process of invention and the process of thinking is that the stages are much more drawn out in time in the case of invention than in the case of thinking. Whereas a simple act of thinking can take place in a split second, the different stages of the same act in inventing can take months or even years.

The difficulty and the challenges of each step are more formidable for inventing than for simple thinking. In thinking we go from one step to the next not wandering very far from known territory. When we are thinking through the process of how to dress in the morning, we consider only a very narrow range of choices. We consider only clothes we own. We do not even consider garments which are not for the season.

Inventing, value systems and ethics

Inventing can be really facilitated with the use of an expressed value system, such as our OVIS. The objective of the invention effort is placed within the total value system in order to visualize exactly what are the surrounding values to this objective.

All lower values to this objective then become possible means to attain the objective. We mentioned that physical, intellectual and moral values are often interchangeable in an accepted range. In invention, the

334

process is usually limited to physical values, with the possibility however to go from one set of physical values to another. Values which belong to the set of biology may be used for the purpose of an invention objective which pertains to the set of mechanical engineering.

An expressed system of values can also be utilized to show that an innovative solution of a problem which may appear unethical is really not. Indeed, the litmus test of an ethical act is the wrongful exchange of a higher value for a lower value.

Therefore, when in Shakespeare's Richard III, the king says "My Kingdom for a Horse", the exchange seems very unethical (which makes it striking to the mind and interesting). A kingdom is of a much higher value than a horse. A straight exchange of the latter for the former would be highly inappropriate and unethical as it would seem to show contempt for human dignity and the proper appreciation of a kingdom with its natural resources and its priceless populations.

However, the values at issues in the Bard's tale are not only the kingdom and the horse. There is a third value which is "the king's survival" or "the king's freedom". He wants a horse in order to escape and to ensure this survival and freedom. When the king says "my kingdom for a horse", he is really making the statement "I'd rather be alive or free than to remain king and be either a dead king or a captive king". He is also not talking about any kingdom in absolute, nor even the intrinsic value of his own kingdom but of the personal advantage that he presently draws from being king.

Oftentimes, the oddity in an inventive solution is based on the fact that the solution incorporates similarly a decision which seems to have taken an ethical risk. Proper analysis of the solution and of the circumstances show that the danger is compromising ethical standards is only apparent and, in last reflection, nonexistent. The ethical risk often conceals many innovative solutions.

A genuine expert in ethics who can hone the innovative skills of a corporation and of its creative people by bringing light to the twilight zone between ethics and creativity can make very substantial contributions.

On the other hand it is certain that some inventions which purport to be innovative are plainly unethical. The debate is still open whether Alexander the Great cutting the Gordian knot (a huge bunch of knots that visitors where invited to try and undo) was really presenting an innovative or an unethical solution to the problem of that terribly entangled knot. Was he really playing by the rules when he cut the knot with his sword? In which case he was brilliant. Or was he simply cheating and abusing his rank of general to silence a possible opposition to his radical solution?

Similarly, innovative solutions may often initially hurt our sense of aesthetics. These automobiles whose bodies were the first to be resolutely different from horse-drawn carriages looked strange to their contemporaries but their forms really followed their true function.

Innovative solutions seem to go against ethics when they challenge a values systems based on the criterion of perceived importance of the values. Innovative solutions seem to go against aesthetics when they challenge a values system based on the criterion of like or dislike of values. These criteria were discussed in the section on values systems.

The management of invention

Organizations have been more or less successful in managing inventions.

They think they manage invention when they delegate the whole inventing effort to a small section of the corporation and call this

336

section names like R&D (for research and development).

They stack these departments with scientists and pour money into them. They also learn that they should not expect too much too soon from these departments. There are instances where scientists have been working for up to seven years on projects without paying back a single cent to the corporation that feeds them and allows them to play with a number of expensive research tools, toys of sort.

The problem is that what these corporations expect from their R&D departments are full blown inventions like Minerva coming out of the thigh of Jupiter with her complete panoply, all her weapons. This naive expectation stems from a lack of appreciation of the process of innovation.

Another tool that organizations use to manage invention is to have imaginative people follow very religiously the different paths of an acceptable process of inventing. One of the processes which has been very successful is called Synectics and was developed at Cambridge, Massachusetts. The process forces would-be inventors in the programs to do things like "imagine you are a spring in that little box, how do you feel and where do you want to go?"

R&D departments and invention methods are useful up to a point. They facilitate invention but do not really replace the need for the virtues associated with the invention process.

Institutionalizing creativity

Studies of inventions which came out of R&D departments show that any major invention has to have someone to fight for it: a champion.

A team of physicists finds many interesting facts when working in a laboratory. Someone has to decide that one of these facts is really an invention, that it is practical in the world outside the lab. This person has to confront his fellow scientists that there is indeed a world outside the lab with functions and standards which are different from the world in the lab.

Often a scientist has to have a notion that one of the new discoveries they made is easily translatable into a marketable object and that there is no need to keep researching it at R&D but that it should come out of R&D and be evaluated by Marketing research, in order to test it on people with an altogether different set of values and standards than the physicists at the lab. It takes virtues to decide: "we have an invention now".

A chemical scientist may know something about electrical engineering and believes that the latter discipline can bring a solution to his team research problem. He would have to bring such an expert from outside the lab and would have to fight his chemical engineers colleagues to succeed in this effort.

The scientific champion of an invention in the setting of organizational research must therefore be courageous, prudent, temperate and just.

Invention or creative techniques, similar to Synectics, which allow for different types of people in the organization to come together and study innovative solutions to organizational problems have also their limits.

These sessions may become rigid in the sense that one problem at a time will be considered at any given the session. Each session must have an agenda and the agenda itself may be constraining: is it the right problem? Couldn't we look at two problems at the same time and look for a single solution to take care of them?

Also, management may decide that no innovative thinking is allowed outside the sessions. After all, there is a lot of operational work to do in a business organization and most of it is much less exciting than looking at creative solutions to a single problem.

Therefore top management may feel that it is sacrificing enough to the need of innovation by scheduling these creative sessions and can therefore demand more tidy and conformist behavior on the part of their managers and employees alike outside the sessions.

Innovation

We have started to use the word "innovation". Invention and Innovation are similar in some respects and different in others.

What the independent inventor who works in his basement alone produces are inventions. What he has to do to have these inventions accepted and utilized by the world at large is innovation. In this case there is a clear cut distinction between invention and innovation.

Invention in this sense is much more the product of personal psychological efforts on the part of the owner of a single brain. Innovation requires that a group of people or society at large be convinced to adopt the invention.

Innovation is therefore much more of a sociological endeavor.

Most independent inventors are faring poorly at the specific phase of innovation. On the one hand they often miscalculate the need for the resources and efforts it takes to innovate, to convince others; often they do not possess these means which may entail the manufacturing of expensive prototypes or the funding of market research.

On the other hand, they often feel that their responsibilities stop at inventing, someone else should pick up the torch and carry the invention through the stages of innovation. They look at corporations, especially large corporations, to assume the tasks of innovating.

But the sad truth is that more often than not corporations are not interested in extending the required efforts to innovate with someone else's invention.

When an invention is the product of an organizational effort, the line between invention and innovation is much more fuzzy. The inventor, or a close friend of the inventor in the organization, should start convincing his team mates, then try to convince the wider department, next they have to win over the corporation as a whole. This is also innovation.

The virtues that need to be exerted here are very much the same virtues that need to be exerted for invention.

The difficulties of innovation

In many ways innovation is more difficult than invention. In the US patent office are deposited millions of inventions, although a very small number are being exploited: 1 or 2%. The innovative effort dispensed for the bulk of the patented inventions has been unsuccessful.

Another way to look at it: inventions have been made which were granted a certificate of invention which were not really ready for dissemination to the public, for industrial, social, economic or aesthetical reasons. In these cases one is entitled to wonder if they were genuine inventions.

On the other hand, the social scene gives us many examples of innovation which are not really based on inventions, in the noble sense of invention. Fashion in the clothing industry provides many examples of innovation. Men's neck ties which do not fulfill any clear and useful need have been around for more than a century.

The '6Os were the age of the wide adoption of blue-jeans, a product that had been available for a century. These blue-jeans have also been adopted by people in many nations of the world. Most blue-jeans makers, even those who were around a hundred years ago, like Levi's, are not really responsible for this recent innovation which was somewhat spontaneous. They just followed a trend and tried to satisfy a market.

Levi's did invent blue-jeans for the market of the Californian gold-rush diggers a century ago. But the company is really not responsible for the adoption of blue-jeans by teen-agers of today the world over.

With a clear recognition that the innovation phase is one of the major hurdles for an invention to be successful, some inventors then seek to invent in areas in which they are reasonably convinced that the process of innovation will be manageable. This may be a very astute decision, or it may be a decision based on a lack of courage.

Corporations have become masters at the game of bringing out new products which are not very inventive. Often what they call new products are very slight improvements on existing successful products: a car of a imperceptibly different design, a packaged good in a different sized box.

Or they bring out a product which is not very different from a competitor's highly successful product. When household and cosmetic products in spray cans were successful marketwise, all the related industries jumped on the band wagon. This is me-tooism in marketing.

On the other hand it is important to have a sense of the signs of the times when inventing. One's invention should be acceptable within the surrounding life-style of people in one's generation. Some inventors tend to be a little asocial and ignore the life-styles around them as they themselves have adopted quite different, if not eccentric, lifestyles. This attitude of triumphant individualism which may be helpful in the invention phase may be an hindrance in the innovation phase.

Breakthroughs

There are cases where the innovation process is not really important. This is the case of breakthrough inventions.

Breakthrough inventions contribute to satisfy human needs is such self-evident manner that there is no real need to prove to anybody who can see it the advantages of the invention.

Penicillin was quickly adopted because there was no substitute for it. As soon as automobiles became affordable they replaced horse-drawn carriages as the vehicles of choice. The telephone was a definite breakthrough for human communications.

However, there are several problems with breakthroughs. 1) There are very few breakthroughs compared to the overall number of inventions. The great majority of inventions are slight improvements on existing inventions. 2) Most inventors or owners of inventions believe they have a breakthrough and prefer to assume that others will fight and beat a pathway to their doors and that they personally can therefore eschew efforts to ensure innovation. 3) Even in the cases of some breakthroughs some additional innovative efforts are needed.

Ford was a great innovator in the automobile industry not because he was a great engineer but because he found a way to increase dramatically the market for automobiles by lowering their price.

The telephone functioned for decades by the means of party lines and public phones. It took much organizational effort, the advent of automatic switchboards, forests of telephone poles, the digging of river of trenches to offer individual numbers to each household.

Light bulbs, on the other hand, came in widespread use quite quickly for they were a great improvement over gas lights and everyone needs a safe and clean source of light in the evening, whereas not everyone felt he could afford the luxury of instant communications by telephone when the post office offered a means of reasonably effective, although delayed, communications.

Innovative management

Innovative management is the quality by which good managers are always on the lookout for better methods to handle the tasks the corporation must fulfill.

Innovative management is not necessarily involved with physical inventions. The introduction of the computer in a department may be a product of innovative management. The development of a new product line is an innovation. But organizational innovations are also very important which may help a business function more effectively. Such innovations may include clarifying the mission of a business, splitting a department into two more specialized departments: e.g. a commercial department into a sales department and a marketing department, etc.

Innovative management requires many of the processes as well as virtues which are associated with the innovation of inventions.

Sometimes "innovative management" is contrasted with "administrative management", implying that administrators only have the responsibility to keep an organization functioning according to the rigid manner in which it has been designed, a maintenance function of sorts.

Actually, no business organization can afford to be an administration. It must perpetually evolve because of the external pressure for new and better services and by the changing society in which it operates, and also by the internal pressure of the business employees who are growing on their job and feel capable of assuming a greater number of more advanced and different responsibilities.

Public administration and government agencies are unnatural establishments. These administrations are necessarily designed according to a rigid system. This system depends on the political mandate by which they have been established and the mandate regarding the responsibilities they are to fulfill, as well as the annual budgetary constraints according to which they are able to operate.

But people within these public administrations are very stifled. They want to grow and they want to develop the administration with them.

The danger is these functionaries will overstep their mandate and therefore use illegitimate powers. They may also agitate to keep open an agency the mandate and function of which are obsolete, therefore creating waste and inefficiency in an economy.

The only avenue for managers of public organizations is to hire more employees and ask for bigger budgets in order to give themselves more importance, thus growing in size but not necessarily in efficiency or effectiveness. Public administrations should be reduced to a strict minimum and severely cut down from their present sizes.

Business organizations may look at these public administrations as living examples of what not to follow if they genuinely want to encourage innovative management.

5. Providing Objects of Admiration - Leadership.

Great Men

Social Scientists consider that pre-scientific ideas of leadership viewed leaders as people with special qualities with which they were born. Leaders were considered to be born not made. This, according to our scientists, was the "great men" theory of leadership.

This approach would have been somewhat improved upon by the modern scientists who restated that leaders have a number of positive psychological traits which are necessary for leadership. The "great men" theory of leadership has now become the "trait theory of leadership".

The traits that were identified were:

- Intelligence (the most prevalent trait observed in all studies on leadership). Studies showed that leaders were more intelligent than their followers, but not much more intelligent than them.

- Social maturity and breadth. Leaders are emotionally stable and have a good "self-concept".

- Inner motivation and achievement drives. Leaders strive for "intrinsic rather than extrinsic rewards".

- Human relations attitudes: leaders, according to these studies, "possess consideration" and are "employee- rather than production-centered".

Other theories

The Group and Exchange theories of leadership come from the small camp of a special brand of social scientists called "social psychologists". They claim that there is a trade-off for members of a group between being led and following their leaders and that the whole secret of leadership is to know when to make that trade-off work.

Sociologists prefer to talk about "role expectations" and state that good leaders create the right expectations in their followers about their roles.

Other scientists are interested in showing that leaders can learn from followers just as followers learn from leaders. This is the "Social Learning" approach to leadership.

Situational Theories

Fred Fiedler came up with another theory of leadership: the situational theory.

Questionnaires were given to all members of a group and each one was asked to tell who was the least preferred member and co-worker of the group. Lenient styles of leadership would be marked by leaders who do not give great importance to the difference between the most preferred and least preferred co-workers. The "hard-nosed" style of leadership would be very conscious of these differences and very critical of least preferred co-workers.

Naturally, such a study may somewhat edify social scientists but they quickly create a divisive mood in any work group when members of the group come out and state their lack of sympathy for some workers who are crushed, and admiration for other co-workers who will be very much tempted to become conceited and arrogant.

Fiedler then, not quite satisfied, developed a "contingency model of leadership".

Leadership to be effective would depend on three dimensions:

1 - the leader-member relationship

2 - the degree of task structure

3 - the leader's position of power or formal authority.

When the three dimensions are high the leadership is very effective, says the theory. However, still toying with his other theory, Fiedler discovered on the basis of his data that both when the dimensions were very good and when they were very bad the "hard-nosed" type of leader functioned very well.

The rationale of that finding is that when a boat sinks, the captain is going to be very effective in having his orders obeyed, whether he is a good person or not. If a group of friends are making plans to decide a picnic site, hard-nosed leadership is not going to work. This is the contingency theory of leadership.

Path-Goal Leadership theory

This theory looks at the effect of leadership on the members of the group. Four styles of leadership are defined:

- Directive leadership: this is the authoritarian leader, the subordinates are not expected to participate.

- Supportive leadership: the leader is friendly.

- Participative leadership: the leader ask for members to contribute ideas.

- Achievement-oriented leadership: "the leader sets challenging goals for subordinates and shows confidence in them to attain these goals and perform well".

This theory accepts that a leader can change his styles according to the circumstances. Research has shown that indeed different leadership styles are more effective than others in different situations. But are leaders capable of changing styles? That's another matter.

Scientists' Angst

Elements of the different theories above presented, as well as those of a few other minor theories, have been synthesized in a single table by Tannenbaum and Schmidt. (39)

The table is a continuum that is to say it displays different gradual types of leadership on a single line.

These types correspond to different leadership behaviors according to a scaling value. The two extremes of the lines are: at one end, the extreme boss-centered leadership (maximum "use of authority by the manager") and, at the other end, the extreme subordinate-centered leadership (maximum "area of freedom for subordinates".)

We will present this line vertically from the most to the least "authoritarian" style:

Extreme Boss-centered leadership

- Manager makes decision and announces it.

- Manager "sells" decision.

- Manager presents ideas and invites questions.

- Manager presents tentative decision subject to change.

- Manager presents problem, gets suggestions, makes decision.

- Manager defines limits; asks group to make decision

- Manager permits subordinates to function within limits defined by superior.

Extreme area of freedom for subordinates.

As we can see from such a table, the issues that are truly in the mind of the different social scientists who are promoting quite a number of different theories of leadership are surprisingly limited in number.

There is basically a single issue, as betrayed by the choice of this continuum and the issue is whether the boss cracks the whip or not. On one hand this simplistic issue reveals the liberal bias of the experts whose ideology professes [but not necessarily supports in practice] a distrust of any "fascist" method of enforcement, and, on the other hand, it also discloses the emotionalism, related to this single issue, on the part

349

of these "experts" whose claim to scientific objectivity is seriously put in doubt. Naturally, whether bosses crack whips or not is a very pertinent question to the matter of leadership. But it is not the central issue. To over-emphasize this point is really to distort the whole matter of leadership as we will see further along.

The Managerial Grid

Management manuals which have little to say about leadership must at least include the Blake and Mouton's managerial grid. (4O)

These scientists' approach to the matter of leadership has been the most wide-spread presentation of accepted wisdom by management scholars.

On one dimension of the grid, is displayed the dimension "concern for production". On the other dimension, the dimension "concern for people" is marked out.

This two dimensional table permits then the definition of 9 types of leadership.

High	Country Club Management	Team Management
Concern		
for	Middle of the Road	
People	Management	
Low		
	Impoverished Management	Task Management
	Low	High
	Concern for Production	

Country Club Management is high in concern for people and low in concern for production. "Production is incidental to good relations. A supervisor's major responsibility is to see that harmonious relationships between people are established and that the work atmosphere is secure and pleasant".

Team Management is high both in concern for people and for production. "Production results from the integration of tasks and human requirements. Good relationships and high production are both attainable, and the supervisor's major responsibility is to attain effective

351

production through participation and involvement of people and their ideas."

Middle-of-the-road Management is average both in concern for people and for production. "A balance between high production and good human relations is the aim. The major responsibility of the supervisor is to find a middle ground so that a reasonable degree of production can be achieved without destroying morale."

Impoverished Management is low both in concern for people and for production. "High production and sound relationships are in conflict, and the supervisor's job is not to get involved in the struggle. Rather, the major responsibility is to stay neutral and see to it that the procedures established in the past are carried out."

Task Management is low in concern for people and high in concern for production. "Good relationships are incidental to high production. A supervisor's major responsibility is to see that production goals are achieved by assuming the task of planning, directing and controlling all work."

This grid is another attempt to describe different leadership situations. It is not normative in the sense that, if it does seem to encourage the Team Management approach, it does not really say how to achieve it.

What this type of grid presentation would like to infer is how to go from "Middle-of-the-road Management" where possibly most of the existing leadership situations are concentrated to the "Team Management" approach.

However Blake and Mouton do not offer any instruction to that effect.

Back to basics

"Leadership" really relates to how a person in authority exercises this authority. Supposedly a "good leader" assumes this authority well; a "bad leader" assumes this authority not so well.

We already covered the issue of authority. Authority is the reality that in any society some people are put above others and are enabled to give orders to their subordinates. They are put in a relation of superiority over other men who are henceforth put in a position of subordination.

As we also mentioned, the very acceptance of this definition is what is often opposed by many on allegedly ideological grounds, even though evidence has shown that a "classless", or authority-less or leader-less, society of the soviet type and an army without ranks of the Communist Chinese type are just myths that cannot be substantiated in reality.

There was a very powerful "aristocracy" in the Soviet Union, called the Nomenklatura. There are generals and sergeants and captains in the Chinese army, whatever the names they are called with.

Authority and Society

However, a corporation is not the Chinese army nor the Soviet society. In particular, employees presumably can leave a company and resign a middle management position. Is the principle of authority affected by the difference? If we wish to investigate that fact, we need to have a closer look at the society component in the relationship between society and authority.

Society is defined as "a stable union of a plurality of persons in pursuit of a common good" by St. Thomas Aquinas [St. Thomas "Contra Impugnantes Dei cultum ac religionem, c.3].

A nation is a society with the very broadest common good, the common good of the whole people of that nation. A soviet citizen cannot easily drop off that society. When he does it is a very serious matter: he is a defector. In a less rigid society than the soviet society, the person who drops off is an expatriate and this is still a serious matter.

Any business organization on the other hand, as it was pesented in a previous chapter, seeks to produce the goods and services that allow a national society to function at the material level. A specific business organization, a single corporation, has a business mission which defines what kinds of goods or services it will provide the broader public society.

These are the "metaphysical", or abstract, definitions of the different societies we are now considering. As we can see, authority does not appear in this definition. However a philosopher states that if authority does not belong to this abstract essence of society, it belong to the physical essence of society. (41)

As soon as a society will take up a concrete form, authority appears; that is to say that practically there cannot be a society without people being put in charge over other people. Authority is the form of society; it gives it shape. Differently stated, authority is the formal element of society.

Authority, Society and Society's goal

However, authority is always in principle dependent on the principle of a society and a society is always defined by its goal.

Therefore authority is always defined by the goal of the society in which it is assumed.

The authority of a manager is dependent on the fact that the corporation in which he works must bring out products and services. The authority of manager has everything to do with being effective at bringing out these products and services. However, the authority will also depend on whether the corporation is producing complex products like automobiles on assembly line production systems or if it is a consulting firm employing professionals. The authority of the manager is not the same in the two instances.

The manager is not morally nor technically free to pick and choose among the broadest styles of leadership. The general style of leadership is imposed on him by the organization for which he has accepted a managerial position. It is even imposed on him by the very type of managerial position, since different managers are supervisors over different tasks and of employees with different backgrounds within the same corporation.

In a sense, a work team of a dozen persons is also a society which is defined by the goals of the team.

The leader's virtues

The first responsibility of a manager is then to understand the immediate goals of the society, or business organization, in which he is to operate. The physical as well as financial goals usually determine, within a given country and stages of development, the process, tools and procedures that will be utilized to achieve these goals. Then, employees will be selected in function of these means so that their skills and formation mesh with the technology.

The manager will have to adapt his leadership ability within these constraints and will have to do it on the basis of the virtue of prudence, that is, an understanding of the proper articulation of means and ends. This virtue of prudence is not really a trait, although it is somewhat stable, but a virtue meaning that it needs to be cultivated.

The leader will also have to exhibit the virtue of justice when he confronts issues of the good of different employees with different levels of abilities, different needs, under his command as well as the good of others in the corporation and even out of the corporation.

The leader will have to exhibit the virtue of courage to spell out difficult orders when necessary, of establishing clear instructions and therefore expectations for his subordinates even when there is some difficulty in doing so. The leader will have often to lead by example and this falls under the need for the leader to exercise the virtue of courage as he is to be often the first to perform a task that is difficult, boring, dangerous, intellectually taxing or challenging in order to show that it can be done and how it can be done.

The leader will show temperance as he will try flexibility in approaching the methods of fulfilling his tasks as well as directing his employees.

The top man in a company will do well to draw the attention of all his supervisors or leaders to the fact that they have to work unceasingly at their leadership skills and the virtues that go with them. He will succeed at this task by creating an atmosphere throughout the company which encourages the development of virtues.

Morale

356

All societies, however, are philosophical representations of what is practically called "organizations" and all organizations have an additional responsibility as we have seen in the related chapter: it is its responsibility towards the spiritual dimension and responsibilities of its people.

The leader has a responsibility to facilitate the moral and spiritual development of his subordinates. This responsibility is superadded to his responsibility to ensure that the technical objectives of the organizations are met, as well as to his responsibilities to ensure that the employees whom he supervises behave in a constructive and productive way under his command.

All the "scientific" theories of leadership stop at the material responsibilities of leaders towards their subordinates. According to these theories, leaders have to make sure that their people are happy, that their quality of work life is high, that their job satisfaction is good, that their morale is high.

However, in truth, "morale" comes from the French and means "Morals". The real secret for a leader to improve the morale of his people is to create a work atmosphere in which moral development is highly encouraged.

The true leader is able to describe and promote a very convincing and appealing goal - a good and a value - which all will appreciate and seek to attain while working constructively and in cooperation with fellow workers at organized tasks. This is the good for which his people will follow him.

Naturally, the Christian leader will have no qualm in establishing that this good is God and the true virtues that motivate him are the Christian virtues of Faith, Hope and Charity. He is not required to promote his faith on the job beyond establishing his position in this matter. Faith is a virtue and the leader will be quick to help develop this faith in his people, given half a chance. But faith is also a gift from God and cannot be forcibly injected in anyone.

The true leader will not be embarrassed, however, to stress the importance to his people of the moral and intellectual virtues organized within the four cardinal virtues that they all should seek to attain, for their own benefit first and only secondarily for the good of the business enterprise.

He will try as much as possible to avoid philosophical abstractions but make every effort to translate what he means into very practical realities relative to the job environment of each of his employees.

Further, he will endeavor to ask nothing of his people that he is not able and willing to undertake himself. The power of virtuous leadership is made or broken on the fact that the leader is showing by example or not what he wants others to do.

In essence, true leadership is moral leadership and this moral leadership must be translated into genuine applied exemplary acts of the leader in order for his subordinates to practically follow him.

Born leaders.

We all know what we mean when we say that someone is a born leader. The problem is that we may talk of a child or of a person who is not a supervisor in any organization.

Some individuals have a natural authority; i.e., nature has placed them in a position of superiority over other people. This is possible as much as nature produces people with a nose that is more or less long, a skeleton which is more or less tall, etc. all according to the plans of the good Lord.

358

But again there are different types of authority as we stated in the chapter on authority.

There is intellectual authority. Someone with such authority will keep his opponents speechless by the proper mastering of facts and the articulation of his convincing argumentation.

There is physical authority where the school bully will get all the lunches and marbles he wants because he has established that he can get them by force if necessary.

There is financial authority according to which the person who pays the piper calls the tune. Financial authority may resort to legal authority which recognizes financial contracts and in turn legal authority may resort to the physical authority of law enforcement agencies when necessary.

And there is also moral authority. That authority consists in the ability of presenting a particular good as attractive and attainable. The military leader tells his men: "We need to get to the top of the hill and place our artillery to gain advantage on the enemy, save the lives of our troops and get closer to winning the war."

The business leader tells his men and women: "We have a great challenge to beat our competition and to do it by providing excellence in our products and services. Each of our people will do his best to try and control his physical weaknesses, to concentrate his intellectual efforts, to be open to the needs of all and to become more aware every day of the tasks to complete and how to better complete them."

An elite force like the Marine Corps and the Boy Scouts use the means of inculcating institutional ethos on which to build morale for the participants.

Leadership is really a combination of these different authorities, especially intellectual authority and moral authority. Physical authority may be necessary in some groups and financial authority in others. Legal authority without any other type of authority is usually pathetic.

With moral authority the leader designates a goal as particularly good and worthy or pursuit; with intellectual authority the leader specifically explains how it can be achieved.

Some people are brighter than others. Some people are more moral than others. When the two are combined, we have people who may well be born leaders. However, their moral abilities would have to withstand the experience of being in leadership position when and where they are effectively leaders.

Their future as leaders as well as the future of societies, political or business societies, depends on whether they will be able to maintain these abilities.

Forming leaders

Leaders are not formed by presenting to them that there are different types of leadership styles and "please pick whatever is going to work for you".

Leaders are formed when they are helped to grow in the virtues of prudence, justice, courage and temperance as applied to leadership. This enhances their moral authority. Leaders are formed when their intellectual authority is also enhanced as they are fully educated in the tasks at hand.

To be able to educate their people and exert their intellectual authority over them, an Organizational Values Information System (OVIS) based value system would be very useful for leaders to make their presentation.

The system of values would help show the connection between, for example, personal salvation and the different tasks to be done in the company, as well as the importance of the virtues, thus helping increase the "morale" of their employees.

Leadership is also the skill to have people act. Two behaviors that need to be vanquished therefore are inaction and procrastination.

One type of inaction results from the inability to be properly motivated by the objective of the action. A leader can show his employee that completing a report, a limited value, can help attain a higher value like a promotion, or like any other higher value that the employee would be more sensitive to. The leader will enhance the motivation of his employee.

Systems of values will help leaders gain many points when they are taught to present to their people that there is no inconsistency between what they want for life and working the best they can for the company that employs them.

Another type of inaction or procrastination is often the result of a conflict in the mind of people between two objectives. The employee has decided to perform one action; however, it is not clear in his mind, whether he should not perform another instead.

Many people are in the position of the Jackass who is placed between a stack of carrots and a pail of water. The Jackass is equally hungry and thirsty and, therefore, equally drawn between the carrots and the water. He is unable to move. He is about to die from thirst and hunger.

Figuratively, thanks to the OVIS-based system of values, the leader will help show his employee that he may be slightly more thirsty than hungry, therefore that he should drink first and then come back for the carrots, when it is the case.

Calvinism and business

Another type of inaction is when it is not clear in the mind of someone whether an action is going to compromise the person's values, defined with a stronger ethical content.

Some people want very much to be successful in business but they are afraid that it would mean they will have to be greedy or ruthless.

On the other hand, other people without those scruples can be very successful, not because they are smarter, nor necessarily because they are unscrupulous, but because they do not have these conflicts. They have resolved these things in their minds.

David Rockefeller has been quoted as stating that Latin American nations will be economically successful when Catholicism is replaced by Protestantism. There is a common perception than Protestants are more business-minded than Catholics. (42)

Calvinism provides a structured solution to the problem of inaction derived from a conflict of value between being an effective, but possible unethical, businessman and a good Christian.

Calvinism states that material success is a sure sign that one is favored by God and is a good Christian. Therefore one must concentrate on being a successful businessman, not worrying too much about issues of ethics, so as to be successful and prove that one is a good Christian; retroactively, if one is successful and therefore a good Christian, one has handled properly the ethical issues confronted on the way.

As it can be shown that the values "justice", "disinterestedness" and "business success" can be articulated in a system of values, thanks to a OVIS presentation, this type of employee inaction will also be removed.

Bishops will also be able to effectively preach how business initiative is compatible with a life of faith and effectively and magisterially help unlock the economic stagnation of many Third World countries.

- 6. Trail Blazing - Entrepreneurship.

The nature of entrepreneurship

Entrepreneurship, as an element of the discipline of management, is the culmination of all the above mentioned concepts and then more.

An entrepreneur must have a keen sense of what is a business. He must perfectly understand what is an organization. He must be able to appreciate the social role of business organizations. The entrepreneur is at ease with "people issues". He is an innovator and a leader.

But the entrepreneur is even more: he is someone with a philosophy of life that is not shared by many and he is following through on this philosophy at the risk of considerable personal costs, but also in the hope of significant personal rewards. He also tends to have a different psychological make up from the rest of the population.

Jean-Baptiste Say, a French economic theorist writing around 1800 coined the term "entrepreneur" and gave it the following definition: "the entrepreneur shifts economic resources out of an area of lower and into an area of higher productivity and greater yield". (43)

363

The entrepreneurial philosophy of life.

Economists from the beginning of their profession have had a difficult time understanding entrepreneurs.

Adam Smith, the author of the Wealth of Nations, the book which was of enormous importance to the development of western economies, considered that the economic system worked when businesses went into competition with each other, thus driving down prices and increasing markets.

Adam Smith and most other economists consider the economy first and postulate that it is roughly operating correctly - they say it is in "equilibrium". All economic agents then, including this special type of economic agents: entrepreneurs, are contributing, in their own capacity, to this equilibrium.

But both Jean-Baptiste Say and Joseph Schumpeter, an Austrian publishing in 1911, came closer to the perspective that entrepreneurs themselves have of economic theory. The economic theory of entrepreneurs is all the more important in that it is also their philosophy of life and of action.

Disequilibrium, not equilibrium, is the rule. The entrepreneur will seek to make the most of a disequilibrium. By doing so, he is the prime driver of the economy. Equilibrium will never be reached. There always will be entrepreneurs building their operations on the premise that a given disequilibrium offers a business opportunity.

Entrepreneurs also tend to see entrepreneurship as the most important reality in the business world and the rest of non- or less-entrepreneurial business organizations as fallen angels from the entrepreneurial ideal.

Bias against entrepreneurs

The problems with entrepreneurs, as with inventors or saints, is for them to convince the rest of the population that, even though they constitute an often tiny minority among businessmen, technicians or scientists or theologians or church-goers, they are more significant in the overall picture than the majority of their confreres. They actually are the prime drivers of the economy, of technology and of spirituality.

The case for struggling entrepreneurs - as opposed to the successful entrepreneurs of history as folk heroes - is becoming all the more difficult these days when statistics have become the science of choice not only in the social sciences but also in many of the "hard sciences" and in management. Statistics claims that any proposition which is true for 95% of the cases can be considered as quasi-certainty. In other words, the 5% of the observations - also known as hard evidence - which do not fit the main proposition can be considered as negligible. There 5% are dismissed by statisticians as "outliers".

When entrepreneurs constitute much less than 5% of the working population they are therefore under the very strong threat to be treated as negligible entity.

Entrepreneurs, on their part, will maintain that they, the less than 5% of the labor force, are more important than the 95% in an economy. Entrepreneurs are totally convinced that economies in which entrepreneurs are shackled are doomed to fail.

Paradoxes and Christianity

Entrepreneurs see themselves as exceptions who are more important than the majority. They tend also to have a business strategy which is typically oriented toward seeking exceptions to a rule.

When, in a given situation, non-entrepreneurial managers see a business impossibility, a "wall" that prevents them to go in a given direction, a market that is fully covered by well-entrenched companies, a technical problem that is insurmountable, the entrepreneur is looking at the wall very closely to find a chink.

Finding this often unimpressive chink the entrepreneur will set up camp and expend much effort until the chink becomes a full-fledged business niche. Such a business niche is thus a chink in the overall economic picture that has been properly exploited by an entrepreneur.

Entrepreneurs thrive on paradoxes. A paradox is a lesson which goes against received wisdom or against regular teaching as given by official schools. It is an apparent inconsistency. The paradox is the chink; the accepted teaching, the wall.

Due to their psychological pre-disposition towards paradoxes, entrepreneurs may be in an ideal situation to understand the teachings of the Church. True teachings of the Church are indeed quite paradoxical: "the first will be last"; "the saints are washed in the blood of the lamb"; "if you seek to save your life you will lose it"; the Virgin Mary, the creature elevated to the highest dignity by her divine Son has no formal function in the Church; "my kingdom is not of this world".

Popular culture is solidly attached to this world. On the other hand, the "good News" of the Gospel proclaims that there is a Kingdom of God and we should prepare to join this kingdom, and for that purpose we need change our attitudes and behavior. This is a very difficult proposition for many.

Unfortunately, not all, nor even probably most, entrepreneurs are saints. However, developing the skills necessary to identify business niches may help one gain a special sensitivity, a different perspective on life, and be able to perceive the lightening rays of grace piercing through the walls of a materialistic world.

Psychological traits of entrepreneurs

Many studies have been conducted to try and isolate what makes an entrepreneur an entrepreneur.

The psychological trait that has been believed to be the most associated with entrepreneurship is a trait called Need for Achievement. People with the greater need to excel will have a greater tendency to create new companies. The Agency for International Development of the US State Department has invested large sums of money on programs based on this theory in order to create more entrepreneurs in the Third World.

A friend of this author, Dr. Jean Schéré, has shown in a scientific study that this trait is really not particular to entrepreneurs. Many managers, school teachers and politicians have a high need for achievement without being entrepreneurs. (44)

The trait that he found to be the best prediction for entrepreneurs is called "Tolerance for Ambiguity".

Entrepreneurs have this quality that they do not need the latest or the most complete information in order to make a decision.

That is not to say that they are happy making decisions in the dark. Some have said that entrepreneurs are risk-seekers but that is a simplified view held by people who need all their i's dotted and t's crossed. Entrepreneurs are not more interested in risk than the next person.

Entrepreneurs come sooner to the conviction that a given situation is clear and are more quickly ready to react to that situation than others in the business population. They tend to rely very much on their intuition.

Two very important traits of entrepreneurs is thus that they perceive situations differently and that they have a need to act to make things happen.

Entrepreneurial Perception

Entrepreneurs tend to have a vision of the world and of business situations which is quasi-artistic. They see a situation drawn out in their minds a little bit like the flow-chart of a computer program with arrows and decision lines and check-points etc. going in all directions. They sometimes even see these situations in a third dimension. Some studies found that the type of perception can be traced to the right side of the brain, the artistic side. The left side of the brain is better at handling a linear approach to thinking; it is much more systematic and logical in its approaches.

Three dimensional images are difficult to describe and communicate since a "picture is worth a thousand words". It may well be that entrepreneurs go into business for themselves because they feel restricted when forced to explain their visions to bosses who have no imagination.

Generalists

Entrepreneurs are generalists. They are very comfortable with the concept of a business being a complicated system. They enjoy and look forward to the challenge of managing an organization with different types of people with different functions and talents. Should they become intemperate and unjust enough to favor some functions over other functions over the good of the whole system, their venture will fail.

Entrepreneurs have a good sense of business. They do not need to be told that a business has to turn out a profit to succeed.

Entrepreneurs also relish studying the economy as a complex system. They are acutely aware of their obligation to please the buying public. Entrepreneurs are also very comfortable with the notion that they need very good people and that they must dedicate themselves to obtaining the best for these people, just as much as they will expect these employees to give the best of themselves to make the new business succeed.

Being a special type of "change agents", entrepreneurs understand they need to fight inertia in order for their customers to buy their products; they have to fight inertia in order for their employees to follow them down a difficult path. They are leaders.

Entrepreneurs have a good sense of the two major imperatives of businesses: the customer or marketing imperative and the employee - or personnel - imperative as discussed in a previous chapter.

Entrepreneurs are innovators rather than inventors, they prefer achieving a success for their businesses rather than to succeed in having their own technological brainchild adopted by society. They sometimes utilize the technical invention of someone else. The real invention of entrepreneurs is the formula of their new business itself.

Krok bought the MacDonald's chain from a man called MacDonald who had invented the restaurant's business formula. Krok made the formula succeed. He was a better entrepreneur than MacDonald. Land who invented Polaroid was an inventor and never managed the whole Polaroid-Land company.

However innovators are not necessarily entrepreneurs.

Corporations may support innovation in their midst but they cannot really support entrepreneurship, that would be self-defeating. Entrepreneurs' projects need to be distinct from those of large organizations. However, efforts are made to instill the entrepreneurial spirt in established corporations under the label of "intrapreneurial".

One possible formula: joint ventures set up between individual entrepreneurs and large corporations, for example, an employee whose project is not accepted by the company that employs him may quit the company in order to set up a joint venture with the company on the project.

But then, it is the large corporation which has a very hard time teaming up with single individuals; corporations are much more at ease signing joint ventures with corporations their own size.

Effectiveness and efficiency

Because of the keen interest in making projects with marginal chances to succeed, entrepreneurs are much more interested in effectiveness than in efficiency. Being effective means being successful in the difficult attempt at entering a niche.

Most likely the successful entrepreneur will find himself alone in that niche; he does not need to worry too much about cutting costs and lowering prices at first, because he will have little competition for a time. When the market matures, there will be competition and it will be very important to be efficient.

But, by then, he will also face the necessity to hire other kinds of people: technicians with advanced degrees and slide-rules and other precise instruments. These are the people who believe in the rule of the 95% being certainty. Entrepreneurs will not find themselves very at ease working with these "efficiency experts". They may even decide to sell out the business and start a new one.

Need to act.

The other principal reason why entrepreneurs make up their minds quickly about a business situation and decide to go into business for themselves is that they also experience an inner need to act, to build, to make a difference and to do it on their own.

Studies have shown that many entrepreneurs come from the fringe of a given society. It is inferred that entrepreneurship is a means to leap-frog conventional patterns of social climbing in order for the entrepreneur to accede quickly to the higher levels of that society, or at least be accepted by it.

The self-image of entrepreneurs as outcasts is paradoxically both what provides fuel to their desire for change (change their own situation and change society so that it will accept them) as well as their source of pride.

Furthermore, the need to act is oftentimes spontaneous and almost unconscious.

An entrepreneur friend was dating a young woman of a Marxist persuasion. He was trying very hard to explain to her the point of view of entrepreneurs. She proposed to him the cliché than entrepreneurs are only interested in monetary gain. Then he realized that both of them had come about the same time into about the same sum of money. With her money she had bought a condo in order to live comfortably. He invested his money to start a company for which he had to spend a whole year on the road presenting his product without making a single sale. Decades later he could afford to buy a yacht.

He was more than willing to invest this money as he felt that it had a productive and constructive potential. He did not feel that his own personal comfort and preference for an elegant condo should go ahead of the necessity he felt for trying his best to bring about the productive potential of his capital. The story finishes well: he became a successful businessman, he converted her to the goodness of entrepreneurship and married her.

Blacks and Koreans

Entrepreneurs are not really interested in seeking to make a sacrifice, to deny themselves the comfort that a little more financial affluence may bring. But they see capital as the key to a better life, as the opportunity to be in business and be productive. They will search very hard for that opportunity and when they have that key they will feel impelled to try it.

In certain neighborhoods of Philadelphia, conflicts were endemic between the black population and Korean shopkeepers. In order to foster mutual understanding, a Korean academic devised a program which supported the employment of young African-Americans in Koreans' businesses. These young blacks gained a first-hand and most valuable experience in entrepreneurship.

The assumptions of the young blacks was that banks were making loans to Koreans much more readily than they would make loans to blacks. The reality is that banks do not treat Koreans in any preferential position compared to blacks.

Korean families save on the paltry incomes of several of the members who enjoy regular jobs outside of the community. Elders of the community meet once a month and decide to invest their combined savings of the month on the project of one of their members. Projects

372

which succeed help the whole community come out of its low socio-economic status.

The black employees learned the lesson very well, as well as gained a much greater respect for their Korean employers.

Capital formation is important for entrepreneurs to succeed but true entrepreneurs eventually find the capital they seek. The amounts of capital needed in order to go in business is oftentimes a matter of perception. What would be ample capital in the Third World or in poor neighborhoods is viewed as pocket money elsewhere.

The parable of the talents

One teaching from the Bible which is often taken to refer to the situation of entrepreneurs is the parable of the talents. Let us recall it now:

"It is like a man about to go abroad who summoned his servants and entrusted his property to them. To one he gave five talents, to another two, to a third one, each in proportion of his ability. Then he set out on his journey. The man who had received the five talents promptly went and traded with them and made five more. The man who had received two made two more in the same way. But the man who had received one went off and dug a hole in the ground and hid his master's money. Now a long time afterwards, the master of those servants came back and went through his accounts with them. The man who had received the five talents came forward bringing five more. "Sir", he said, "you entrusted me with five talents; here are five more that I have made." His master said to him "Well done, good and trustworthy servant; you have shown you are trustworthy in small things; I will trust you with greater; come

373

and join in your master's happiness." Next the man with the two talents came forward. "Sir", he said, "you entrusted me with two talents; here are two more than I have made." His master said to him, "Well done, good and trustworthy servant; you have shown you are trustworthy in small things; I will trust you with greater; come and join in your master's happiness." Last came forward the man who had the single talent. "Sir", said he, "I had heard you were a hard man, reaping where you had not sown and gathering where you had not scattered; so I was afraid, and I went off and hid your talent in the ground. Here it is; it was yours, you have it back." But his master answered him, "You wicked and lazy servant! So you knew that I reap where I have not sown and gather where I have not scattered? Well then, you should have deposited my money with the bankers, and on my return I would have got my own money back with interest. So now, take the talent from him and give it to the man with the ten talents. For to everyone who has will be given more, and he will have more than enough: but anyone who has not, will be deprived even of what he has. As for this good-for-nothing servant, throw him into the darkness outside, where there will be weeping and grinding of teeth". (Mat. 25:14-30)

In this parable there seems to be at least two prominent lessons. The first lesson is that we are entrusted with good things in our lives, talents. And we are expected to make something out of them.

The second lesson is that the principal attitudes which prevents the exercise of good stewardship is sloth, or laziness and a false sense of fear. The man who had a single talent was incorrect in his knowledge of God He thought God was a hard God and therefore feared Him.

Different sorts of talents

It is quite interesting that people with talents other than the possession of money, such as artistic talents, are quite willing to cultivate them. The whole culture and educational system support them in this endeavor.

On the other hand people with monetary advantages are frowned upon when they invest their money and act as entrepreneurs, especially in a mass consumer society as that of the US in the end of this millennium. Popular culture accepts very well that people with a little bit of money use the money to buy themselves the things that make for a comfortable life.

Most entrepreneurs, nevertheless, come from amidst these people who only have a little bit of money and deny themselves these basics of a comfortable life when they invest their money in a business venture.

Popular culture also expects people with a lot of money to be generous and to spread it around. Parenthetically, people with substantial sums of money, apart from going in business for themselves or from funding entrepreneurs, are in a unique position to do certain things with their money such as funding the arts by sponsoring the new productions of contemporary artists. But that is not really what the populace expects of them.

This apparent paradox - the middle class is expected to keep its money, the rich to give it away - may be explained as popular culture sees money as a potential which is depleted when exercised.

Popular culture understands that most people want to keep their money rather than see it vanish away. On the other hand, popular culture wants to take money away from those it judges to have too much, because in this case it sees money as power which can be shared around, and tough luck if, by distributing it, it will mean that there will be less of it for the rich.

Entrepreneurs see money in a way that is dynamic, as financial resources. Non-entrepreneurs see money in a way that is static.

Liberalitas

Entrepreneurs, because of their own experiences or inner confidence, see money as something dynamic because they see it as a commodity in flux which can be made and which can be lost. Non-entrepreneurs see money as a limited pie and their principal concern about money therefore becomes how the pie should be divided.

Perceiving money as a dynamic commodity can be cultivated. St. Thomas Aquinas tells us that the ability not to be attached to money or wealth is a virtue. It is called "liberalitas" or liberality.

First let us state that liberality is different from what "liberals" see as a virtue as in liberalism. Liberality is the ability to detach ourselves from the money we have.

Liberals promotes the virtue of cultivating the habit of being quick to distribute money to other people or causes but they do not mean their own money. Only when liberality is associated with the reasoned and charitable willingness to give to others out of one's own wealth, then there is generosity, a virtue the Church teaches to acquire and to practice through "alms-giving".

virtue   --------liberality----->

non virtue   ------liberalism-------->

virtue   -------------- generosity --------------------->

Ourselves   Others
376

Liberality, by itself, naturally is the first virtue necessary to perform the evangelic counsel of voluntary poverty. That does not mean that entrepreneurs are monks but that they do share something with monks. Like monks, they are willing to forego the immediate benefits of money.

Individuals who are willing to grow in the virtue of liberality may at the same time acquire some talents for entrepreneurship as well as appreciate the spiritual qualities to be derived from self-denial if not of ascetic practices.

Cultivating the economic talents.

As we are all materialistic and cling to our possessions, liberality is a rare virtue which explains that popular culture does not reflect it and therefore does not support the cultivation of economic talents.

However, it is only a first step on a road to the spiritual life. On that road we need to detach first from the things exterior to ourselves (the counsel of voluntary poverty) then from our own body (the counsel of chastity), and then from our own will (the counsel of obedience), the most difficult.

We are all invited to live a spiritual life and become saints. Poverty, chastity and obedience constitute the "evangelical counsels". One true and tested method to lead a spiritual life is try and follow these counsels.

Fear and entrepreneurship.

That entrepreneurs seem confident in themselves does not mean that they do not agonize over a decision. The magazine of upcoming new businesses, "Inc. Magazine", had an article researching the number one feeling experienced by entrepreneurs during the first months and the first years with a new venture; they that that this feeling is a feeling of terror. Starting entrepreneurs wake up at night in a cold sweat.

Entrepreneurs are always wondering if they are going to succeed, if the market is going to accept their product and service, if they will be able to make a profit at it, if they are going to have enough cash to keep paying the good people who work for them and to stay in business. Also, as this feeling lingers on for a long time, entrepreneurs need be very persistent.

"Corporate entrepreneurs", by the way, are never faced with the same type of fear: the proper management of innovation in a large business requires that the corporation accepts failures from its innovative employees. Innovative managers of a well-managed corporations need not experience fear.

To withstand these most uneasy feelings, entrepreneurs need to be quite courageous.

Often what has the potential to break an entrepreneur is the effect of his new business on his family. Members of the family of an entrepreneur are prone to be even more in a state of panic as they are not necessarily entrepreneurial themselves. The panic of the family often takes the concrete form of fear of losing a home. Most new businesses are financed by mortgages which entrepreneurs take on their own homes. An entrepreneur may feel more pain witnessing the anguish of his family than from his own sense of financial insecurity.

Some entrepreneurs are blessed with a very strong backing on the part of their wives and children. Many entrepreneurs, unfortunately, like J. Paul Getty just put their businesses before their family life. Getty changed wives often. Other entrepreneurs remain single.

Providence and entrepreneurship

The Christian can alleviate the fear associated with entrepreneurship who places a great trust in God's Divine Providence.

The individual who feels a great compulsion to start a business and, after prayerful reflection, concludes that this compulsion is genuine, sincere and reasonable, must conclude that he has received this compulsion from God himself. This inner prompting is not altogether different from the reception of a call or vocation to the religious or priestly life. Everyone has his calling and a special plan of life that God wants him to follow.

Entrepreneurs sometimes overstate their case. After all, God only wants a tiny minority to be successful entrepreneurs and offer jobs to the rest of the working population.

But definitely God wants entrepreneurs and if He chooses any one of us to be one of these entrepreneurs we can trustfully follow the prompting he places in our heart. We can expect that if along the road of the entrepreneurial struggle the situation appears bleak at times, these are periods of trial specifically designed for our benefit and for our spiritual development; His Providence is with us and will not abandon us.

The entrepreneurial imperative

But we are required to cultivate our talents. Some have substantial sums of money and they are expected to be good stewards of that money. Others have simply an entrepreneurial spirit and are expected to be diligent and look for opportunities to exercise this entrepreneurial spirit.

Others know they have no money and believe they have no entrepreneurial spirit. But as this spirit, in many instances, can be cultivated, we are all expected to grow in each and every virtue of entrepreneurship. We are further expected to remain vigilant and do our utmost to see if there are not entrepreneurial opportunities available to us.

For many businesses, 90% of the products they market today did not exist 10 years ago. However, 95% of new products that are brought to market fail. 90% of new businesses go in bankruptcy before they are 2 years old.

Entrepreneurship is certainly a very necessary function for society but not always well accepted socially.

If successful entrepreneurs can make ten times more money than they would as simple managers, we must recall that for one who succeeds nine have failed. Or the one entrepreneur who succeeds may have failed nine times previously. These gains are part of the total picture of entrepreneurship as wanted by God.

We should not be envious of them. We should not surmise that those entrepreneurs are necessarily greedy as only a minority are financially very successful.

As a society we must ensure that our economy accommodates entrepreneurship; we must help entrepreneurs cultivate their talents. We must allow for a cultural climate which allows others in the labor force to cultivate their virtues as workers, virtues which may lead them to become entrepreneurs.

Relying on God's Providence and conquering the fear of material want, an entrepreneurial society would have to curtail the cancerous growth of its public sector agencies who appear to mimic Providence and pretend to be able to protect all citizens from material needs. Christians know that these extravagant promises of the welfare state are both silly and impossible.

Only God is in control and can protect us from lacking. And God has stated that he would primarily satisfy our material needs by sanctioning our work, not by providing us with a Welfare State.

CONCLUSION

Perfection, efficacy and the business life

"Let no man therefore imagine that there is any opposition between these two things so that they cannot be properly reconciled: namely, the perfection of one's own soul and the business of this life, as if one had no chance but to abandon the activities of this world in order to strive for Christian perfection, or as if one could not attend to these pursuits without endangering his own dignity as a man or as a Christian."

"However, it is in full accord with the designs of God's providence that men develop and perfect themselves by exercise of their daily tasks, for this is the lot of practically everyone in the affairs of this mortal life."

Pope John XXIII Mater et Magistra, par. 255-256

We have similarly developed the thesis here that man's professional duties as a businessman, manager or a corporate employee is not in opposition with his spiritual life. We have, in addition, shown how by performing his duties in the right spirit and according to the proper respect for the virtues, man can grow spiritually on the job.

But we went further, following the good pope John:

> "As often, therefore, as human activity and institutions having to do with the affairs of life, help toward spiritual perfection and everlasting beatitude, the more they are to be regarded as an efficacious way of obtaining the immediate end to which they are directed by their very nature. Thus, valid for all time is that noteworthy sentence of the divine Master: 'Seek first the kingdom of God and His justice, and all these things will be given you besides (Matt. 6:33)'"

> Pope John XXIII Mater et Magistra, par. 257

Precisely when man takes on the whole challenge of being a true Christian businessman, manager or employee, he becomes much more effective at his job of businessman, manager, employee. By seeking to be virtuous at his work, he becomes much more effective at being a businessman or manager than he would have even dreamed of becoming before taking the narrow road to follow Our Lord. (45)

We have thus provided a practical demonstration, for the world of work and business, of the great teaching of the New Testament where Jesus tells us: "Trust me, follow me and all your necessities will be provided for".

Management and morality.

There is another conclusion to be drawn from the previous pages: All of the principles of management are related to principles of morality. These principles, furthermore, are not necessarily Christian, since as we saw above the Cardinal virtues first appeared in history under the pen of a pagan philosopher: Plato.

This means that businessmen and managers are embarked on a great adventure at work, as is practically everyone else, where they all strive to perform practical implementations of ethical standards.

On the other hand, as we have listed all the virtues it takes to ensure that the most humble management function will be performed properly, and as the economic systems on the whole function properly, it is clear that most managers and workers, in the course of their daily tasks, are fulfilling properly many such ethical obligations.

Ethics offers a necessary descriptive conceptual framework for management. Ethics helps understand what management really is. But ethics is also descriptive in a different plane: most managers, most of the time, and as they perform most of their tasks are quite ethical.

Ethics, on the other hand, also offers a necessary prescriptive norm for management: the more a businessman, manager or employee is ethical at work, the more he will be effective.

And this is a direct challenge to Capitalism.

Capitalism

Unlike Communism for which there is a central Communist party (at least per Communist nation) where one can ask what it is they are trying to do, nobody pretends to hold for Capitalism a definition of its underlying philosophical concept with total authority.

There is not even really a grandfather of Capitalism we can turn to since the term was essentially coined by Karl Marx, in his book "Das Kapital". Marx did not precisely expound the concept for the purpose of promoting Capitalism. Indeed he defined Capitalism as "the exploitation by private ownership of the means of production."

Max Weber, in "Protestant Ethics and the Spirit of Capitalism", wrote that Capitalism is "identical with the pursuit of profit, and forever renewed profit, by means of continuous rational, capitalistic enterprise". Weber was very supportive of Capitalism; it is regrettable therefore that he does not offer a more useful definition.

In the absence of a precise definition, we must consult popular opinion on the subject. Most people who think of Capitalism are in fact thinking of an economic "laissez-faire" system and more specifically of Adam Smith's proposal for a free-market system where competition is all the policing that is needed to ensure an effective operation of the system. Adam Smith used the term of "invisible hand" to describe the regulatory effects of business competition.

Cardinal Ratzinger -Pope Benedict XVl

An official promoter of the teachings of the Church, after the Pope who named him, was Joseph Cardinal Ratzinger, Prefect of the Congregation of the Doctrine of the Faith, the future Pope Benedict the 16th. a Bavarian who is steeped in the social teachings of the Church as only a German can be since most of the studies that influenced the writings of the most important encyclicals in modern history, including Rerum Novarum, the first such encyclical, were written by Germans.

Then Cardinal Ratzinger, at a conference in Rome in 1985 on the matter of the Church and the Economy, expressed his difficulty in accepting the principle of the "invisible hand", on the ground that this principle is too deterministic.

Indeed, Adam Smith states that:

"As every individual, therefore, endeavors as much as he can both to employ his capital in the support of domestic industry, and so to direct that industry that its produce may be of greatest value; every individual necessarily labours to render the annual revenue of the society as great as he can. He generally, indeed, neither intends to promote the public interest, nor knows how much he is promoting it. By preferring the support of domestic to that of foreign industry in such a manner as its produce may be of greatest value, he intends only his own gain, and he is in this, as in many other cases, led by an invisible hand to promote an end which was no part of his intention. Nor is it always the worse for the society that it was not part of it. By pursuing his own interest he frequently promotes that of the society more effectually than when he really intends to promote it. I have never known much good done by those who affected to trade for the public good. It is an affectation, indeed, not very common among merchants, and very few words need be employed in dissuading them from it."

Adam Smith, "Wealth of Nations" (46)

As this economic theory, often called "classical theory of economics" is usually understood to work without the theoretical necessity of any moral contribution on the part of the economic agents who are businesspeople and managers, it is deterministic.

Capitalism, as it is most often understood to correspond with this interpretation, is therefore also deterministic. Cardinal Ratzinger reminds us that its determinism it is an insult to man's dignity as it does not recognizes man's moral responsibilities and freedom to choose.

The Church and Capitalism

The Church has no problem with the principle that men can contribute to economic activity at different levels with their capital and their labor. The Church recognizes private property.

The Church has no problem with the fact that private business enterprises who will attempt to simultaneously satisfy consumer demand will find themselves in a position of competition. The Church would like, however, to see ethical limits on the manner that competition is carried out between different businesses.

The Church does have problems with an economic system where freely competing businesses are all that there is. There must be a mechanism and a center of authority which ensures that the common good is protected and promoted.

What Adam Smith really said.

Adam Smith who wrote a study on ethics, "The Theory of Moral Sentiments", was not prone to dismiss the importance of morality without giving very serious care to what he was saying in that regard.

"The Wealth of Nations" is really looking at a very specific issue. Paul Samuelson, not particularly a friend of free-markets, wrote in his textbook, the most widely utilized basic textbook of economics:

> "What Smith did do in his great book was to enumerate countless cases of follies by government. He mined ancient and contemporary history for valuable illustrations of the harmful effects that well-meaning government interference had on nations".

388

"His book is a masterpiece. It is a practical handbook that might be entitled, 'How to Make the GNP Grow'."

Two justices

These latter arguments of The Wealth of Nations are still valid. When governments try to develop a master plan for the economy these attempts are complete failures, are an embarrassment for the governments and a disaster for the populations who do not see their material needs met and may go hungry.

An old joke says that the Soviet Union has had adverse agricultural conditions for the last 70 years of its existence.

But to develop a master plan for the economy is not the only way a government may try to promote the common good in a nation's economy.

We have seen in our section on the virtue of justice that there are three types of justice: legal or general, distributive and commutative. We will look in this section at the last two.

To try to design and implement a master plan for the economy belongs to the distributive type of justice: justice that flows from the state, or the leadership of society, towards each of the constituents of that society.

But government plans which endeavor to specifically determine what a nation will produce (product policy - manufacturing policy) and how these products will be distributed (marketing policy - retailing policy) are attempts to perform actions of distributive justice in the economic sphere at levels which are totally improper as they disobey the principle of subsidiarity and bankrupt in practicality. Adam Smith and decades of socialism have shown that these efforts are to be abandoned.

This conclusion established, we must then recognize the validity of the basic principle that businessmen should be granted an essential freedom of action.

But competition should not be an excuse for all sorts of unsavory activities. The state should preserve fairness in competition. The role of the state can technically then be described as preserving commutative justice between competing businesses.

The state should also defend economic participants other than businesses, namely employees and customers, in a free-market society who might be hurt by too extreme a business competition. In a sense the protection of employees and customers may be viewed as ensuring distributive justice in the population. In another sense it may be rather viewed as a continuation of ensuring commutative justice between businesses for certain businesses will not be permitted to gain an unfair advantage over their competitors by taking advantage of their employees and customers.

All this, we believe, Adam Smith as a teacher of moral philosophy had in mind when he wrote the "Wealth of Nations" as he stated:

"Every man, as long as he does not violate the laws of justice, is left perfectly free to pursue his own interest his own way, and to bring forth his industry and capital into competition with those of any other man, or order of men".

Adam Smith, "An Inquiry into the Nature and Causes of the Wealth of Nations", 1776

However, if Adam Smith believed in the importance of the exercise of commutative justice by businessmen and the ensuing obligation for the state that such principles of justice be respected in business, his belief does not seem to have been included in the popular and modern understanding of Capitalism.

This is one point where popular wisdom is wrong on Adam Smith.

General Justice

Adam Smith did not seem very concerned about the fact that business people should cultivate the virtue of general justice. And this is where we depart from him principally.

Naturally, a businessman on the brink of starting a business, or more simply to invest his capital, cannot substitute himself for the state or for some sort of private national economic planner and try to evaluate where his money be most wisely invested so that the common good be best satisfied and the general economy most surely made to grow. Individual entrepreneurs have a subjective, but not necessarily inappropriate, view of their own opportunities and capabilities as well as of the needs of the general economy.

If government after government, year after year, has not been able to solve the problem of how to maximize national production, neither can a single businessman. It really is unreasonable to expect him to.

But that does not preclude businessmen from cultivating the virtue of general justice. The businessman should desire the good of the state as a whole in the economic sphere, as an expression of the common good, and should look forward to apply this virtue, whenever possible, as shown in this study.

Businessmen should care very much about the quality of the political and economic institutions of the country as they often do. And that is part of general justice.

The above quoted words of Adam Smith as representative of other statements he made in that vein, as they are tinged with irony and cynicism, lead us to the conclusion that he indeed did not put much stock in the usefulness of the virtue of general justice in businessmen.

The public and modern understanding of the principles of Capitalism does not seem to give much weight either to these virtues in businessmen.

Popular wisdom has correctly understood Adam Smith on this point. But this is the very point where Adam Smith is wrong.

A new economic theory

We are strongly opposing the view that businessmen need not be particularly eminent in the virtue of general justice. One cannot be truly virtuous if one is strong in one of the virtues but sorely lacking in another.

Essentially, virtues are one. One cannot be truly hard working, possess business good judgment, a sense of the market and a knack to lead people at work and not possess to a certain degree the virtue of general justice.

A blatant disregard for the common economic good of their nation on the part of businessmen cannot be accepted as an normal element of a system which pretends to describe how a good economy works, recommend how economic forces should function and how an economic policy should be conducted.

Our main proposition for a new economic theory: the more businesspeople, managers and employees are ethical, are well versed in the ethical content of all business decisions and are actively seeking to perfect themselves in the virtues on the job, the more successful their personal businesses, the better working the economic system and the more prosperous a country.

This is all the more true when the government possesses the required wisdom to ensure that competition is fair and effectively prevents unfair practices to pay off in the short turn. And, in view of past failure of governments to display such wisdom, it is preferable that governments utilize a light rather than an heavy hand in that exercise.

Competition is not primarily what makes the free-market system work. Virtues are what make the system work.

Competition explains that a business will try to maintain its activities within boundaries defined by the market and the activities of other businesses. Competition – as demonstrated by Adam Smith - explains why a businessman reacts to business threats and opportunities for he is thus contributing to the good of the whole economy.

However, competition does not explain entrepreneurs.

Competition does not explain that human beings in business are not only able to display attitudes which are re-active, but they are also able to display attitudes which are pro-active. It does not explain why a businessman would start a company and struggles with it for years when the odds of succeeding at it are so poor.

If competition cannot explain entrepreneurs and entrepreneurship, it cannot explain the wider reality of the free-market system.

Conclusions for policy

Economics is a strange discipline where there are only generals and no soldiers. The soldiers belong to fields other than economics. Economists seem to have no compunction about deciding what businessmen should do, because businessmen are the soldiers economists play with on their theoretical economic game boards.

It often seems that economists, taken individually, are not primarily interested in assisting directly the economic growth of a nation. They would be in business if they did. All indications tend to show that economists, on a personal level, are mostly interested in articulating policy which will affect the economic sphere.

A sane economy depends on the ethics of businessmen. Economists have to accept that essential importance of moral forces in the economy and factor them into the policies of nations.

This stated, it is a sobering moment when we realize than some economists have little understanding of the truly ethical. John Maynard Keynes, on whose ideas Paul Samuelson tells us that "modern mainstream economics" have essentially been based since the end of WWII, was an arrogant, asocial individual who did not hesitate to utilize as one of his maxims of economic policy: "Foul is fair and fair is foul". Keynes' lack of temperance as an homosexual certainly impaired the balance of his intellect.

Economies will gain a great boost in vitality when the field of economics will have been subjected to an energetic scrubbing both of people and ideas.

Economists will have to learn humility and accept that they cannot design a master plan of economic development. Economists will have to learn that the main economic actors in a nation are its business leaders and employees, and that they necessarily operate in an environment where ethical decisions are quite common. They will have to learn that on the quality of these decisions rests the strength of an economy, and that these economic actors should be encouraged and supported to make decisions of the highest ethical quality.

Economists should consequently learn that their role is to be the servants of these business leaders and employees and to devise policies which encourage the proper formulating of these decisions and discourage the improper development of these decisions.

Politicians will also have to change and promote the ethical development of business leaders and workers and of future or potential business men and women. Political science will have to change and grant much more room for the exercise of religion, as well as return the family to its natural autonomy as both religion and family are widely recognized as the prime incubators of ethical formation.

Modern political science will have to reverse its attitude from seeing governments as "administrators of things" to re-instating them as "managers of people".

The notion that Providence is a divine force, the notion that the essential function of government is not to replace divine Providence have to be returned to popular culture. Then business leaders will be permitted to function in the proper frame of mind as they take economic risks and need feel they are protected by an entity greatly superior to the uncertain authority of political economists.

Business schools, especially business schools attached to Christian universities, should stop teaching "business ethics" as an elective course to be offered at the end of a curriculum when all other managerial principles of decision have already been taught. Instead of presenting ethics as an afterthought, Management and Marketing, the two academic subjects dealing with human beings, namely employees and customers, need to be revised in their philosophical and sociological assumptions, as they are usually dangerously antithetical to principles of morality, as we have shown the dangerous influence of behaviorists to be.

Churchmen

Churchmen in general should start studying seriously the social teachings of the Church and believe in their practical relevance.

They would find there that "Man is older than the state" (Leo XIII's encyclical Rerum Novarum) and that therefore, "it is wrong to withdraw from the individual and commit to a group what private enterprise and private industry can accomplish" (John XXIII's encyclical Mater et Magistra).

They would not be surprised to find that free markets, as a first principle of economics, come directly from the teachings of the Church. Free-markets are good things in themselves - not as a device to promote competition - but because they put the businessman in the position to grow in the virtues and gain his salvation.

Churchmen should also resign themselves to the fact that business people are the prime actors on the economic game board, not politicians. Churchmen should unlearn the manners of hushed civility that one can cultivate in the hallowed and musty halls of governmental offices and start preaching about the virtues of work and of business.

They should stop being satisfied with promoting the most worthy but sadly limited policy of a "preferential option for the poor" which they can play safely and ritualistically with political dignitaries without really engaging their own authority with their flock. They should realize that by limiting themselves to the marginalized in society, as far as economics is concerned, they render their own teaching and influence marginal in that society and in these matters, when they should be universal.

The poor as an individual should have our preference over the non-poor. However, the poor as a segment of the population cannot have precedence over the population as a whole. The good of the poor cannot take precedence over the common good as the latter already includes the good of the poor. To promote the interests of the poor as a class in the general economy ahead of the common good – the interest of all - will impair the design of a healthy economic policy and the good economic development of the nation as a whole and the betterment of each group composing that nation, including the poor, and will therefore be self-defeating.

Churchmen should, on the contrary, confront systematically and on a sustained basis the secular state which has limited to such an extent the range of authority of religious leaders to carry out their sacred duties to teach the true Gospel. They should fight also, the State's unrelenting fight to limit the importance of the sacred in the life of citizens. They should fight with all their strength policies which are the most destructive of human dignity, as their own leadership in these matters is such an important educational tool for business people to grow in the virtues.

They would find that, despite many warnings made by Pope Leo XIII against Socialist views in politics, a horrifying number of these views have in fact been reduced to practice and are well entrenched in modern politics.

Finally and most importantly, Churchmen should acknowledge the enormous significance and depth of their responsibility, in the economic sphere as in any other sphere, as pastors. Their flocks need to be instructed in the teachings of the Church, to be provided the sacraments and to be protected from the wolves outside and inside the Church. Christians deserve a vigorous program of moral and spiritual direction on the part of their pastors and are entitled to the full wine of the teachings of the Magisterium, not an amateurish concoction.

Business people need be presented with the teaching that the social body is a representation of the body of the Church and therefore that it cannot be made secular and fulfill at the same time and adequately its promises.

Further, they need to accept that the concept of "individualism" - which is attached to that of Capitalism - is quite opposed to the spirit of Christian solidarity.

Consequently "competition" should not be expected by Christians to bring about quasi magical effects. Social relationships need not be adversarial, neither between managers and employees as in the "class struggle", nor between businesses as in "competition".

Furthermore it has been shown that cooperation in civic activities between companies in the same line of business can be a strong element favoring economic development. William Ouchi, in the M-Form Corporation, showed examples of this for the city of Minneapolis.

W. Edwards Deming, the grandfather of Japanese quality circles arrived in Japan with the team put in place by General MacArthur. He taught Japanese quality manufacturing so well that today the top award in Japan for excellence in industry is called the "Deming Prize". Deming has strongly argued the case for corporations to establish strong ties of cooperation with a limited number of suppliers, instead of creating an atmosphere of cut-throat competition between a large number of possible suppliers.

Churchmen should understand that the choice is clear: either business people would have to learn the importance of morals in their professional activities, or governments will have to keep increasing the heavy burden of regulations. Burden that is not auspicious of the common good as it undermines economic prosperity for all citizens as well as political harmony. Churchmen therefore have the grave responsibility to delve in the principles and practical suggestions exposed in this book to evangelize the business world with solid Christian values and, on the other hand, stop concentrating on their present limited, ideological, self-defeating and naïve understanding of "social justice".

Antonism

We propose to call this new economic theory "antonism", after St. Antoninus, archbishop of Florence.

This Dominican friar of the fourteenth and fifteenth centuries was not interested in ecclesiastical honors, as he had to be threatened with excommunication by the pope to make him accept the charge of archbishop. He was not impressed by the political powers as he once kicked out of his Church Cosmo de Medici, the most powerful man in the republic and his principal benefactor. He loved the poor and designed and managed a program to help them which is operating to this day. When he died, his body, which can be seen in the convent of San Marco in Florence today, remained incorrupt.

Antoninus was also a great scholar, an influencing pastor, a pioneer historian, a lawyer, a philosopher and theologian. He commented on the teachings of his elder Dominican confrere, St Thomas Aquinas as they related to the economic sphere. His teachings did not consist in telling the folks of this rich city of merchants that they all should give their money to the poor and become monks. No. He told them how to be good merchants and, at the same time, how to follow the Lord by conducting their business according to sound moral principles.

This makes him a true theologian for our time of affluence when all Christians should be taught a proper Christian attitude towards things produced by our vibrant economy and towards their responsibilities at work on jobs which provide for much more than the bare essentials of life.

His advice to the businessmen of the time is based on the exercise of the virtues (47):

"The object of gain is that by its means man may provide for himself and others according to their state. The object of providing for himself and others is that they may be able to live virtuously"

and, expanding to a whole economy, could justify the success of an economy also only on the predominance of virtues:

"If the object of the trader is principally cupidity, which is the root of all evils, then certainly his trading will be evil. But that trade (as natural and necessary for the needs of human life) is, according to Aristotle, in itself praiseworthy which serves some good purpose - i.e. supplying the needs of human life. If, therefore, the trader seeks a moderate profit for the purpose of providing for himself and his family according to the condition becoming to the state of life, or to enable him to help the poor more generously, or even if he goes into commerce for the common good (lest, for example, the State should be without what its life requires), and consequently seeks a profit not as an ultimate end but merely as a wage of labor, he cannot in that case be condemned."

The fact that St. Antoninus is almost forgotten in our days speaks more of our day that of St. Antoninus. For, excepted for the immediate past, the renown of St. Antoninus was well established and much credit given him even by a famous non-Catholic British author, R.H. Tawney, as recently as 1926:

400

"The elements of the social theory of the Middle Ages were equally various, and equally changing. Even if the student confines himself to the body of doctrine which is definitely associated with religion, and takes as typical of it the Summae of the Schoolmen, he finds it in constant process of development. The economic teachings of St. Antoninus in the fifteenth century, for example, was far more complex and realistic than that of St. Thomas in the thirteenth, and down to the very end of the Middle Ages the best established and most characteristic parts of the system - for example, the theory of prices and of usury - so far from being stationary, were steadily modified and elaborated."

REFERENCES AND FURTHER READINGS

1. Aquinas, St. Thomas Summa Theologica Westminster, MD: Christian Classics, Inc. 1948. and,

Brennan, Robert Edward, OP, Thomistic Psychology - A Philosophic Analysis of the Nature of Man, New York: McMillan 1941 and

Maher, Michael, Psychology, New York: Magi Books Inc. 1982. and

Glenn, Paul J., A Tour of the Summa, London: Herder Book co., 1960.

2. Luthans, Fred, Organizational Behavior, New York: McGraw Hill 1981.

3. Maritain, Jacques, An Introduction to Philosophy, Westminster, MD: Christian Classics, Inc. 1989. and

Wallace, William, OP, The Elements of Philosophy, New York: Alba House, 1977. and

Kaplan, Abraham, The Conduct of Inquiry - Methodology for Behavioral Science, New York: Harper and Row, 1964.

4. Webber, Ross A., Morgan, Marilyn A. and Browne, Paul C., Management - Basic Elements of Managing Organizations, Homewood, Ill.: Richard Irwin, 1985.

5. Luthans, op. cit.

6. Brennan, op. cit.

7. Maritain, Jacques, Moral Philosophy - An Historical and Critical Survey of the Great Systems, New York: Scribner's, 1947.

8. Aumann, Jordan, OP, Spiritual Theology, Westminster, MD: Christian Classics, 1987.

9. Brennan, op. cit.

1O. Aquinas, op. cit. and

Pieper, Joseph, The Four Cardinal Virtues, Notre Dame, Ind.: University of Notre Dame Press, 1966. and

Dent, N.J.H., The Moral Psychology of the Virtues, Cambridge, England: Cambridge University Press, 1984.

11. Clark, J.W., S.J., Religion and the Moral Standards of American Businessmen, Cincinnati: South-Western Publishing, 1966 and

Baumhart, R., S.J., An Honest Profit, New York: Holt, Rinehart, 1968.

12. Orsini, Jean-François, A Research in Application of Cognitive Dissonance Theories to the Teaching of Business Ethics, Philadelphia: Doctoral Dissertation, University of Pennsylvania, Wharton School, 1984.

13. Finnis, John, Natural Law and Natural Rights, Oxford: Clarendon Press 198O.

14. Dunnette, Marvin D., "Mishmash, Mush, and Milestones in Organizational Psychology", APA Convention Proceedings, 1974.

15. Pope John Paul II, Encyclical On Human Work (Laborem Exercens), 1981.

16. Ozbekhan, Hasan, "Planning and Human Action", in Hierarchically Organized Systems in Theory and Practice, Paul A. Weiss (Ed.), New York: Haffner Publishing, 1971. and

Mintzberg, Henry, The Structuring of Organizations, Englewood Cliffs:

Prentice-Hall, Inc., 1979. and

Deming, W. Edward, Out of Crisis, Cambridge: MIT Press, 1982. and

Scherkenbach, William W., The Deming Route to Quality and Productivity, Washington, D.C. : Ceep Press, 1988. and

Pugh, D.S. ed., Organization Theory, New York: Penguin Books, 1971-1982.

17. Tarrant, John J., Drucker - The Man Who Invented the Corporate Society, New York, Warner Books, 1976. and

Drucker, Peter, Management - Tasks, Responsibilities, Practices, New York: Harper and Row, 1974.

18. Lorange, Peter, Corporate Planning - An Executive Viewpoint, Englewood-Cliffs, NJ: Prentice Hall, 1980.

19. Clausewitz, Carl von, On War, New York: Pelican Classics, 1968-79.

20. Ackoff, Russell L., Creating the Corporate Future, New York: John Wiley, 1981. and

Ansoff, H. Igor, ed., Business Strategy, New York: Penguin, 1969-1978.

21. Brusk, Edward C. and Chapman, John F., editors, New Decision-Making Tools for Managers- Mathematical Programming as an Aid in the Solving of Business Problems, New York: New American Library, 1963.

22. Clément, Marcel, Le Chef d'Entreprise, Paris: Nouvelles Editions Latines, 1956. and

Clément, Marcel, La Doctrine Sociale de l'Eglise est-elle Applicable?,

Paris: L'Escalade, 1985.

23. Grenier, Henri, OP, Thomistic Philosophy, Charlottetown, Canada: St. Dunstan University, 1950. four volumes.

24. Vitz, Paul C., Psychology as Religion- The Cult of Self Worship, Grand Rapids, Mich: Eerdmans Publishing, 1977. and

Vitz, Paul C., "Secular Personality Theories: A Critical Analysis" in Burke, Thomas J., editor, Man and Mind: A Christian Theory of Personality, Hillsdale College Press, 1987.

25. Drucker, op. cit.

26. Peters, Tom, In Search of Excellence, New York: Harper and Row, 1982 and

Peters, Tom, Thriving on Chaos, New York: Alfred A. Knopf, 1987.

27. Webber, op. cit.

28. Luthans, op. cit.

29. Orsini, Jean-François, "A Thomistic Theory of Values with Application in the Management Sciences", in Social Justice Review, Nov-Dec. 1983 and

Rokeach, Milton, The Nature of Human Values, New York: The Free Press, 1973. and

Laszlo, Erwin, The Systems View of the World, New York: George Braziller, 1972. and

Emery, E.F., ed., Systems Thinking, New York: Penguin, 1969-1978 and

Churchman, C. West, The Systems Approach, New York: Delta, 1968. and

Ackoff, Russell, L. and Emery, Fred E., On Purposeful Systems, Chicago: Aldine- Atherton, 1972. and

Boulding, Kenneth, The Image - Knowledge and Life in Society, Ann Arbor: University of Michigan Press, 1956. and

Orsini, Jean-François, "Artificial Intelligence: A Way Through the Strategic Planning Crisis?" in Long Range Planning, Great Britain: Pergamon Journals, Vo. 19, 1986.

3O. Luthans, op. cit

31. Skinner, B.F. Skinner, Beyond Freedom and Dignity, New York: Vintage Books, 1971.

32. Scott, William G. and Hart, David K., Organizational America, Boston: Houghton Mifflin, 1979.

33. Benis, Warren G. Organizational Development: Its Nature, Origins, and Prospects, Reading, Massachussetts: Addison-Wesley, 1969.

34. Frenh Wendell L. and Bell, Jr., Cecil H., Organization Development, Englewood Cliffs, NJ: Prentice Hall, 1978.

35. Benne, Kenneth, Bradford, Leland and Lipitt, Ronald, "The Laboratory Method" in Bradford, Leland, Gibb, Jack R., and Benne, Kenneth (eds.) T-Group Theory and Laboratory Method, New York: Wiley, 1964.

36. Benne et al., op. cit.

37. Greiner, Larry E. "Evolution and Revolution as Organizations Grow" in Harvard Business Review, July-Aug. 1972.

38. Staff of the Wall Street Journal, The Innovators - How Today's Inventors Shape Your Life Tomorrow, Princeton, NJ: Dow Jones Books, 1968. and

Mansfield, Edwin et al. Research and Innovation in the Modern Corporation, New York: W.W. Norton, 1971. and

Drucker, Peter, Innovation and Entrepreneuring - Practice and Principles, New York: Harper and Row, 1985. and

Gordon, William J.J., Synectics : The Development of Creative Capacity, New York: Collier, 1961.

39. Tannenbaum, Robert and Schmidt, Warren H., "How to Choose a Leadership Pattern" in Harvard Business Review, March-April 1958.

4O. Blake, Robert R. and Mouton, Jane S., The Managerial Grid, Houston: Gulf Publishing, 1964.

41. Grenier, op. cit.

42. Ratzinger, Joseph Cardinal in "Market Economy and Ethics", in Roos, Lothar (ed.) Church and Economy in Dialogue : A Symposium in Rome, Cologne: Ordo Socialis, 1990. and

Weber, Max The Protestant Ethics and the Spirit of Capitalism, New York: Scribner's, 1958 and

Tawney, R.H., Religion and the Rise of Capitalism, New York: Mentor Books, 1926. and

Fanfani, Amintore, Catholicism, Protestantism and Capitalism, New York: Sheed and Ward, 1935. and

Orsini, Jean-François, "The Sacrament of Confirmation and the Social Doctrine of the Church" in Social Justice Review, Nov-Dec 1990. and

Orsini, Jean-François, "The Achievements and Aftermaths of RERUM NOVARUM", in Social Justice Review, May-June 1991.

43. Drucker, Innovation and Entrepreneurship, op. cit. and

Pinchot, III, Gifford, Intrapreneuring, New York: Harper and Row, 1985.

44. Schéré, Jean Loup, Tolerance of Ambiguity as a Discriminating Variable Between Entrepreneurs and Managers, Doctoral Dissertation, University of Pennsylvania, Wharton School, 1981.

45. Ratzinger, Joseph Cardinal, "Church and Economy: Responsibility for the future of the world economy", in Communio, Notre Dame, Ind., special issue: Church and Economy, Fall 1986. and

Calvez, Jean-Yves, SJ and Perrin, Jacques, SJ, The Church and Social Justice, Chicago: Henry Regnery, 1961. and

Chafuen, Alejandro A., Christians for Freedom: Late-Scholastic Economics, San Francisco: Ignatius Press, 1986. and

Keller, Rev Edward A., C.S.C., Christianity and American Capitalism, Hinsdale, Ill: Heritage Foundation, published for the Council of Business and Professional Men of the Catholic Faith, 1984. and

Kristol, Irving, Two Cheers for Capitalism, New York: New American Library, 1978. and

Flannery, Austin, OP, (ed.) Vatican Council II - The Counciliar and Post Counciliar Documents, Northport, NY: Costello Publishing, 1975.

46. Smith, Adam, An Inquiry into the Nature and Causes of the Wealth of Nations, Indianapolis: Liberty Classics, 1976.

47. Jarrett, Bede, OP, St. Antonino and Medieval Economics, St. Louis, Mo: B. Herder, 1914. and

Jarrett, Bede, OP, Social Theories of the Middle Ages 1200-1500, London: Ernest Benn, 1926.

48. Tawney, R.H., opus cit.

INDEX

5-Need model, 53

ability, 74, 100, 103, 108, 212, 213, 244, 251, 275, 311, 318, 331, 332, 333, 356, 359, 373, 376

abnormal, 55, 56

aborted babies, 245

abortion, 36, 90, 166, 245, 314

abstract, 44, 85, 152, 354

academic, xix, xxii, 85, 90, 131, 152, 186, 215, 254, 372, 395

accounting, 80, 107, 114, 139, 322

achievement, vi, 54, 57, 348, 367

Ackoff, xxiii, 185, 186, 405, 407

act, xiii, 29, 33, 34, 35, 36, 44, 45, 60, 69, 74, 75, 91, 110, 122, 129, 152, 178, 208, 209, 210, 255, 257, 270, 280, 308, 309, 334, 335, 361, 368, 371, 375

action, v, 29, 34, 44, 45, 46, 48, 49, 73, 74, 75, 79, 80, 98, 154, 177, 184, 186, 192, 211, 212, 222, 223, 277, 294, 295, 305, 306, 310, 311, 312, 317, 318, 323, 361, 362, 364, 390

acts, 33, 34, 35, 36, 45, 60, 68, 71, 75, 76, 85, 103, 166, 219, 277, 358

Actual Grace, 67

Adam and Eve, 205

adrenaline, 33, 103

advertising, x, 107, 164, 175, 191, 192, 244, 246, 247, 248, 296

aesthetics, 46, 336

affiliation, 54, 57

Agathon, 72

Agency for International Development, 367

agent, 36, 45, 67, 310, 311, 317, 318

aggressiveness, 108, 147

Albigentianism, 110

Alexander the Great, 336

America, xxiii, 42, 309, 407

analysis, 85, 97, 105, 170, 196, 214, 217, 220, 227, 233, 274, 335

anger, 32, 33, 103, 205

Anhaueser-Busch, 186

Animal, 27

animal soul, 31, 32

anti-business, 85

anti-intellectualist, 152

anti-religious bias, 37

antonism, 399

apartheid, 79

appetite, 33, 35, 49, 50, 68, 77

Appetite for aggression, 77

Appetite of flesh, 77

Appetite of the intellect, 35

Aquinas, xviii, xix, 41, 46, 66, 88, 90, 95, 109, 110, 111, 209, 243, 334, 354, 376,

411

399, 403, 404
Argentina, 328
Aristotle, 30, 44, 45, 46, 47, 61, 76, 90, 110, 218, 400
Art, 38
astronomy, 39
Atheism, 233
attitude, xxi, 59, 80, 91, 93, 99, 101, 106, 112, 117, 128, 131, 162, 175, 179, 191, 200, 205, 207, 208, 215, 216, 228, 235, 236, 250, 267, 271, 274, 277, 278, 289, 313, 327, 330, 331, 342, 395, 399
Austrian, 364
authoritarian, 94, 195, 228, 347, 348
authoritarianism, 194
authority, ix, xx, 25, 26, 94, 95, 122, 143, 155, 156, 165, 166, 171, 174, 214, 218, 219, 221, 222, 223, 224, 225, 226, 227, 228, 229, 230, 264, 269, 270, 271, 326, 347, 348, 353, 354, 355, 358, 359, 360, 385, 388, 395, 396, 397
automation, 148
autonomy, 177, 228, 321, 395
babies, 243, 245, 246
badness, 85
bankruptcy, 116, 133, 258
beatific vision, 46, 47, 60
behavior, xi, xxi, 37, 39, 41, 42, 43, 44, 47, 48, 50, 51, 53, 55, 56, 58, 79, 84, 90, 100, 103, 133, 166, 168, 198, 228, 241, 282, 283, 290, 291, 297, 308, 310, 313, 314, 339, 366
behavioral, xvii, 37, 38, 39, 41, 43, 51, 52, 53, 54, 56, 137, 152, 308, 312
behavioral sciences, 37, 38, 39, 41, 43, 152
belief, 42
Bennis, Warren, 310
Bentham, Jeremy, 234
bias, 38, 56, 109, 115, 152, 170, 232, 241, 242, 245, 349
Bible, 40, 67, 72, 125, 143, 144, 145, 227, 373
Bishops, 363
Blake and Mouton, 350
Blame, 74
Blessed Sacrament, 66
blue-jeans, 341
boast, 248
body, xvii, xviii, 27, 30, 31, 33, 58, 64, 105, 108, 109, 110, 111, 139, 145, 155, 190, 203, 237, 238, 274, 299, 377, 397, 399, 401
boldness, 183, 184, 185, 186
boring, 105, 148, 356
boss, 156, 214, 217, 222, 224, 226, 227, 231, 260, 281, 348, 349
Brain, 31, 35
breakthrough inventions, 342
bribes, 168, 169
Buddhist, 284

buggy-whip, 99
bureaucracies, 175, 204
business, vii, viii, xi,
   xii, xiii, xv, xvii,
   xviii, xix, xxi, xxii,
   xxiii, 37, 42, 51, 55,
   60, 80, 81, 82, 83, 84,
   86, 97, 98, 99, 100,
   105, 106, 107, 114,
   116, 122, 124, 125,
   126, 127, 128, 129,
   130, 131, 132, 133,
   134, 135, 137, 138,
   139, 140, 141, 147,
   150, 151, 152, 153,
   156, 157, 159, 160,
   161, 162, 164, 166,
   167, 170, 171, 172,
   173, 174, 175, 176,
   179, 180, 182, 183,
   184, 185, 186, 187,
   189, 190, 191, 204,
   207, 218, 219, 220,
   225, 229, 230, 241,
   247, 250, 259, 267,
   268, 269, 270, 272,
   273, 282, 283, 285,
   294, 296, 298, 309,
   313, 314, 315, 316,
   318, 323, 325, 326,
   339, 343, 344, 354,
   355, 358, 359, 360,
   362, 363, 364, 365,
   366, 367, 368, 369,
   371, 372, 373, 375,
   378, 379, 383, 384,
   386, 388, 390, 391,
   392, 393, 394, 395,
   396, 398
Business Ethics, viii
business schools, xxii, 37,
   42, 86, 204, 207, 250,

395
Business units, 322
Calvinism, xii, 362
Cambridge, 337, 404
capabilities, 58, 100, 216,
   279, 300, 391
capital, 107, 116, 160, 372,
   373, 387, 388, 390, 391
Capitalism, xiii, 385, 386,
   387, 388, 391, 392,
   398, 408, 409
capitalist democracy, 162
Cardinal virtues, 72
career, 48, 100, 105, 256
cases, 54, 55, 83, 85, 87,
   97, 98, 169, 170, 180,
   184, 198, 213, 274,
   298, 340, 342, 365,
   387, 388
casuistry, 85
Catholic, xxiii, 164, 256,
   283, 400, 409
cause, xv, 69, 72, 81, 89,
   92, 98, 162, 164, 165,
   184, 218, 219, 313
caution, 212
CEO, 145, 174, 178, 179,
   181, 286, 300, 324, 327
challenges, 75, 309, 310,
   334
change, xi, 36, 43, 99,
   105, 116, 137, 138,
   151, 166, 173, 188,
   198, 205, 207, 223,
   245, 248, 283, 285,
   292, 293, 301, 302,
   303, 304, 305, 307,
   309, 310, 311, 314,
   316, 317, 318, 348,
   349, 366, 369, 371, 395
changes, 67, 99, 100, 105,
   113, 141, 147, 188,

200, 235, 285, 300,
302, 304, 307, 317
charity, 69, 70, 71, 78,
100, 101, 172, 236,
238, 239, 303, 357
chastity, 110, 377
chemistry, 39
children, 90, 378
choices, v, 31, 34, 35, 47,
48, 59, 81, 129, 210,
262, 269, 334
Christ, vi, 38, 47, 48, 62,
63, 64, 65, 66, 101,
104, 120, 121, 207,
228, 238, 239, 277
Christian, v, vi, vii, viii,
ix, xi, xviii, xix,
xxi, xxii, xxiii, 25,
29, 30, 37, 39, 43, 46,
47, 48, 55, 59, 60, 61,
62, 71, 72, 78, 79, 86,
89, 91, 95, 100, 101,
103, 104, 116, 119,
120, 121, 122, 158,
159, 160, 161, 163,
168, 172, 174, 186,
188, 198, 199, 213,
219, 225, 226, 227,
228, 232, 235, 236,
239, 241, 247, 248,
250, 256, 257, 258,
260, 261, 271, 280,
281, 282, 283, 357,
362, 379, 383, 384,
385, 395, 398, 399,
403, 404, 406
Christian perfection, 71
Christianity, xiii, 61, 233,
365, 409
Church, xiii, xv, xxii,
xxiii, 70, 72, 84, 96,
97, 116, 171, 172, 184,

218, 227, 260, 281,
366, 376, 386, 388,
396, 397, 399, 408, 409
Churchmen, xiii, 396, 397
circumspection, 212
civilization, 60
clarification, 311, 312
class struggle, 89, 398
Clausewitz, Carl von, 183, 184,
405
Clement, Marcel, 218, 220
clients, 56, 114, 121, 240
Cognitive psychologists, 208
collaboration, 92, 197, 323
Commandments, 47, 61
commerce, 400
common sense, xv, 40, 72,
152, 153
communications, 84, 150,
155, 208, 240, 286,
296, 301, 320, 322,
324, 342, 343
Communism, 38, 94, 206,
385
Communists, 156
commutative, 92, 98, 164,
389, 390
Commutative Justice, 92
competence,, 54
competent, 42, 271, 326
competition, xxi, 57, 98,
131, 138, 146, 173,
182, 189, 190, 270,
359, 364, 370, 386,
388, 390, 393, 396, 398
competitive, 80
computer, 206, 208, 270,
300, 305, 343, 368
Comte, Auguste, 37
concupiscence, 50
confessors, 85
conflict reduction, 152

conflicts, x, 114, 232, 264, 265, 266, 267, 268, 269, 270, 271, 362, 372
conglomerate, 176, 323
conscience, 83, 174, 187
consensus, 51, 56, 185
consent, 211
constraint, 176
consultant, 152, 186
Contingency Theory of Management, 304
contracts, 82, 164, 219, 220, 283, 359
contractual agreements, 93
control, 26, 33, 108, 109, 125, 129, 142, 144, 147, 148, 149, 155, 160, 176, 189, 190, 191, 193, 198, 224, 232, 236, 240, 259, 282, 294, 307, 322, 326, 333, 359, 381
controls, 34, 49, 128, 129, 186, 188, 189, 191, 192, 193, 196, 197, 198, 199, 200
co-optation, 156
coordination, 148, 326
core activity, 125, 138
corporation, 99, 106, 107, 112, 113, 114, 115, 128, 146, 147, 151, 152, 153, 162, 163, 170, 180, 188, 190, 192, 194, 196, 199, 214, 215, 216, 218, 229, 257, 258, 259, 260, 283, 284, 286, 297, 300, 301, 313, 315, 320, 322, 324, 326, 327, 336, 337, 340, 343, 353, 354,

355, 356, 370, 378
corrections, 190, 195
Corsican, 183
cortisone, 328, 329, 331
cost, 81, 107, 176, 193, 216, 283
counsel, 67, 68, 211, 213, 377
courage, 75, 78, 82, 101, 102, 103, 104, 105, 106, 107, 108, 135, 138, 149, 183, 191, 192, 197, 251, 269, 333, 341, 356, 360
courageous, 56, 80, 102, 103, 105, 106, 145, 191, 281, 305, 332, 338, 378
Course of action, 29, 34
Coward, 76
cowardice, 55
creation, 36, 47, 62, 65, 91, 117, 120, 132, 133, 134, 170, 205, 226, 242
creative, xx, 58, 135, 336, 338, 339
creativity, 54, 57, 320
Creator, 47, 49
Creature, 28
credit, xxiii, 74, 127, 265, 266, 267, 269, 270, 400
crime, 54
Crusades, 186
cultural imperialism, 42
culture, xxii, 56, 60, 89, 90, 101, 109, 170, 171, 173, 222, 284, 286, 300, 310, 312, 333, 366, 375, 377, 395
cupidity, 400
curiosity, 111, 112, 249

customers, 55, 59, 97, 114, 125, 126, 127, 128, 129, 130, 131, 132, 134, 135, 137, 138, 141, 161, 162, 189, 190, 247, 265, 266, 267, 270, 292, 369, 390, 395
cut-throat tactics, 173
cynicism, 392
damnation, 228, 252
dangerous, xxiii, 60, 105, 110, 115, 135, 151, 175, 176, 215, 225, 315, 356, 395
Das Kapital, 386
data, 38, 40, 100, 135, 223, 235, 305, 322, 347
deal, 51, 56, 59, 81, 125, 126, 127, 166, 168, 177, 201, 202, 203, 240, 293, 295, 297, 307
death, xx, 31, 71, 101, 102, 141, 156, 318
Decalogue, 47
Decentralization, x, 262
decision, xv, xvii, xx, 29, 42, 48, 49, 56, 57, 60, 80, 82, 83, 86, 107, 113, 114, 129, 133, 143, 151, 152, 153, 157, 163, 168, 190, 195, 196, 201, 202, 203, 204, 205, 206, 207, 208, 209, 210, 211, 213, 214, 216, 217, 219, 225, 259, 268, 269, 270, 271, 273, 277, 281, 306, 312, 321, 334, 335, 341, 349, 367, 368, 378, 392, 394, 395

Decision Sciences, 206
decision-making, 80, 203, 206, 208, 209, 210, 217
delegate, 321, 324, 336
deliberation, 80, 211
Deming, W. Edward, 398
democracies, 168, 169
deontological, 90
Deontology, 90
design, 32, 33, 58, 125, 140, 143, 165, 166, 185, 186, 189, 190, 192, 196, 197, 198, 200, 245, 264, 294, 295, 325, 341, 389, 394, 397
desire, 32, 35, 49, 50, 70, 71, 81, 83, 100, 102, 280, 282, 326, 330, 371, 391
despair, 70, 199
devil, 103
dictatorship of the proletariat, 94
dignity, xviii, 87, 89, 97, 100, 122, 154, 155, 156, 158, 161, 196, 205, 219, 227, 261, 309, 318, 335, 366, 383, 387, 397
discounts, 114
disequilibrium, 364
disobedience, 205
disorganization,, 143
disposition, 73, 91, 138, 213, 219, 366
distributive, 92, 93, 94, 95, 98, 389, 390
distributive justice, 92, 94, 98
Divine Providence, 121, 133, 138, 230, 277, 379
Divini Redemptoris, 172
division of labor, 117

docile, 68
docility, 212, 227
doctrine, 67, 85, 86, 164,
    226, 256, 312, 401
Dodge, 189
domain of reference, 297, 298
Dominican, xxiii, 399
drink, 80, 109, 111, 361
Drucker, Peter, xvii, 156,
    157, 159, 176, 250,
    255, 256, 405
drudgery, 120
drug cartels, 166
drug problem, 170
Durkheim, Emile, 37
duty, xviii, xix, 60, 61,
    90, 93, 97
dynamic, 206, 285, 375,
    376
eagerness, 147, 274, 316
earth, 28, 29, 64, 70, 122,
    226, 228, 261
Ease, 73
Ecclesiasticus, 212
ecologists, 164
economic, xiii, xv, xx,
    xxi, 43, 126, 133, 139,
    157, 165, 170, 171,
    172, 173, 174, 196,
    203, 219, 234, 247,
    277, 278, 284, 325,
    326, 327, 340, 363,
    364, 366, 373, 377,
    385, 386, 387, 388,
    389, 390, 391, 392,
    394, 395, 396, 397,
    398, 399, 401
economics, 37, 172, 327,
    387, 388, 394, 396
economy, xv, xviii, xx,
    66, 116, 117, 132, 136,
    150, 197, 219, 247,
    344, 364, 365, 369,
    380, 389, 391, 392,
    393, 394, 397, 399,
    400, 409
economy of grace, 66
ecstatic, 263
education, 79, 134, 151,
    159, 262, 316
effective, xv, 42, 43, 50,
    74, 92, 96, 100, 104,
    122, 139, 141, 174,
    182, 195, 199, 206,
    216, 222, 223, 245,
    259, 268, 274, 305,
    306, 308, 310, 343,
    347, 348, 351, 355,
    362, 370, 384, 385, 386
effectiveness, 43, 131, 157,
    193, 200, 263, 271,
    312, 344, 370
efficiency, xiii, 192, 263,
    318, 325, 344, 370, 371
efficient, 40, 80, 96, 169,
    195, 218, 219, 278,
    293, 295, 306, 325, 370
efficient cause, 218
effort, xxi, 74, 91, 101,
    104, 105, 106, 107,
    113, 121, 135, 136,
    137, 151, 154, 174,
    178, 180, 195, 196,
    197, 199, 200, 216,
    222, 223, 226, 238,
    240, 257, 260, 270,
    274, 280, 308, 310,
    317, 318, 326, 330,
    334, 336, 338, 339,
    340, 342, 343, 358,
    359, 366, 390
elective course, 395
elitist, 179
emotional, 228, 273, 278,

311
Emotionalism, 34
empathy, 100
empire building, 114, 215
employee, xv, 26, 48, 59,
   97, 122, 134, 135, 138,
   150, 157, 158, 159,
   160, 166, 170, 181,
   182, 185, 188, 197,
   199, 200, 224, 225,
   240, 241, 248, 258,
   259, 260, 263, 272,
   279, 280, 281, 283,
   297, 300, 306, 307,
   324, 327, 345, 361,
   363, 369, 370, 383,
   384, 385
Employee participation, 157
employees, xv, xx, xxiii,
   25, 26, 54, 97, 98,
   100, 104, 105, 106,
   107, 121, 132, 134,
   135, 137, 138, 141,
   144, 147, 148, 149,
   151, 153, 156, 157,
   158, 159, 160, 161,
   163, 165, 172, 174,
   178, 179, 180, 181,
   182, 184, 185, 187,
   188, 196, 197, 198,
   199, 200, 201, 214,215,
   224, 225, 227, 229,
   230, 231, 232, 240,
   241, 248, 250, 253,
   254, 256, 257, 258,
   259, 260, 261, 262,
   263, 264, 272, 273,
   279, 280, 282, 283,
   284, 286, 300, 301,
   304, 307, 309, 313,
   317, 318, 323, 324,
   326, 327, 339, 344,
   353, 355, 356, 357,
   358, 361, 369, 373,
   378, 390, 392, 394,
   395, 398
Employees Stock Ownership Plans,
   258
encouragement, 48
end, v, xvii, xxi, 36,
   44, 45, 46, 47, 48, 49,
   52, 59, 60, 63, 69, 70,
   72, 80, 122, 128, 139,
   182, 186, 192, 210,
   213, 218, 252, 254,
   268, 289, 294, 295,
   309, 328, 332, 348,
   375, 384, 387, 394,
   395, 400, 401
ends, 222, 356
endurance, 102
energy, 68
engineering, 114, 115, 141,
   214, 267, 301, 335, 338
engineering department, 114
enjoyment, 46, 210, 217
entertainment, 46, 112
enthusiasm, 149, 263
entrepreneurial, xii, xiii,
   135, 320, 325, 364,
   366, 378, 379, 380
entrepreneurs, xii, xiii,
   xxi, 325, 327, 364,
   365, 366, 367, 368,
   369, 370, 371, 373,
   375, 376, 377, 378,
   379, 380, 391, 393
Entrepreneurship, 363, 408
envious, 380
environment, 89, 99, 114,
   117, 125, 137, 138,
   141, 143, 146, 147,
   153, 163, 164, 189,
   240, 258, 261, 270,

358, 394
epistemology, 207, 208
EPS, 175
equilibrium, 364
equipment, 138, 211
ERG model, 51, 52, 53, 54
ESOPs, x, 258, 259, 260
Esteem, 52
eternal, 64, 65, 66, 116,
   155, 225, 227, 228,
   261, 316
ethics, x, xii, xv, xvii,
   41, 42, 43, 44, 45, 60,
   61, 62, 84, 85, 86, 90,
   91, 122, 164, 166, 167,
   168, 225, 230, 246,
   282, 283, 286, 291,
   313, 314, 334, 336,
   362, 385, 386, 388,
   394, 395
eudaimonia, 46
Europe, 42
evangelical counsels, 377
evangelization, 184, 316
evil, xi, 35, 36, 62, 91,
   98, 102, 110, 163, 166,
   205, 206, 213, 222,
   237, 251, 303, 306,
   313, 315, 400
Evil acts, 35
excommunication, 399
existence, 28, 40, 41, 44,
   51, 54, 70, 76, 78, 86,
   109, 110, 145, 154,
   186, 228, 251, 258,
   271, 303, 389
Exodus, 145
expense, 328
experience, xx, xxi, 37, 38,
   40, 82, 102, 103, 156,
   233, 234, 265, 270,
   273, 275, 279, 296,

315, 360, 371, 372,
   376, 378
exploited, 56
faith, 37, 47, 67, 69, 70,
   71, 78, 84, 199, 236,
   241, 249, 250, 281,
   303, 305, 315, 316,
   357, 363, 386, 409
Fall, 91, 120, 226, 303,
   409
family, xxi, 112, 241, 249,
   266, 289, 315, 378,
   395, 400
Father, 30, 63, 64, 68, 78,
   104
fatigue, 105
fear, 32, 33, 67, 102,
   108, 151, 205, 251,
   272, 282, 325, 374,
   378, 379, 380
Fear of the Lord, 67, 68
Fiedler, Fred, 346, 347
final cause, 218
finance, 107, 114, 115,
   139, 315
financing, 81, 82, 125, 127
Finnis, John, 92
firmness, 101
First principles, 77
Fleming, 333
flexibility, 137, 138, 160,
   197, 235, 255, 295,
   325, 332, 356
Florence, 399
food, 32, 33, 34, 49, 50,
   52, 53, 109, 110, 194,
   195, 295, 309
Ford, 37, 165, 188, 189,
   190, 195, 342
Ford foundation, 37
Foreign Corrupt Practice Act, 168
foresight, 212, 213

419

formal cause, 218
formalization, 320
fortitude, 68, 72, 77, 78
founder, 140, 141, 145,
    174, 320
Free act, 35
free will, 48, 49
freedom, xx, 30, 35, 66,
    83, 86, 215, 255, 261,
    309, 335, 348, 349,
    387, 390
Freedom of choice, 30
Freedom of will, 66
free-market, xx, 386, 390,
    393
French, 183, 218, 357
Freud, Sigmund, 37, 204, 233,
    234
friendship, 50, 61, 66, 70,
    234
full employment, 133, 134
function, vii, ix, xvii,
    26, 30, 31, 32, 51, 60,
    67, 68, 127, 128, 129,
    130, 131, 132, 133,
    137, 138, 141, 144,
    145, 147, 156, 157,
    158, 159, 160, 179,
    180, 186, 187, 192,
    194, 195, 201, 214,
    222, 224, 225, 226,
    237, 243, 247, 257,
    260, 262, 272, 285,
    286, 306, 328, 336,
    343, 344, 349, 354,
    355, 366, 380, 385,
    392, 395
functional departments, 114,
    131, 139, 141, 321
gain, xx, xxii, 37, 46,
    116, 122, 188, 195,
    225, 231, 236, 238,

239, 249, 252, 262,
    282, 289, 359, 361,
    366, 371, 387, 390,
    394, 396, 400
Garbage Can, 204
generalists, 368
generosity, 277, 376
geology, 39
Germans, 183, 291, 328,
    386
Getty, J. Paul, 378
Gift of God, 69
gifts, 67, 68, 69, 303
Gifts of the Holy Spirit, 67
glory, 64
GM, 158, 176, 177, 189
Gnosticism, 236, 241
goals, x, xvii, xx, 46,
    222, 267, 268, 269,
    270, 271, 311, 312,
    330, 348, 352, 355
God, vi, ix, xix, xxi,
    29, 30, 36, 40, 41, 46,
    47, 49, 59, 60, 61, 62,
    63, 64, 65, 66, 67, 68,
    69, 70, 71, 72, 78, 84,
    87, 96, 108, 111, 117,
    121, 122, 133, 143,
    144, 165, 198, 213,
    222, 225, 227, 228,
    230, 234, 237, 239,
    242, 250, 255, 271,
    277, 278, 283, 288,
    289, 291, 293, 295,
    303, 305, 308, 314,
    326, 327, 357, 362,
    366, 374, 379, 380,
    381, 383, 384
good, viii, xix, xxii, 26,
    34, 35, 36, 38, 39, 42,
    43, 44, 45, 46, 47, 48,
    49, 57, 61, 64, 66, 69,

70, 76, 79, 81, 82, 84, 85, 88, 90, 91, 92, 93, 94, 96, 97, 98, 99, 101, 102, 105, 106, 110, 113, 134, 136, 156, 162, 163, 170, 172, 173, 179, 188, 189, 192, 197, 198, 200, 204, 206, 208, 209, 210, 213, 222, 223, 224, 225, 226, 234, 237, 239, 245, 253, 258, 262, 264, 265, 266, 267, 269, 271, 274, 276, 277, 286, 289, 291, 293, 295, 299, 302, 303, 304, 305, 308, 321, 324, 325, 330, 331, 332, 341, 343, 345, 346, 347, 351, 352, 353, 354, 356, 357, 358, 359, 360, 362, 366, 369, 373, 374, 378, 379, 384, 387, 388, 389, 391, 392, 393, 396, 399, 400

goodness, 49, 69, 70, 85, 209, 372

Gordian knot, 336

Gospel, 366

government, xviii, 87, 88, 94, 95, 96, 129, 149, 165, 168, 169, 171, 173, 175, 176, 283, 298, 326, 328, 329, 331, 344, 388, 389, 391, 393, 395

grace, 47, 63, 64, 65, 66, 67, 71, 73, 227, 261, 295, 303, 366

greed, 95, 151, 293

greedy, 50, 293, 362, 380

Greek, 30, 46, 47, 178

Greiner, Larry, 319, 323

growth, xi, 31, 51, 54, 59, 62, 63, 64, 70, 71, 73, 117, 120, 131, 132, 135, 138, 146, 149, 150, 159, 175, 188, 227, 318, 319, 320, 323, 380, 394

guild, 172

Gulag, 249

habit, 73, 74, 75, 76, 83, 85, 126, 137, 152, 184, 188, 228, 239, 243, 256, 257, 266, 277, 302, 303, 321, 325, 326, 376

handicapped, 90, 180, 238

happiness, xviii, xix, 46, 47, 60, 62, 374

Hard work, 104

harmonious, 227, 238, 255, 319, 351

health, 36, 43, 46, 53, 104, 164, 288

heresy, 110

hierarchical, xxiii, 52, 53, 141, 150, 154, 157, 175, 181, 222, 223, 226

hierarchical levels, 141, 154, 181, 182

hiring, 132, 133, 150, 211, 272, 273, 276, 280, 281, 282

Hitler, Adolph, 309

holiness, 63, 64, 120, 159

holy, 64, 67, 88

Holy Father, 28

Holy Grail, 186

Holy Spirit, 30, 64, 67, 69, 78

homosexuals, 84, 314
honesty, 97, 287, 288, 289, 291
honor, 64, 65, 93, 108
Hope, 69, 70, 71
Housework, 118
Human soul, 31
human actions, 44, 46
Human acts, 34
human being, 29, 31, 32, 34, 35, 39, 42, 52, 87, 116, 117, 135, 145, 156, 158, 159, 165, 178, 180, 227, 239, 243, 252, 255
human beings, xi, xv, 29, 56, 60, 63, 72, 86, 87, 88, 89, 96, 97, 116, 117, 126, 134, 145, 153, 154, 155, 156, 158, 159, 161, 165, 167, 176, 205, 219, 226, 227, 234, 236, 237, 239, 240, 242, 252, 254, 271, 285, 286, 301, 302, 304, 309, 393, 395
human engineering, 41
human nature, 29, 36, 43, 49, 50, 52, 59, 84, 111, 145
human person, 29
human rights, 87
Human soul, 31
Human species, 73
humanists, 79, 284
Humanity, 28
humility, 198, 328, 333, 394
hunger, 46, 49, 361
hypocrites, 284
ideas, xx, xxi, xxii, xxiii, 31, 37, 38, 60,

101, 113, 156, 170, 183, 205, 235, 240, 247, 256, 276, 314, 345, 348, 349, 352, 394
ignorance, 48
illuminative, 63
Image of God, 29
imagination, 75, 99, 191, 237, 280, 368
immaturity, 86
immortal, 31, 154, 155, 158, 161, 165
immortal souls, 154, 165
impartial, xx, 195, 326
implementation, 82, 100, 201, 202, 203, 255, 269, 324
Inc. Magazine, 378
Incarnation, 64, 252
incentive, 59, 195, 199, 253, 260
incentive system, 59
income, 94, 95, 128
inconsistency, 366
independence, 127, 131, 322, 326
in-depth testing, 137
indifference, 249
individual, xviii, xix, xx, xxi, xxii, 29, 32, 34, 43, 52, 56, 57, 58, 66, 68, 74, 85, 90, 91, 92, 93, 95, 97, 106, 107, 110, 128, 133, 136, 144, 145, 150, 160, 161, 171, 180, 185, 186, 187, 189, 200, 205, 219, 223, 226, 227, 229, 236, 239, 240, 245, 255, 262, 264, 266, 274, 276, 280, 285, 286, 291, 297, 298, 299, 312,

317, 343, 370, 379,
387, 394, 396
industrial psychologists, 104
industry, 80, 82, 83, 98,
160, 164, 174, 176,
177, 247, 259, 267,
289, 328, 332, 341,
342, 387, 390, 396, 398
inertia, 150, 182, 203, 204,
369
influence, 156, 168, 170,
172, 208, 216, 221,
223, 240, 286, 395, 396
information, 80, 98, 100,
115, 132, 164, 193,
196, 204, 208, 231,
232, 233, 242, 243,
244, 245, 249, 261,
262, 270, 271, 272,
278, 296, 302, 323,
324, 326, 367
infused virtues, 68, 69
initiative, 28, 105, 113,
149, 160, 177, 181,
182, 184, 248, 256, 363
Injustice, 33
injustices, 62, 168, 169,
170, 197, 298
Innocent life, 36
innovation, xii, 99, 137,
138, 328, 337, 339,
340, 341, 342, 343,
370, 378
innovative, 106, 137, 323,
325, 328, 335, 336,
338, 339, 340, 343,
344, 378
Instinct, 32
instinctive, 84, 196
institutionalization, 106
integrity, 109, 171, 180,
228, 289, 292

intellect, 30, 31, 32, 33,
35, 49, 63, 67, 68, 70,
71, 76, 77, 80, 87,
108, 109, 116, 159,
187, 209, 210, 211,
227, 261, 279, 298,
302, 309, 394
intellectual, xx, 31, 39, 50,
68, 71, 73, 74, 75, 76,
78, 82, 83, 105, 112,
179, 180, 204, 205,
206, 212, 213, 223,
224, 234, 237, 243,
253, 257, 289, 292,
293, 295, 302, 304,
308, 332, 334, 358,
359, 360
Intellectual habit, 73
Intellectual powers, 76
Intellectual virtues, 76
intelligence, 180, 212, 222,
255, 259, 275, 277
intelligent, 70, 117, 178,
184, 237, 255, 345
intemperate, 114, 369
intention, 36, 84, 98, 104,
210, 293, 312, 387
Intention of the agent, 36
interact, xxi, 109, 147,
257, 280, 285
interview, 274, 275
intuition, 67, 190, 270,
272, 330, 368
inventor, 82, 330, 331,
332, 333, 339, 340, 369
investor, 127
invisible hand, 386, 387
irony, 104, 392
Isaiah, 67
Japan, 43, 297, 398
Japanese, ix, xxi, 43, 152,
182, 201, 202, 203,

284, 398
jeans, 56, 341
Jesse, 67
Jewish, 283
Jews, xv, 72, 156
job, xv, 25, 26, 40, 43,
  54, 59, 74, 81, 87,
  100, 106, 112, 113,
  121, 129, 133, 134,
  135, 146, 152, 157,
  166, 170, 203, 241,
  246, 250, 254, 262,
  272, 275, 276, 277,
  278, 279, 280, 281,
  282, 284, 288, 292,
  297, 298, 300, 301,
  316, 327, 344, 352,
  357, 358, 384, 393
job-creating, 133
jobless, 165
John Paul II, Pope, 28, 29, 117
John XXIII, Pope, 383, 384,
  396
Judas, 290
judge, 67, 68, 168, 213,
  293
judgment, 79, 80, 81, 85,
  211, 213, 392
Judgment Day, 30
Jupiter, 337
Just, 76
justice, xiii, xix, 72, 76,
  78, 79, 84, 87, 88, 90,
  91, 92, 93, 94, 95, 97,
  98, 99, 100, 102, 121,
  134, 138, 149, 163,
  164, 167, 168, 169,
  170, 172, 197, 227,
  230, 235, 306, 326,
  332, 356, 360, 362,
  384, 389, 390, 391, 392
Kant, Immanuel, 60, 61, 90,

234
Keynes, John Maynard, 394
Kingdom, 66, 91, 335, 366
knowledge, xxi, 38, 39, 41,
  64, 67, 82, 97, 111,
  126, 179, 212, 222,
  242, 244, 263, 264,
  293, 300, 374
Kohlberg, Lawrence, 79
Koreans, xiii, 372
Krok, 369
labor, xviii, 116, 117,
  160, 172, 173, 174,
  365, 380, 388, 400
Laborem Exercens, 28, 29
laissez-faire, 386
Land, 369
law, xviii, 61, 82, 87,
  88, 115, 167, 219, 228,
  235, 359
laziness, 104, 200, 205,
  251, 253, 254, 257, 374
LBO, 175
leader, xii, 94, 140, 143,
  153, 184, 258, 263,
  314, 318, 321, 345,
  346, 347, 348, 353,
  355, 356, 357, 358,
  359, 360, 361, 363,
  369, 397
leadership, 27, 130, 149,
  316, 320, 345, 346,
  347, 348, 349, 350,
  352, 353, 355, 356,
  357, 358, 359, 360,
  361, 389, 397, 408
Legal Justice, 92
legitimacy, 156, 166
Leo XIII, Pope, 396, 397
Levi's, 341
liberalism, 376
liberality, 376, 377

424

liberals, 222, 376
life, xii, xiii, xviii,
  xix, xxi, xxii, 34, 36,
  38, 47, 51, 54, 56, 59,
  62, 63, 64, 65, 66, 67,
  70, 72, 89, 92, 102,
  107, 112, 120, 129,
  138, 156, 188, 219,
  225, 229, 236, 241,
  249, 250, 254, 255,
  261, 265, 276, 278,
  288, 289, 292, 293,
  294, 295, 296, 298,
  305, 307, 326, 330,
  331, 342, 357, 361,
  363, 364, 366, 372,
  375, 377, 378, 379,
  383, 384, 397, 399, 400
lifestyle, 189
Light bulbs, 343
line, 27, 28, 52, 104, 105,
  124, 125, 126, 143,
  144, 149, 150, 179,
  184, 188, 194, 209,
  214, 215, 217, 218,
  235, 267, 273, 294,
  321, 323, 327, 340,
  343, 348, 355, 398
liturgy, 84
Lobbyists, 169
Lord, xxi, 47, 63, 67, 68,
  91, 102, 111, 120, 207,
  248, 250, 291, 293,
  358, 384, 399
love, xix, xxi, 30, 35,
  44, 47, 49, 50, 52, 53,
  54, 56, 61, 62, 63, 65,
  66, 68, 69, 70, 71, 72,
  95, 100, 102, 108, 230,
  234, 238, 239, 251,
  263, 283, 289, 293,
  316, 331

loyalty, 97, 149, 150, 291
lust, 50
Luthans, Fred, 275, 308, 309
MacArthur, General, 398
MacDonald, 297, 369
Mafia, 166
Magisterium, 397
Magnanimity, 106
Magnificence, 107
malfeasance, 97, 98
malice, 48
Mammon, xxi, 143
man, xviii, xix, xxii,
  28, 29, 30, 32, 33, 34,
  39, 40, 41, 44, 46, 47,
  69, 73, 76, 78, 86, 88,
  90, 102, 104, 107, 109,
  110, 115, 117, 122,
  134, 155, 162, 183,
  184, 204, 212, 308,
  309, 312, 325, 326,
  356, 369, 373, 374,
  383, 384, 387, 390,
  399, 400
management, xi, xii, xv,
  xvii, xviii, xix, xxii,
  25, 26, 37, 38, 39, 42,
  44, 51, 59, 72, 80, 98,
  99, 104, 106, 114, 119,
  122, 134, 135, 141,
  143, 148, 149, 150,
  152, 156, 159, 160,
  163, 172, 173, 174,
  175, 183, 184, 187,
  188, 191, 194, 195,
  201, 202, 203, 204,
  205, 206, 207, 208,
  214, 215, 216, 217,
  225, 226, 229, 230,
  231, 232, 251, 255,
  256, 258, 259, 263,
  264, 272, 280, 284,

286, 300, 301, 304,
307, 308, 309, 310,
313, 314, 315, 320,
321, 322, 324, 325,
326, 327, 328, 336,
339, 343, 344, 350,
353, 363, 365, 378, 385
manager, x, xv, 25, 26,
37, 39, 42, 48, 97, 98,
100, 105, 106, 112,
113, 114, 122, 135,
144, 145, 165, 174,
175, 177, 178, 188,
190, 191, 193, 200,
209, 210, 211, 214,
215, 217, 219, 227,
229, 240, 241, 248,
255, 257, 260, 261,
262, 263, 269, 270,
272, 274, 278, 279,
280, 281, 282, 320,
348, 355, 356, 383,
384, 385
managerial grid., 350
managerial style, 177, 178, 286
managers, xv, xx, xxiii,
25, 26, 37, 42, 43, 51,
59, 72, 97, 98, 106,
107, 112, 113, 122,
131, 132, 134, 138,
143, 144, 146, 147,
148, 149, 150, 151,
152, 153, 156, 157,
158, 159, 176, 178,
179, 182, 185, 186,
187, 188, 189, 193,
199, 204, 214, 217,
218, 231, 240,242, 257,
261, 262, 264, 271,
273, 276, 278, 280,
281, 282, 283, 284,
304, 307, 313, 318,

320, 321, 322, 323,
325, 326, 327, 339,
343, 344, 355, 366,
367, 378, 380, 385,
387, 392, 395, 398
Manichean, 110
manufacturing, 82, 114, 115
market, 137, 141, 160,
173, 186, 267, 284,
320, 341
market place, 99, 101
market segment, 59
marketing, 58, 82, 114,
115, 127, 128, 129,
130, 131, 133, 139,
140, 141, 146, 157,
164, 189, 190, 191,
195, 202, 214, 216,
217, 240, 244, 275,
279, 295, 296, 299,
341, 343, 369, 389
martyrdom, 101
Marx, Karl, 386
Marxist, 230, 259, 260, 371
Mary, 65, 366
Maslow, Abraham, 233, 255,
256
Mater et Magistra, 383, 384
material cause, 218, 219
materialism, 38
materialistic, 157, 158, 283,
299, 367, 377
mathematical, 27, 206, 207,
208, 275
Mathematician, 76
McGregor, Douglas, 250, 255
means, x, xvii, 33, 36,
46, 54, 59, 60, 70, 80,
81, 85, 88, 94, 101,
106, 107, 109, 113,
121, 122, 128, 129,
131, 132, 133, 134,

135, 152, 157, 161,
162, 166, 171, 172,
180, 182, 196, 209,
210, 211, 217, 220,
226, 246, 247, 254,
255, 257, 258, 259,
260, 261, 264, 268,
269, 270, 271, 276,
287, 289, 294, 306,
311, 314, 317, 330,
331, 332, 334, 339,
343, 355, 356, 357,
358, 370, 371, 385,
386, 400
Measuring work, 27
media, 89, 170, 223, 313
mediating organizations, 171
mediatrix, 65
Medici, 399
Meekness, 103
memory, 30, 76, 212
mental, 36, 43, 183, 231,
 237, 238, 241
merchants, 387, 399
Merck, 328, 331
method, xx, 27, 38, 40,
 58, 85, 86, 152, 179,
 182, 223, 243, 246,
 278, 289, 300, 312,
 317, 328, 329, 330,
 349, 377
military, 130, 182, 183,
 184, 359
mind, 31, 63, 68, 78,
 105, 106, 109, 155,
 172, 189, 198, 207,
 208, 210, 211, 212,
 217, 233, 236, 237,
 243, 249, 263, 275,
 277, 335, 349, 361,
 362, 390, 395
Minerva, 337

miscommunication, 143
mission, xxii, 139, 140,
 141, 142, 147, 163,
 165, 175, 176, 177,
 186, 187, 267, 323,
 326, 343, 354
mobility, 31, 32, 146
moderation, 72
money, 53, 94, 122, 127,
 163, 164, 166, 168,
 211, 225, 231, 237,
 277, 283, 296, 315,
 319, 331, 333, 337,
 367, 371, 372, 373,
 375, 376, 377, 379,
 380, 391, 399
money-making, 122, 164, 231
moral, x, xx, 33, 35, 36,
 69, 70, 72, 76, 78, 79,
 83, 85, 86, 90, 91,
 183, 206, 217, 220,
 224, 225, 235, 237,
 241, 246, 247, 253,
 257, 269, 289, 316,
 319, 324, 334, 357,
 358, 359, 360, 387,
 390, 394, 397
Moral dimension, 35
moral law, 33
Moral quality, 36
Moral virtue, 76
morale, 200, 352, 357, 361
moralistic, 86
morality, xiii, 34, 36, 76,
 83, 213, 220, 224, 227,
 246, 286, 384, 385,
 388, 395
Mortal sin, 66
Moslem, 199, 283
motivation, x, 91, 96, 134,
 143, 147, 200, 245,
 250, 252, 258, 259,

260, 262, 263, 307, 345, 361
mystery, 64, 65, 252
Mystical, 64
Napoleon, 183
National Organization for Women, 165
national security, 43
natural law, 33, 87, 88, 94
Naturalism, 233
Nazis, 89, 156
neck ties, 341
needs, v, 31, 33, 42, 43, 44, 46, 51, 52, 53, 54, 55, 57, 58, 59, 63, 81, 83, 89, 99, 100, 102, 121, 125, 126, 127, 128, 132, 135, 137, 140, 144, 147, 163, 167, 171, 176, 177, 188, 195, 198, 203, 206, 221, 226, 240, 251, 257, 258, 272, 277, 279, 280, 292, 311, 320, 327, 328, 330, 342, 343, 356, 359, 380, 381, 389, 391, 400
negative, 98, 105, 109, 119, 120, 163, 176, 246, 251, 254, 273, 278, 301, 303, 312
neuro-physicists, 208
new age philosophies, 235
New Testament, 384
new wine, 125
Newman, John Henry Cardinal, 236
niche, 267, 366, 370
Nichomachean, 44, 45
Noblesse Oblige, 93
Nomenklatura, 94, 353
non-Aryans, 89

normal, 53, 54, 55, 56, 58, 105, 153, 155, 293, 295, 300, 392
Nourishment, 31
novelty, 244
OArtIS, 300, 301, 312, 317, 324, 334, 360, 361, 363
obedience, 101, 377
objectives, 26, 28, 80, 90, 113, 128, 132, 163, 165, 177, 180, 181, 187, 188, 192, 194, 197, 202, 222, 224, 257, 261, 264, 280, 289, 305, 306, 307, 317, 330, 332, 357, 361
objectivity, x, 62, 89, 189, 274, 279, 280, 350
obligation, xviii, 47, 61, 63, 90, 91, 98, 228, 262, 369, 390
OD, 310, 311, 313, 316, 317
On Human Work, 28, 29
operation, 31, 33, 34, 36, 69, 132, 187, 320, 321, 386
operational, 142, 143, 146, 147, 148, 149, 153, 185, 187, 192, 193, 214, 216, 224, 275, 339
opinion, 30, 81, 89, 314, 386
orders, 114, 143, 144, 203, 211, 214, 222, 223, 224, 225, 229, 231, 232, 347, 353, 356
organization, viii, ix, xi, xx, 26, 37, 91, 96, 97, 100, 116, 118, 125, 134, 135, 138, 139,

428

140, 141, 142, 143,
144, 145, 146, 147,
149, 150, 151, 152,
153, 155, 158, 159,
160, 161, 163, 165,
166, 170, 173, 179,
180, 181, 185, 186,
187, 188, 189, 190,
191, 192, 193, 195,
196, 197, 203, 219,
221, 224, 225, 229,
245, 253, 265, 266,
267, 268, 271, 280,
285, 298, 299, 304,
306, 310, 311, 315,
317, 318, 319, 322,
325, 326, 338, 339,
340, 343, 344, 354,
355, 358, 363, 368
organization behavior, 37
Organization Design, 195
Organization Development, xi,
310, 313, 407
organize., 25
original sin, 91, 120, 205,
226
Ouchi, William, 398
Our Mother, 293
owner, 96, 100, 162, 258,
260, 339
ownership, 96, 122, 157,
160, 162, 163, 166,
229, 230, 259, 260, 386
parable, xiii, 373, 374
paradise, 88, 111, 205
paradox, 183, 366, 375
passions, 31, 32, 33, 48,
63, 77, 103, 108, 109,
147, 228
patent, 81, 82, 140, 141,
340
pathological abnormality, 55

patience, 103, 105, 165,
192, 333
Penicillin, 333, 342
perception, xiii, 242, 243,
244, 245, 246, 249,
250, 308, 362, 368, 373
perfection, vii, 59, 71, 75,
130, 131, 134, 135,
136, 138, 280, 383, 384
Perseverance, 107
persistent, 378
person, xx, 28, 29, 30, 31,
33, 34, 35, 45, 60, 61,
62, 63, 70, 72, 73, 76,
83, 86, 87, 91, 93,
102, 106, 109, 111,
116, 117, 122, 128,
140, 143, 155, 180,
212, 219, 222, 223,
224, 227, 231, 233,
236, 237, 239, 244,
248, 249, 251, 253,
256, 257, 263, 268,
270, 274, 277, 279,
280, 281, 291, 292,
304, 338, 347, 353,
354, 358, 359, 362, 367
personality, 59, 178, 231,
232, 233, 237, 238,
239, 240, 241, 275, 281
personality., 231, 281
personnel, 82, 100, 114,
126, 134, 165, 200,
216, 272, 273, 276,
278, 321, 324, 369
Peters, Tom, 254
pets, 245, 246
Philadelphia, 372, 404
philosopher, 30, 34, 37, 44,
46, 55, 60, 61, 72, 78,
88, 92, 207, 208, 282,
354, 385, 399

philosophy, xii, xix, xxii, 37, 38, 39, 40, 41, 42, 47, 53, 79, 85, 87, 110, 116, 117, 119, 151, 152, 158, 160, 182, 207, 234, 255, 264, 283, 306, 312, 313, 314, 327, 363, 364, 390

phobias, 54

Physical authority, 224, 359

physics, 27, 39, 208

Physiological, 52

Pieper, Joseph, 78, 86, 108, 404

Piety, 68

Pius XI, Pope, 172

Pius XII, Pope, 218, 219

plan, 48, 49, 58, 64, 82, 104, 127, 129, 147, 160, 162, 163, 178, 179, 180, 181, 182, 184, 185, 188, 211, 230, 258, 259, 260, 289, 294, 295, 305, 309, 317, 347, 358, 379, 389, 394

Planned Parenthood, 163, 166

planning, 106

Plato, 61, 72, 385

Pleasure, 73, 75

pluralistic societies, 42

Polaroid, 369

policy, xiii, 99, 112, 113, 129, 131, 133, 134, 151, 165, 188, 195, 199, 253, 267, 269, 270, 271, 321, 389, 392, 393, 394, 396, 397

political science, 37, 395

poor, xv, 72, 84, 89, 94, 189, 209, 224, 229, 230, 236, 253, 266, 289, 326, 373, 393, 396, 399, 400

poorer countries, 133

pope, 29, 384, 399

pornographic, 163

positive, 109, 119, 120, 173, 199, 208, 239, 246, 251, 254, 258, 265, 278, 307, 345

positivist, 38

Poverty, 377

power, xix, xx, 27, 44, 46, 49, 53, 54, 68, 83, 135, 152, 184, 190, 209, 221, 222, 223, 236, 259, 276, 277, 298, 307, 308, 347, 358, 375

powers, xx, xxi, 73, 74, 76, 80, 88, 108, 179, 280, 309, 344, 399

POWs, 249

practical, xxii, 37, 80, 82, 83, 95, 99, 105, 152, 213, 216, 232, 250, 260, 270, 275, 338, 358, 384, 385, 389, 396

practicality, 152, 389

practice, 69, 84, 132, 133, 179, 186, 224, 229, 234, 254, 273, 314, 349, 376, 397

praise, 62

pray, 64, 91, 303

prayer, 120, 250, 277, 293, 295

preferential option, 396

president, 115, 139, 177, 181, 265, 267, 268, 269, 270, 329, 331

prestige, 44, 189, 207, 215

Presumption, 70
price, 81, 151, 162, 267, 287, 296, 342
prince of the world, 103
principles, xvii, 33, 67, 69, 82, 83, 85, 88, 98, 110, 131, 144, 157, 164, 167, 170, 213, 219, 227, 230, 235, 241, 312, 332, 385, 390, 392, 395
private property, 95, 96, 97, 162, 229, 388
private sector, 129, 132
privilege, 65, 176, 215
problem, 53, 60, 89, 114, 149, 150, 151, 152, 161, 166, 168, 170, 171, 173, 174, 176, 180, 188, 190, 191, 192, 196, 204, 206, 225, 228, 232, 237, 280, 299, 310, 316, 323, 325, 330, 331, 333, 335, 336, 337, 338, 339, 349, 358, 362, 366, 388, 391
problems, xi, xxi, xxii, 28, 104, 148, 149, 150, 151, 152, 153, 156, 173, 174, 204, 205, 206, 225, 250, 270, 301, 309, 312, 318, 327, 338, 342, 365, 388
procedures, 54, 105, 138, 188, 189, 191, 195, 196, 206, 225, 270, 271, 320, 330, 352, 355
process, xii, 38, 63, 67, 74, 75, 80, 89, 113, 117, 122, 139, 157, 163, 167, 180, 181,

182, 184, 185, 186, 187, 188, 193, 197, 203, 205, 208, 209, 210, 211, 216, 217, 223, 233, 238, 244, 252, 270, 271, 272, 273, 274, 276, 278, 279, 283, 286, 293, 295, 300, 302, 305, 308, 311, 318, 329, 330, 331, 333, 334, 335, 337, 341, 342, 355, 401
procrastination, 143, 361
product, 81, 107, 114, 129, 131, 137, 141, 162, 164, 209, 210, 217, 225, 240, 246, 267, 296, 320, 325, 326, 329, 339, 340, 341, 343, 371, 378, 389
production, 114, 116, 139, 140, 141, 142, 154, 167, 193, 195, 200, 214, 217, 258, 259, 260, 268, 294, 345, 350, 351, 352, 355, 386, 391
professional interaction, 155
professional recognition, 150
profit, 81, 114, 121, 128, 131, 132, 160, 165, 166, 175, 176, 259, 322, 333, 369, 378, 386, 400
profit margin, 114
proof, xv, 38, 72, 101, 102, 110
propaganda, 244, 249, 330
Propensity, 75
prosperous, xv, 393
Protestant, 236, 283, 386,

408

Providence, vii, xiii, 121, 122, 213, 277, 379, 380, 395

prudence, 72, 77, 78, 79, 80, 81, 82, 83, 84, 85, 86, 88, 102, 105, 149, 166, 169, 212, 213, 306, 332, 333, 356, 360

prudent, 33, 54, 80, 145, 213, 307, 338

psychiatrists, 55

psychiatry, 55

psychology, xxii, 37, 39, 41, 53, 55, 204, 206, 208, 232, 235, 236, 241, 242, 243, 308

Psychometric, 55

purgative, 63

Puritanism, 110

purpose, xxii, xxiii, 35, 39, 41, 58, 61, 62, 63, 81, 97, 112, 132, 172, 173, 177, 178, 181, 187, 188, 212, 213, 216, 217, 240, 244, 262, 272, 278, 281, 289, 291, 294, 307, 311, 335, 366, 386, 400

Quadragesimo Anno, 172

qualitative, 80, 181

quality, 126, 133

Quality of the act, 36

quantitative, 80, 181

questionnaires, 58, 137

R&D, 99, 107, 177, 202, 214, 216, 301, 337, 338

R.O.E, 175

R.O.I, 175

Rational, 29, 73

Rational soul, 30

Rationality, 33

Ratzinger, xiii, 386, 387, 408, 409

reality, 34, 56, 70, 80, 83, 104, 105, 107, 169, 173, 194, 207, 222, 229, 233, 237, 242, 243, 248, 256, 273, 274, 297, 300, 319, 353, 364, 372, 393

Reason, 31, 33, 69

reasoning, 212

Recruitment, 272

redemption, 104, 120, 205, 252

reductionism, 38, 234

reformers, 84, 111

Reincarnation, 30

relatedness, 51, 54

relativism, 235

religion, xv, xx, 43, 47, 72, 101, 110, 158, 236, 256, 314, 315, 316, 395, 401

repetition, 75, 244

reproduction, 31, 34, 146

Rerum Novarum, 386, 396

research, 38, 39, 41, 58, 135, 144, 183, 186, 206, 215, 216, 217, 265, 301, 310, 311, 317, 318, 328, 329, 330, 331, 332, 337, 338, 339

resolve, 107, 183

resources, 92, 99, 100, 107, 118, 120, 134, 169, 173, 176, 177, 179, 182, 193, 195, 199, 237, 267, 268, 277, 280, 290, 300, 305, 318, 335, 339, 363, 376

respect, xxii, 59, 71, 87,

432

93, 100, 115, 154, 155, 163, 165, 166, 189, 216, 227, 230, 235, 239, 260, 261, 267, 270, 271, 373, 384

responsibilities, xvii, 26, 47, 48, 106, 122, 126, 130, 131, 134, 135, 148, 149, 153, 161, 163, 166, 167, 170, 194, 214, 227, 256, 259, 264, 271, 279, 315, 321, 327, 328, 340, 344, 357, 387, 399

responsibility, xvii, xviii, 25, 36, 48, 130, 132, 133, 142, 143, 144, 147, 149, 153, 155, 163, 170, 180, 197, 214, 219, 227, 230, 255, 261, 262, 269, 271, 316, 326, 343, 351, 352, 355, 357, 397

responsive, 129, 142, 147, 321

responsiveness, 131

resume, 272

resurrection, 30

retirement fund, 162

return on investment, 175, 191

revelation, 30, 38, 40, 41

rich, 89, 94, 95, 97, 182, 229, 230, 247, 249, 293, 375, 399

riches, 46

right, xviii, xix, 33, 36, 47, 82, 84, 85, 86, 87, 94, 96, 99, 116, 139, 165, 185, 224, 241, 260, 261, 278, 294, 312, 314, 332, 338, 346, 368, 384

Right and wrong, 36

rights, 86, 87, 88, 93, 94, 97, 98, 100, 154, 161, 166, 220, 326

risk-seekers, 367

Robinson Crusoe, 130

robotization, 148

robots, 153

Rockefeller, David, 362

Rockefeller, John D., xviii

rogues, 284

role, 156

Rome, 314, 408

sabotage, 179, 203, 326

sacraments, 64, 295, 397

sacrifice, xix, 289, 372, 377

safety, 52, 54, 148

salaries, 104, 160, 259, 261, 320

salvation, 47, 60, 62, 63, 68, 112, 116, 158, 188, 227, 236, 240, 249, 261, 295, 361, 396

Samuelson, Paul, 388, 394

San Marco, 399

sanctification, 62, 63, 68

Sanctifying grace, 65

sanctity, 64, 289, 292

sanity, 56, 312

Sartre, Jean-Paul, 306

Satan, 205

Say, Jean-Baptiste, 363

Schéré, Jean, 367

Scholarship, 72

Schoolmen, 401

Schumpeter, Joseph, 364

science, xvii, xxii, 27, 39, 40, 41, 42, 53, 73, 76, 85, 86, 183, 205, 208, 215, 234, 237, 242, 293, 296, 310,

315, 365, 395
secular, xv, xxi, 61, 72,
   79, 85, 104, 119, 232,
   233, 234, 284, 313,
   314, 397
security, 44, 46, 54, 55,
   58, 59, 224, 279, 301
self-actualization, vi, 52, 53,
   57, 236
self-actualize, 52, 53
self-confidence, 274
self-esteem, 52, 54
self-starter, 257
self-supporting, 128
Sensitivity Training, 311, 315
Sensual powers, 76
sensuality, 108
Serendipity, 333
servants, 130, 373, 395
service, 128, 225, 296
sex, 109, 110, 204, 234
Sexual desire, 32
Sexual revolution, 34
Shakespeare, 335
shelter, 52, 53, 95
Shintoist, 43, 284
shrewdness, 212
Significant work, 253
Simon, Herbert, 204
sin, 48, 63, 64, 71, 85,
   86, 110, 206, 236
skills, 80, 116, 117, 120,
   136, 215, 216, 294,
   302, 320, 361
Skinner, B.F., 308, 309
slack, 128, 200
Smith, Adam, 364, 386, 387,
   388, 389, 390, 391,
   392, 393
social destination of privately-owned
   goods, 97

Social nature, 33
social sciences, 37, 205, 313,
   365
social teachings, 116, 218,
   281, 386, 396
social-esteem, 54
Socialist, 397
socializing, 56
society, xii, 41, 56, 60,
   84, 90, 91, 93, 94, 95,
   96, 97, 99, 101, 103,
   117, 118, 126, 129,
   130, 132, 133, 134,
   135, 136, 137, 142,
   147, 150, 155, 156,
   157, 159, 167, 170,
   171, 172, 173, 213,
   215, 218, 219, 222,
   225, 226, 227, 240,
   247, 253, 309, 313,
   314, 325, 339, 344,
   353, 354, 355, 369,
   371, 375, 380, 387,
   389, 390, 396
sociologists, 56
sociology, xxii, 37, 41,
   206, 219
soldier, 185
solidarity, 26, 92, 121, 173,
   218, 247, 271, 398
solutions, 149, 192, 204,
   205, 207, 323, 333,
   335, 336, 338, 339
solving, 85, 174, 176, 310
soul, xix, 30, 31, 32, 34,
   47, 63, 65, 69, 72,
   107, 110, 111, 116,
   145, 146, 147, 154,
   160, 161, 165, 180,
   204, 255, 302, 303,
   317, 324, 383
span of control, 144

434

Species, 73
spiritual, xx, xxi, 53, 59,
    62, 63, 65, 66, 68, 70,
    71, 73, 89, 92, 110,
    112, 120, 121, 160,
    218, 219, 220, 233,
    234, 235, 239, 241,
    249, 278, 284, 289,
    290, 293, 295, 324,
    328, 357, 377, 379,
    383, 384, 397
spirituality, 62, 365
spokespeople, 143
St. Ambrose, 102
St. Antoninus, 399, 400, 401
St. Augustine, 49
St. Paul, 108
St. Thomas, xix, xxiii, 46,
    209, 334, 354, 376,
    401, 403
St.Catherine of Siena, 239
stability, 128, 148
Stable disposition, 73
staff, 107, 134, 144, 165,
    179, 181, 196, 214,
    215, 216, 217, 218, 300
stake-holders, 185
Stalin, Joseph, 309
standardization, 146, 148,
    173, 189
State of grace, 66, 71
state of life, 400
static, 206, 376
statistical methods, 40, 206
statistics, 365
status, 97, 150, 156, 157,
    158, 159, 160, 161,
    180, 204, 309, 373
stock, 151, 160, 176, 258,
    305, 392
stockholders, 163
strategic, xvii, 82, 99, 106,
    140, 141, 142, 143,
    146, 147, 148, 149,
    151, 152, 153, 158,
    169, 174, 175, 177,
    178, 179, 180, 181,
    182, 184, 185, 186,
    187, 188, 192, 214,
    225, 274, 304
strategic plan, 178, 179, 182
strategy, 81, 99, 107, 143,
    151, 182, 183, 187,
    188, 191, 192, 310, 365
strenuous, 105
structure, xviii, xxii, 78,
    143, 144, 146, 147,
    149, 150, 190, 196,
    240, 256, 310, 327, 347
subjective, xvii, 29, 38,
    60, 119, 120, 189, 235,
    236, 271, 278, 391
Subjective being, 29
Subjectivism, 235
subjectivity, 189, 241, 272,
    273, 274, 278
subsidiarity, 389
subsistence, 117, 121
success, 80, 81, 82, 99,
    100, 134, 150, 180,
    191, 227, 256, 258,
    291, 326, 332, 362,
    369, 400
successful, xv, xxii, 72,
    81, 82, 105, 106, 138,
    258, 291, 325, 332,
    336, 337, 341, 362,
    365, 370, 372, 379,
    380, 393
suffering, 68
Summa Theologicae, 110
supernatural, 65, 66, 67, 70,
    154, 155
Supernatural life, 66

supervise, 25, 139
Supervision, 26
supervisor, 26, 144, 274,
    279, 351, 352, 358
suppliers, 97, 98, 121, 126,
    127, 161, 240, 398
Supreme good, 70
survival, 100, 220, 335
Synectics, 337, 338, 408
system, xv, xviii, xix,
    xx, 49, 60, 61, 80, 94,
    96, 107, 108, 109, 128,
    139, 140, 167, 168,
    169, 185, 189, 190,
    198, 200, 218, 249,
    284, 286, 290, 291,
    292, 294, 295, 298,
    299, 300, 301, 304,
    305, 306, 307, 312,
    317, 321, 322, 324,
    334, 335, 336, 344,
    360, 361, 362, 364,
    368, 369, 375, 386,
    388, 392, 393, 401
talents, xiii, 116, 117,
    119, 120, 121, 122,
    136, 252, 368, 373,
    374, 375, 377, 379, 380
tasks, xv, xvii, 119, 143,
    144, 146, 147, 148,
    149, 159, 160, 186,
    196, 200, 208, 255,
    256, 257, 258, 262,
    263, 278, 279, 293,
    330, 340, 343, 347,
    351, 352, 355, 356,
    357, 359, 360, 361,
    383, 385
Tawney, R.H., 400
tax rates, 94
taxation, 95
teaching, 41, 62, 85, 97,

120, 168, 198, 277,
    316, 366, 373, 384,
    395, 396, 397, 398
team, 81, 114, 116, 140,
    201, 202, 203, 257,
    260, 280, 317, 323,
    325, 326, 329, 338,
    340, 355, 398
technology, 106, 124, 164,
    185, 202, 264, 268,
    310, 324, 332, 355, 365
tedious, 148, 330
teenagers, 56
teleological, 90
telephone, 272, 342, 343
temperance, 69, 77, 78,
    108, 109, 111, 112,
    113, 114, 138, 149,
    332, 333, 356, 360, 394
temperate, 109, 112, 114,
    145, 151, 215, 326, 338
temptation, 85, 89, 150,
    175, 179, 240
terror, 102, 378
tests, x, 58, 137, 227,
    237, 275, 276, 279, 328
T-group, 311
theodicy, 40
theologian, xxiii, 37, 44,
    399
theological, xxii, 40, 69,
    71, 72, 205
Theological virtues, 69
theology, xxii, 36, 37, 38,
    40, 41, 42, 85, 86,
    205, 236, 314, 316
Theory of Moral Sentiments, 388
Theory X and Theory Y, x, 250
Thinking, 29
third world nation, 169
threat, 48, 220, 365
threats and opportunities, 99,

100, 147, 393
toil, 119, 185
tolerance, 111, 235, 237, 314
Tolerance for Ambiguity, 367
torture, 48
totalitarian, 87
touchy feely, 236, 312
trade, 167, 168
training, xi, 26, 40, 74, 85, 134, 138, 175, 198, 211, 262, 276, 311, 312, 313, 315, 316
Training Group, 311
trait, 54, 59, 237, 345, 356, 367
Transactional, 146
transactual, 141, 143, 147
transitive, 117
Trinity, 66
truth, xix, 28, 47, 49, 56, 64, 67, 70, 84, 207, 208, 228, 232, 235, 250, 313, 316, 340, 357
TV, 45, 112, 144, 324
ultimate end, 44
unborn children, 165
understanding, 25, 26, 30, 36, 37, 38, 42, 43, 49, 51, 67, 77, 79, 84, 101, 107, 133, 138, 145, 167, 169, 170, 186, 207, 209, 212, 213, 221, 222, 223, 231, 232, 237, 239, 243, 245, 254, 256, 263, 275, 281, 298, 305, 324, 330, 332, 356, 364, 372, 391, 392, 394
Uniformity, 75
Unique Selling Proposition, 240

unitive, 63
unity of command, 143, 157
universal destination, 96
universe, 40, 41, 66, 70, 110, 243
Upjohn, 329, 331
use, vi, 26, 32, 33, 35, 48, 56, 58, 61, 73, 76, 81, 96, 104, 110, 170, 179, 184, 193, 197, 199, 203, 211, 223, 224, 229, 236, 240, 244, 259, 284, 298, 303, 306, 307, 310, 314, 328, 334, 337, 339, 343, 344, 348, 375
Utilitarianism, 234
utility, 38
valid, 38, 56, 58, 104, 112, 223, 230, 244, 246, 256, 264, 268, 275, 276, 279, 281, 308, 309, 330, 384, 389
value, xi, xii, xvii, xviii, 45, 57, 81, 85, 91, 101, 111, 112, 114, 116, 117, 119, 120, 138, 158, 160, 161, 167, 176, 188, 196, 205, 207, 219, 221, 234, 235, 246, 255, 262, 274, 276, 286, 287, 288, 289, 290, 291, 292, 293, 294, 295, 296, 297, 298, 299, 300, 301, 304, 305, 306, 307, 312, 313, 317, 319, 320, 324, 334, 335, 348, 357, 360, 361, 362, 387
Value Theory of Management, 301
values, xi, xvii, xviii,

xxi, 42, 43, 79, 112,
117, 156, 157, 161,
166, 171, 174, 185,
227, 228, 247, 254,
279, 281, 283, 284,
286, 287, 288, 289,
290, 291, 292, 293,
294, 295, 296, 297,
298, 299, 300, 301,
304, 305, 306, 307,
310, 311, 312, 313,
314, 317, 334, 335,
336, 338, 361, 362
vegetative, 31, 32, 146
vegetative soul, 31, 32, 146
venture, 169, 369, 370,
375, 378
Verne, Jules, 330
vice, 56, 76, 104, 110,
111, 112, 115, 139,
177, 181, 228, 249,
251, 265, 267, 268,
269, 270, 301, 302
Vietnam, 249
Vinci, Da, 330
virtue, 69, 70, 71, 76, 78,
79, 80, 82, 85, 86, 88,
89, 90, 91, 97, 99,
100, 101, 102, 103,
104, 106, 108, 111,
113, 117, 119, 121,
148, 183, 198, 211,
212, 213, 237, 249,
251, 253, 305, 314,
317, 318, 331, 332,
333, 356, 357, 376,
377, 380, 389, 391, 392
virtues, xi, xii, xv, 68,
69, 70, 71, 72, 73, 76,
78, 79, 84, 85, 86, 88,
89, 91, 101, 110, 116,
117, 120, 122, 135,

136, 137, 138, 148,
150, 158, 159, 183,
198, 208, 212, 213,
228, 241, 251, 256,
295, 302, 303, 304,
305, 307, 318, 324,
326, 327, 333, 334,
337, 338, 340, 343,
355, 356, 357, 358,
360, 361, 380, 384,
385, 392, 393, 396,
397, 399, 400
virtuous, 47, 68, 103, 107,
135, 138, 188, 290,
295, 318, 326, 358,
384, 392
vision, xviii, 36, 43, 47,
107, 184, 185, 186, 368
Vitz, Paul, 232, 233
vocation, 60, 328, 379
volition, 180, 209
voluntary act, 34, 35
volunteer, 118, 128, 165
wages, 97, 160
wants, 44, 45, 46, 50, 61,
66, 83, 137, 171, 225,
266, 280, 281, 331,
335, 358, 359, 375, 379
wealth, xix, 81, 237, 247,
289, 291, 376
Wealth of Nations, 364, 387,
388, 389, 390, 409
Webber, Ross, xxiii, 44, 264
Weber, Max, 386
Welfare State, 381
Weltanschauung, 291
Wharton, xxiii, 186, 264,
404, 409
whistle-blowing, 98
Will, 31, 34, 70, 77
wisdom, xv, xix, 50, 64,
67, 72, 80, 212, 246,

250, 278, 350, 366,
391, 392, 393
witchcraft, 235
wives, 315, 378
women, 33, 165, 245, 314,
359, 395
work, xii, xv, xix, xxi,
xxii, 25, 26, 27, 28,
29, 34, 37, 41, 42, 43,
45, 57, 59, 68, 76, 82,
88, 96, 104, 105, 106,
116, 117, 118, 119,
120, 121, 122, 125,
126, 128, 129, 130,
132, 134, 135, 136,
140, 142, 143, 144,
148, 149, 151, 152,
153, 158, 173, 178,
180, 183, 187, 192,
193, 196, 199, 200,
202, 208, 214, 215,
216, 217, 219, 220,
221, 224, 226, 227,
240, 244, 249, 250,
251, 252, 253, 254,
255, 256, 257, 258,

259, 261, 262, 263,
264, 266, 273, 276,
279, 281, 285, 286,
289, 300, 301, 307,
308, 310, 311, 314,
317, 318, 320, 321,
324, 326, 327, 328,
329, 330, 339, 346,
347, 351, 352, 355,
356, 357, 360, 378,
381, 384, 385, 387,
392, 393, 396, 399
worker, x, 42, 43, 104,
105, 106, 118, 122,
134, 135, 136, 141,
142, 144, 148, 149,
196, 219, 248, 251,
252, 253, 254, 255,
256, 257, 258, 260,
262, 263, 315, 346,
357, 380, 385, 395
works of mercy, 95, 121
wrong, 36, 45, 48, 60, 89,
115, 122, 189, 391,
392, 396
zeal, 130, 131

ABOUT THE AUTHOR

For 20 years, Jean-Francois Orsini has run the *St. Antoninus Institute for Catholic Education in Business*. During this time, he wrote, in addition to monthly newsletters and several annual versions of the Pro-Life Shopping Guide, *Virtue Based Management* a complete handbook of Management treated from a Thomistic perspective, explaining how to faithfully implement Catholic Social Teachings in all the very details of management. He edited that manuscript in 2017. For 15 years, he has been teaching business courses at the university level, including courses of business ethics, finance and general management. He has written a book on politics and another in theology *Love is God*. He has also founded several small businesses. He was granted 6 patents of invention. After high school courses including Latin and Greek as well as the heaviest quota of mathematics and science, he graduated from a top French business school, ESCP Europe, and later earned an MBA and a Ph.D. from the Wharton School. He is a third order Dominican and served two terms as prior of his Dominican lay chapter. He is a Knight of the Holy Sepulcher. Also, father of 6 daughters, he is, so far, grandfather of 7 grandchildren. He was born in Vietnam and grew up in Morocco and France.

Made in the USA
Middletown, DE
28 October 2022